LANGUAGE AN

Dorothy S. Stric
Celia Genishi and Donn
ADVISORY BOARD: *Richard Allington,*
Anne Haas Dyson, Carole Edelsky, Mary Juz..., ... Lyn, Django Paris, Timothy Shanahan

MW01125652

Literacy Leadership in Changing Schools:
10 Keys to Successful Professional Development
SHELLEY B. WEPNER, DIANE W. GÓMEZ, KATIE EGAN CUNNINGHAM,
KRISTIN N. RAINVILLE, & COURTNEY KELLY

Literacy Theory as Practice:
Connecting Theory and Instruction in K–12 Classrooms
LARA HANDSFIELD

Literacy and History in Action: Immersive Approaches to
Disciplinary Thinking, Grades 5–12
THOMAS M. MCCANN, REBECCA D'ANGELO, NANCY GALAS, & MARY
GRESKA

Pose, Wobble, Flow:
A Culturally Proactive Approach to Literacy Instruction
ANTERO GARCIA & CINDY O'DONNELL-ALLEN

Newsworthy—Cultivating Critical Thinkers, Readers, and
Writers in Language Arts Classrooms
ED MADISON

Engaging Writers with Multigenre Research Projects:
A Teacher's Guide
NANCY MACK

Teaching Transnational Youth—
Literacy and Education in a Changing World
ALLISON SKERRETT

Uncommonly Good Ideas—
Teaching Writing in the Common Core Era
SANDRA MURPHY & MARY ANN SMITH

The One-on-One Reading and Writing Conference:
Working with Students on Complex Texts
JENNIFER BERNE & SOPHIE C. DEGENER

Critical Encounters in Secondary English:
Teaching Literary Theory to Adolescents, Third Edition
DEBORAH APPLEMAN

Transforming Talk into Text—Argument Writing, Inquiry,
and Discussion, Grades 6–12
THOMAS M. MCCANN

Reading and Representing Across the Content Areas:
A Classroom Guide
AMY ALEXANDRA WILSON & KATHRYN J. CHAVEZ

Writing and Teaching to Change the World:
Connecting with Our Most Vulnerable Students
STEPHANIE JONES, ED.

Educating Literacy Teachers Online:
Tools, Techniques, and Transformations
LANE W. CLARKE & SUSAN WATTS-TAFFEE

Other People's English: Code-Meshing,
Code-Switching, and African American Literacy
VERSHAWN ASHANTI YOUNG, RUSTY BARRETT,
Y'SHANDA YOUNG-RIVERA, & KIM BRIAN LOVEJOY

WHAM! Teaching with Graphic Novels Across
the Curriculum
WILLIAM G. BROZO, GARY MOORMAN, & CARLA K. MEYER

The Administration and Supervision of Reading Programs,
5th Edition
SHELLEY B. WEPNER, DOROTHY S. STRICKLAND,
& DIANA J. QUATROCHE, EDS.

Critical Literacy in the Early Childhood Classroom:
Unpacking Histories, Unlearning Privilege
CANDACE R. KUBY

Inspiring Dialogue:
Talking to Learn in the English Classroom
MARY M. JUZWIK, CARLIN BORSHEIM-BLACK,
SAMANTHA CAUGHLAN, & ANNE HEINTZ

Reading the Visual:
An Introduction to Teaching Multimodal Literacy
FRANK SERAFINI

Race, Community, and Urban Schools:
Partnering with African American Families
STUART GREENE

ReWRITING the Basics:
Literacy Learning in Children's Cultures
ANNE HAAS DYSON

Writing Instruction That Works:
Proven Methods for Middle and High School Classrooms
ARTHUR N. APPLEBEE & JUDITH A. LANGER, WITH KRISTEN CAMPBELL
WILCOX, MARC NACHOWITZ, MICHAEL P. MASTROIANNI, & CHRISTINE
DAWSON

Literacy Playshop: New Literacies, Popular Media, and
Play in the Early Childhood Classroom
KAREN E. WOHLWEND

Critical Media Pedagogy:
Teaching for Achievement in City Schools
ERNEST MORRELL, RUDY DUEÑAS, VERONICA GARCIA,
& JORGE LOPEZA

A Search Past Silence: The Literacy of Young Black Men
DAVID E. KIRKLAND

The ELL Writer:
Moving Beyond Basics in the Secondary Classroom
CHRISTINA ORTMEIER-HOOPER

Reading in a Participatory Culture:
Remixing *Moby-Dick* in the English Classroom
HENRY JENKINS & WYN KELLEY, WITH KATIE CLINTON, JENNA
MCWILLIAMS, RICARDO PITTS-WILEY, & ERIN REILLY, EDS.

Summer Reading:
Closing the Rich/Poor Achievement Gap
RICHARD L. ALLINGTON & ANNE MCGILL-FRANZEN, EDS.

Real World Writing for Secondary Students:
Teaching the College Admission Essay and
Other Gate-Openers for Higher Education
JESSICA SINGER EARLY & MEREDITH DECOSTA

Teaching Vocabulary to English Language Learners
MICHAEL F. GRAVES, DIANE AUGUST, &
JEANETTE MANCILLA-MARTINEZ

Literacy for a Better World:
LAURA SCHNEIDER VANDERPLOEG

Socially Responsible Literacy
PAULA M. SELVESTER & DEBORAH G. SUMMERS

Learning from Culturally and Linguistically Diverse
Classrooms: Using Inquiry to Inform Practice
JOAN C. FINGON & SHARON H. ULANOFF, EDS.

continued

For volumes in the NCRLL Collection (edited by JoBeth Allen and Donna E. Alvermann) and the Practitioners Bookshelf Series
(edited by Celia Genishi and Donna E. Alvermann), as well as other titles in this series, please visit www.tcpress.com.

LITERACY LEADERSHIP in CHANGING SCHOOLS

10 Keys to Successful Professional Development

Shelley B. Wepner
Diane W. Gómez
Katie Egan Cunningham
Kristin N. Rainville
Courtney Kelly

TEACHERS COLLEGE PRESS

TEACHERS COLLEGE | COLUMBIA UNIVERSITY
NEW YORK AND LONDON

Published by Teachers College Press, 1234 Amsterdam Avenue, New York, NY 10027

The authors would like to express gratitude for permission to use the following:

Figure 3.1 from *The Learning Leader: How to Focus School Improvement for Better Results,* by Douglas B. Reeves. © 2006 by the Association for Supervision and Curriculum Development, Alexandria, Virginia.
Figure 4.2 from *Performance Standards Speaking and Writing, K–12,* by Wisconsin Center for Education Research. © 2014 by Wisconsin Center for Education Research/WIDA/University of Wisconsin-Madison
Figure 8.4 from *Word Journeys Assessment: Guided Phonics, Spelling, and Vocabulary Instruction* (2nd ed.), by K. Ganske. © 2013 by Guilford Press, New York.

Library of Congress Cataloging-in-Publication Data

Wepner, Shelley B., 1951-
Literacy leadership in changing schools : 10 keys to successful professional development / Shelley B. Wepner [and four others].
pages ; cm. — (Language And Literacy Series)
ISBN 978-0-8077-5713-0 (paperback)
ISBN 978-0-8077-7418-2 (ebook)
1. Literacy. 2. Educational leadership. I. Title.
LC151.W36 2015
372.6—dc23   2015033792

ISBN 978-0-8077-5713-0 (paper)
ISBN 978-0-8077-7418-2 (ebook)

Printed on acid-free paper
Manufactured in the United States of America

23 22 21 20 19 18 17 16   8 7 6 5 4 3 2 1

To our loved ones,

who remind us daily how to use challenges as opportunities for growth

and keep us anchored to essential principles for honoring individuality

From Shelley:

To my husband, Roy; and daughters, sons-in-law, and grandchildren—
Leslie, Marc, Teddy, and Sloane Regenbaum; and Meredith,
Judd, Eliza, and Sydney Grossman—who remind me that, with
unconditional love and support, mountains indeed can be moved

From Dee:

To my husband, David, who reminds me to lead by listening; daughters,
Cris, Julia, and Tori, and son-in-law, Ivan, who inspire me daily

From Katie:

To my husband, Chris, whose leadership in schools is a constant
model and inspiration to me; and sons, Jack and Matthew, who
remind me of the power of story and the importance of play

From Kristin:

To my sons, Joey, Dylan, and Tyson DeSabia, who remind me to
be curious, live in the moment, and release my imagination

From Courtney:

To my son, Jack, who reminds me that every student is someone's child,
and that no learner should be on the periphery of a classroom community

Successful leaders see the opportunities in every difficulty rather than the difficulty in every opportunity.

—Reed Markham, Professor, Daytona State College

The quote was shared in a leadership speech to undergraduate students at California State Polytechnic University Pomona, September 1996.

Contents

Acknowledgments

We are eternally grateful to an anonymous donor who urged our college to wake up to the challenges that school districts in our surrounding suburban communities are facing. As this donor watched her own suburban town change, she became increasingly concerned that the schools did not know what to do with the growing achievement gap. This donor asked quite pointedly, "Are you preparing your teachers for these changing districts?" She understood that, indeed, the urban schools need resources, but feared that the changing suburban schools with many of the same challenges would be overlooked and ignored. She gave us a small grant to study the work of demographers and sociologists on the changing suburban phenomenon so that we could shift our conceptual paradigm about disadvantaged schools. Within 6 months of intensive data analysis, we identified 10 school districts within a 25-mile radius of our college that had moderate to significant increases in culturally and linguistically diverse students. This donor challenged us to assume a leadership role within these schools to assist with students' achievement needs. Her generous support of our efforts led to the development of the Changing Suburbs Institute®, which led to the birth of this book.

We are equally indebted to Emily Spangler from Teachers College Press, who understood from our first conversation that the phenomenon of the changing suburbs was becoming widespread across the United States. She appreciated the impact of these changes on teachers' ability to help with students' literacy development. She encouraged us to write a proposal that would focus on helping literacy leaders in changing schools to work with teachers to help them shift their instructional practices so that they could be successful with a different type of learner. Emily served as a critical conduit between the reviewers and us so that we knew how to prepare a manuscript that used the changing reality in schools as the impetus for presenting practical ideas, strategies, and guidelines for literacy leaders to use for themselves and with their teachers. Emily's sharp eye for analyzing and synthesizing information, balanced perspective, kindhearted support, and patient guidance enabled us to eventually produce this book. We are grateful to our talented production editors, Aureliano Vazquez and Jennifer Baker at Teachers College Press, who transformed our well-intentioned draft into a conceptually clean and well-crafted presentation of our ideas We also are appreciative of our publicist, Emily Renwick, at Teachers College Press, who helped us to generate ideas for presenting our message to our audience.

We acknowledge our colleagues at Manhattanville College for all that they already have done and will continue to do to prepare teacher and leader candidates for the changing landscape of K–5 schools. We thank them for allowing us to represent their work related to the Changing Suburbs Institute®.

We recognize our rather extensive and certainly impressive village of K–6 teachers and administrators in the changing schools in our area who are experiencing inexplicable challenges with student achievement. For every step forward, they find themselves two steps behind their goals for students' literacy development. Their willingness to work with us has helped test new ideas and envision new possibilities for working with culturally and linguistically diverse students. Those who have been particularly helpful in sharing their experiences include Andrew Patrick, Susan Ostrofsky, Kweon Stambaugh, and Loretta Butler from the Bedford Central School District; and Kimmerly Nieves from New Rochelle City School District. We are grateful to the classroom teachers at Mount Kisco Elementary School, Bedford; Jefferson Elementary School, New Rochelle; and full-service community schools, Thomas A. Edison and Park Avenue Elementary School, Port Chester, who invited us into their classrooms, engaged in learning with us, and modeled a culture of student-driven learning.

We thank three literacy leaders who allowed us to interview them for this book so that we could better understand their perspective on serving in their roles in a changing school: Karen Brenneke, Laurie Pastore, and Mary Shannon. Their personal stories about their daily lives as change agents gave us the needed insight to understand what could work with different types of teachers, administrators, and school communities. We acknowledge other literacy leaders and classroom teachers from Connecticut, New York, and New Jersey, whose experiences are highlighted throughout the book.

We recognize those affiliated with Manhattanville who assisted during different phases of this book's preparation with research, brainstorming, writing, editing, graphic design, and overall organization. These faculty, administrators, graduate students, and consultants inspired us to stretch our imaginations, rethink our positions, write more clearly, and attend to critical details: Pledger Fedora, Caitlin Miller, Danielle Scalera, Marilyn Scribner, and Lauren Wedeles. We also thank Sandra Priest Rose, founder of the Rose Institute for Learning and Literacy at Manhattanville College, whose lifelong commitment to children's literacy learning is an inspiration to us.

Finally, we acknowledge our families with immeasurable love and eternal gratitude for believing in what we do so much so that they completely understood when we needed time away from family responsibilities to work on this book project. We are especially indebted to our own young children, adult children, and grandchildren for constantly reminding us about the challenges of becoming literate, the importance of appreciating learners' individualized needs for developing literacy, and the artistic skill needed by teachers to use just the right mix of instructional methodologies and resources to help create literate beings. We feel blessed to have this inside track on the power of teachers' influence on children, and know that it has helped us to support literacy leaders as they assist their teachers to grow professionally.

LITERACY LEADERSHIP in CHANGING SCHOOLS

Introduction

Literacy Leadership in Changing Schools: 10 Keys to Successful Professional Development is written for literacy leaders in changing K–6 schools to promote teachers' professional development. With a focus on *leadership*, this book uses literacy basics to suggest concrete ideas that literacy leaders can use to help teachers improve their instruction in response to standards with culturally linguistically diverse students.

A literacy leader is an agent for change responsible for the oversight, implementation, and evaluation of a school or district literacy plan; for example, reading specialists, literacy specialists, literacy consultants, literacy coaches, principals, vice principals, assistant superintendents, curriculum and instruction directors, and teacher leaders. Changing schools are those schools that have seen significant increases in the diversity of their student population because of geographical mobility and immigration. Such changes exist in all types of schools, but are particularly acute in suburban school districts.

With an emphasis on empowering literacy leaders to offer sound professional development opportunities and options for teachers, *Literacy Leadership in Changing Schools: 10 Keys to Successful Professional Development* acknowledges the assets that cultural, linguistic, and socioeconomic diversity brings to schools and communities. While we recognize teachers' and students' extraordinary capabilities, we also recognize that there are challenges that literacy leaders and teachers face in changing schools and other school contexts, including but not limited to high-stakes testing and increasing failure rates; rigorous teacher and principal evaluations that are partially based on the results of high-stakes test results; the motivation, knowledge, and skills needed for improved teacher practice; the potential lack of family engagement in the schools; having to do more with less; and inexperience with how to instruct culturally and linguistically diverse students.

The ideas presented in this book come from our own firsthand experiences and research, and our college's model, the Changing Suburbs Institute® (CSI), for partnering with literacy leaders, teachers,

1

students, and parents in changing schools. All five of us have been involved with teachers' professional development, and bring to the forefront strategies and guidelines for working successfully with teachers. Two connecting themes throughout the book are the Common Core State Standards (CCSS) and data-driven instruction.

Literacy Leadership in Changing Schools: 10 Keys to Successful Professional Development does the following:

- Uses each chapter to discuss an essential component for serving as a literacy leader, and then "puts it all together" in the 10th and final chapter
- Uses community, teacher, and student characteristics of changing schools as a framework for providing professional development about curriculum, programs, materials, and instructional techniques
- Focuses on essential attributes of literacy leaders for helping teachers adjust to their changing student populations as they implement the CCSS and use data-driven instruction to help students achieve
- Uses vignettes about literacy leaders to define who they are, describe what they do, and demonstrate the varied ways in which they function

RATIONALE FOR WRITING
LITERACY LEADERSHIP IN CHANGING SCHOOLS:
10 KEYS TO SUCCESSFUL PROFESSIONAL DEVELOPMENT

America's classrooms are increasingly diverse. Forty-eight percent of P–12 students are students of color (National Center for Education Statistics, 2012) and 20% come from homes where native languages other than English are spoken (United States Census Bureau, 2001). Yet, fewer than 20% of America's teachers are teachers of color (Council for the Accreditation of Educator Preparation, 2013). The suburbs in particular are at a crossroads because of the influx of African Americans, Hispanics, and Asians (Wells & Ready, 2014). In fact, American suburbs are experiencing an identity crisis because the number of Americans living below the federal poverty line in the suburbs is nearly the same as in the cities (Strauss, 2014). Since 2000, the number of people living in poverty in the suburbs has grown by

105%, to 4.9 million, compared to the number of people living in poverty in the cities, which is 5.9 million (Kneebone, 2014). Suburban school districts that were once able to provide ample services for their students now are struggling to identify and provide suitable services (e.g., bilingual staff, translation services, summer school support, and newcomer programs).

Today's teachers are trying to figure out how to adjust and adapt instruction in appropriate ways for their diverse students (Council for the Accreditation of Educator Preparation, 2013). Even if they are aware of and supportive of individual circumstances, they nevertheless are struggling to provide relevant class materials that help their students with curriculum requirements (Bracco & Rabinovitch, 2014). Teachers' professional development is more important than ever if they are to succeed with this changing student population at a time when the literacy landscape is also changing. Teachers need ideas, strategies, and guidelines for targeted literacy instruction in response to standards to promote students' success with high-stakes testing while developing their love for literacy and learning. Literacy leaders are important for fulfilling teachers' professional development needs.

Although many books address the roles and responsibilities and professional development of literacy leaders, they do not home in on what literacy leaders need to do in changing schools with increasingly diverse student populations. For instance, suburban schools of the 21st century do not resemble the suburbs of the past, which were populated by predominantly White, middle-class students whose primary language was English. Today, suburban students come to school with varied racial, ethnic, cultural, linguistic, and economic backgrounds. These students are often challenged by local, state, and national standards for literacy achievement. Literacy leaders need to be able to assist teachers by knowing which programs, materials, and instructional techniques to use with diverse students. Literacy leaders themselves need to know "what works" with planning, instruction, and assessment so that they can offer appropriate professional development opportunities and options.

Unlike other books, this practical text gives specific ideas, strategies, and guidelines for addressing this new and growing phenomenon in K–6 schools. The basis for this book comes from our backgrounds and experiences with literacy coaching, teaching of English learners, and administrative oversight of literacy programs. We also have been

involved with the implementation of the Changing Suburbs Institute®
(CSI) in 13 schools that are located in the New York suburbs.

CSI is a grassroots, school-university-community collaborative
that was established in recognition of the increasing diversity in suburban school districts and the need to ensure that practicing and pro-
spective teachers would be prepared to teach an increasingly diverse
student population. CSI focuses on four major areas: (1) teacher leadership and development, (2) collaboration, (3) dissemination of information, and (4) parent education. Figure I-1 provides a graphic
depiction of the components of CSI.

To address *teacher leadership and development,* CSI established professional development schools (PDSs) in school districts that were
experiencing changing demographics. PDSs focus on the professional
development of teachers, teacher candidate preparation, and student
learning. Our college provides each school with a PDS liaison who
resides at the PDS a minimum of 2 days each week to serve as the conduit between the school and the college. PDS liaisons work primarily
with practicing teachers and teacher candidates to support their development so that they in turn can enhance student learning. Three of us
(Diane, Katherine, and Kristin) have served as PDS liaisons.

The PDSs have developed unique initiatives for their schools—
for example, reading and writing workshops in which faculty members work directly with teachers to help them modify instructional
practices; a special foundations of literacy program for K–2 students;
after-school literacy programs for English learners (ELs); family
literacy nights; Spanish book clubs for K–6 students; and literacy
book clubs for teachers. PDSs are entitled to special discounts for the
teaching staff *and* parents for coursework, conferences, and special
events. High school students from a PDS district who are accepted
to our college are entitled to at least a 50% tuition discount for all
4 undergraduate years. Quantitative and qualitative data indicate
changes in teachers' instructional methodologies, changes in teacher
candidates' level of confidence for first-time teaching, and changes
in K–6 students' learning (Cunningham, 2014; Flaitz, 2013; Wepner,
Gómez, & Ferrara, 2013).

CSI holds an annual educational forum that brings renowned
experts as keynote speakers to present current research about and
practices for working effectively with diverse student populations.
Workshop presenters showcase accomplishments in CSI schools, and
help attendees develop new insights about diverse students' culture,

Figure I.1. Changing Suburbs Institute® (CSI)

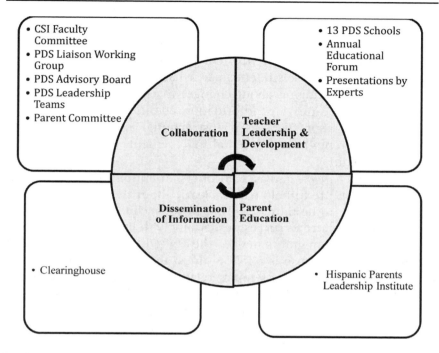

* CSI Faculty
  Committee
* PDS Liaison Working
  Group
* PDS Advisory Board
* PDS Leadership
  Teams
* Parent Committee

* 13 PDS Schools
* Annual
  Educational
  Forum
* Presentations by
  Experts

Collaboration

**Teacher
Leadership &
Development**

**Dissemination
of Information**

**Parent
Education**

* Clearinghouse

* Hispanic Parents
  Leadership Institute

background, behavior, and immigration experiences. CSI also sponsors presentations by experts on ways to work with ELs in relation to national and state assessment mandates.

To address *collaboration*, there are five different CSI teams of school-, university-, and community-based teachers, administrators, and leaders that get together to focus on a specific task, initiative, or challenge related to helping the changing student and parent population better acclimate to school expectations. The CSI Faculty Committee determines the overall goals for the institute, plans professional development opportunities at the college, and oversees special projects. The PDS Liaison Working Group oversees the general direction of the PDSs, discusses each PDS's progress and challenges, and helps to organize and implement the PDS assessment system. The PDS Advisory Board, which includes all the PDS principals and their liaisons, exchanges ideas and assesses progress within and across schools. The PDS Leadership Teams are based at each to determine annual goals and plan activities to address these goals. The Parent Committee of district administrators, teachers, and parents plans the parent conferences and determines strategies for engaging parents. More than 100 people are involved in some type of collaboration related to CSI.

To address *dissemination of information*, a clearinghouse has been developed to serve as a public resource regarding the composition and complexity of changing suburbs, challenges and successes in meeting the needs of diverse students, particularly Hispanic students, and mechanisms for bringing about changes in classrooms and schools. The clearinghouse provides information about successful programs, research studies, practice-based instructional methodologies, and methods for strengthening parental involvement. It can be found at www.mville.edu/.

To address *parent education*, CSI offers an annual Hispanic Parents Leadership Institute to help parents learn about the U.S. educational system in order to be more involved in their children's education to promote their children's success, especially with literacy skill development. Hispanic immigrants new to the United States are included in this institute. There also is a follow-up to the annual conference for Hispanic parents to address topics related to, for example, children with special needs and expectations for college admission. The parent conferences are held entirely in Spanish (Wepner, Ferrara, Rainville, Gómez, Lang, & Bigaouette, 2012). These conferences are in addition to the parent outreach initiatives in each of the PDSs that focus on both the Hispanic and non-Hispanic parents.

Although CSI focuses on the suburbs that have seen a rise in the Hispanic population, we understand that the suburbs across the country are facing significant increases in many different racial, ethnic, and cultural groups. This book addresses cultural and linguistic diversity in general, not just changes with the Hispanic population.

DESCRIPTION OF LITERACY LEADERSHIP IN CHANGING SCHOOLS: 10 KEYS TO SUCCESSFUL PROFESSIONAL DEVELOPMENT

Every chapter includes the following:

- A three-bullet anticipation guide that highlights the chapter's major points
- An introductory vignette that describes a situation with a cultural and linguistically diverse student, a literacy leader in a changing school, or a teacher in a classroom. These

vignettes highlight the various roles and responsibilities of literacy leaders as a result of their context, their teachers' professional development needs, and their students' literacy challenges
- Figures, charts, or graphics to support specific ideas and concepts
- A Literacy Leadership Toolkit at the end of each chapter with exercises that include checklists, surveys, leadership activities, assessment charts, questions, and prompts to use for self-assessment when coaching in the classrooms

Chapter 1 (Know and Cultivate Yourself as a Leader) discusses the knowledge, skills, and dispositions that are essential for serving as a literacy leader. Chapter 2 (Know Your Community and Your School) describes important elements for literacy leaders to consider in learning about the complexities of their communities and schools. Chapter 3 (Know Your Teachers) provides ideas for getting to know teachers to provide appropriate professional development. Chapter 4 (Know Your Students) explores ways for literacy leaders to get to know students in general and understand their speaking, listening, reading, and writing abilities. Chapter 5 (Know Professional Development Options) discusses different professional development options that literacy leaders can use to help teachers continue to grow professionally. Chapter 6 (Know the Link Between Curriculum and Standards) offers specific ideas on ways to support teachers to connect standards with curriculum. Chapter 7 (Know Instructional Techniques) discusses how literacy leaders can help teachers use sound instructional practices to support all levels of readers and writers. Chapter 8 (Know Approaches and Programs to Language and Literacy Instruction) provides literacy leaders with essential guidelines for considering programs and approaches for the development of students' language and literacy skills. Chapter 9 (Know Materials and Resources to Support and Deepen Learning) provides direction on ways that literacy leaders can take the lead with the quality of materials and resources that are used in a school. Chapter 10 (Putting It All Together) discusses how literacy leaders can use the information from the preceding nine chapters to provide effective professional development for a K–6 teaching staff.

Clearly, politicians, legislators, and educational spokespersons have brought national attention to the challenges of educating students in urban schools with achievement, language, and socioeconomic pressures, and the need to pour more money and resources into such schools. It now behooves these same nationally prominent individuals to take a hard look at some of the same achievement challenges in changing suburban school districts, especially with diverse students' literacy development, and promote the importance of literacy leadership.

In the meantime, literacy leaders need to help teachers modify their instructional understandings and practices in response to standards to accommodate their changing student population. This book helps prepare literacy leaders to do just that so that today's culturally and linguistically diverse students view themselves as capable, confident literacy learners prepared for tomorrow's real-world demands.

CHAPTER 1

Know and Cultivate Yourself as a Leader

- A literacy leader needs to possess knowledge and skills about literacy in general, be a competent coach, and have the right disposition for the job.
- Leadership inventories and leadership tips (or dos and don'ts) can help literacy leaders self-reflect about their potential strengths and skills for helping teachers develop.
- Literacy leaders benefit from using specific strategies (e.g., environmental scans and differentiated leadership) to promote teachers' professional development.

Morgan wonders how she is going to develop into a literacy leader who can influence the teachers in her K–6 building to change the way they develop students' literacy skills. Having spent 7 years as a 3rd-grade classroom teacher in the same building, she has enjoyed a wonderful relationship with the other teachers. She knows she was selected for this position because of her newly acquired master's degree and reading specialist certification, her students' success on the statewide reading assessment, and her experience with implementing the Common Core State Standards. Although she has had some experience coaching teachers through her university's practicum course, she is very concerned about having to find out through direct observation what her colleagues are really doing, convincing them to change, and working with them to make those changes. Morgan has hunches about her colleagues, based on students' performance and comments by others, but she now is the one responsible for working closely with the teachers and the principal to help improve the overall performance of students in her school. Having just learned that only 30% of her school's students are considered proficient in reading on the new, more rigorous statewide test, she must figure out ways to emerge as a leader who can help her teachers help their students become more proficient with reading.

DEFINITION OF LITERACY LEADER

What does Morgan need to do to emerge as a literacy leader in her school? First and foremost, she needs to gain enough trust from her colleagues so that they allow her to learn about and help them with their instructional practices in relation to student achievement. This is much easier said than done because Morgan's colleagues need to believe she has the ability to do this on their behalf. Morgan must understand herself as a potential leader before she can expect others to accept the idea that her new role can work for them.

A literacy leader usually is credentialed as a reading specialist so that he or she can work with both teachers and administrators to develop and implement curriculum and special initiatives, develop and lead short- and long-term professional development programs, identify and select reading material, evaluate the literacy program in general, assess the reading strengths and needs of students, coordinate the reading and writing program across grade levels, engage in systemic changes that occur across the school or district, and collaborate with various school personnel such as special educators, psychologists, and speech therapists (International Reading Association, 2010). However, literacy leaders do not necessarily have the same credentials or roles and responsibilities because of varying state and national requirements and school and school district interpretations of such professionals.

Nevertheless, one important type of professional development that a literacy leader should provide is *coaching*. Coaching is a form of instruction where there is an ongoing relationship between an experienced and a less experienced person in which the coach provides training, guidance, advice, support, and feedback to the protégé. Coaching helps teachers learn to use new ideas, tools, and strategies, and practice what they learn within their own contexts. Practicing within their own contexts allows teachers to see whether such ideas and techniques are relevant for their unique teaching situations. Literacy leaders' success with coaching seems to occur when they make time in their schedules to be available for collaborative work with teachers, follow clearly established guidelines, and focus on data-driven student learning (Guth & Pettengill, 2005; Rodgers & Rodgers, 2014; Wepner & Quatroche, 2014).

Morgan's success in getting her master's degree and certification means that she has enough knowledge and skills to pass the requisite exams, but it does not necessarily mean that she can apply such knowledge and skills to her current situation. Because of her own set of experiences thus far, she may find she is more comfortable in some areas than others. It is important for her to assess her own knowledge and skills so that she knows in which areas she can truly help teachers. Other literacy leaders need to do the same because, though Morgan may be representative in some ways of literacy leaders, subsequent profiles of literacy leaders in this book will illustrate other roles, skills, and responsibilities.

KNOWLEDGE AND SKILLS ABOUT LITERACY

In order to serve as a competent literacy leader, you should understand the theoretical and evidence-based foundations of reading and writing processes and instruction, know how to use instructional approaches and materials to promote student learning in reading and writing, know how to use a variety of assessment tools and practices to plan and evaluate effective reading and writing instruction, and be able to create a literate environment that fosters reading and writing (International Reading Association, 2010).

The skills that accompany such a knowledge base are numerous. For example, appropriate use of instructional approaches and materials to promote student learning implies that you have experience and expertise in using varied methodologies to develop concepts of print, phonemic awareness, phonics, vocabulary, comprehension, fluency, critical thinking, motivation, and writing. You know how to use a wide range of texts (e.g., narrative, expository, and poetry) that come from traditional print, digital, and online resources (International Reading Association, 2010).

These competencies need to be applied in different ways to accommodate the diversity of abilities, languages, and cultural backgrounds that exist in classrooms. For instance, with the increased number of English learners (ELs), literacy leaders need to help teachers understand the role of first language and culture in learning, how such differences in language and culture affect students' classroom participation, and ways to provide comprehensible instruction for such students so that they can learn to read and write in general and across content areas (Appalachia Regional Comprehensive Center, 2009; Clair, 1993; Linan-Thompson & Vaughn, 2007; Menken & Look, 2000; Walqui, 1999).

It is daunting to think about the wide array of knowledge and skills that a literacy leader should possess. It actually is nearly impossible for any one person to know and be able to do everything imagined. Take Morgan from the opening vignette, who has current knowledge about the field and has practiced certain skills along the way. Her experiences have been with 3rd-graders only. She knows what her 2nd-grade teacher colleagues are doing to prepare the students for 3rd grade, and she knows what she needed to do to prepare the students for 4th grade with word analysis, fluency, vocabulary, and reading comprehension; however, she has had little experience with the other grades in her building. She does not really have in-depth knowledge of their curriculum standards, and she has not used their instructional materials to meet such standards. Morgan also knows that, as successful as she has been, she has been somewhat frustrated by her ability to use cutting-edge technology tools with her students.

Morgan's situation typifies most literacy leaders' experiences, capabilities, and interests. Even veteran literacy leaders, with years of experience working with students and teachers from different grade levels and content areas, cannot keep up with the changes in curriculum standards, assessment instruments, instructional materials, and technological innovations, let alone the changing student population.

Your first step as a literacy leader is to acknowledge what you know, what you need to learn, what can be postponed, and what can be delegated. A self-assessment checklist can help you take stock of your knowledge and skills (Coskie, Robinson, Riddle Buly, & Egawa, 2005). Figure 1.1 provides an example of such a tool that can help you determine areas of strength and areas in need of development.

COMPETENCIES WITH COACHING

In addition to possessing knowledge and skills about literacy in general, you must also be a competent coach to help teachers achieve specific professional development goals. As a literacy leader, you need to know how to observe, model, and provide feedback about instruction. You should be able to co-plan and co-teach lessons, assist teachers in analyzing student work and identifying instructional resources, facilitate team meetings, conduct teacher study groups or teacher book clubs, make professional development presentations for teachers, and be able to reflect on and adapt your own practices so that others learn how to do the same (International Reading Association, 2004). Figure 1.2 provides a checklist of items to consider.

Figure 1.1. Self-Assessment Checklist of Literacy Knowledge and Skills

	Strong	Developing	Not Yet Developing
Theory and research			
Standards and curriculum			
Common Core State Standards			
Instructional approaches			
Instructional materials			
Multicultural literature			
Formative and summative assessment			
Program evaluation			
Data-driven instruction			
Language acquisition			
Differentiating instruction			
Response to Intervention			
Grouping practices			
Technology integration			
English learners			
Special-needs students			
Parent outreach			

Morgan's experience with coaching activities has been limited to her work in a practicum course. When she took the self-assessment in Figure 1.2, she discovered that she has had limited experiences with teacher observation, co-planning, locating resources, providing supportive feedback, facilitating team meetings, conducting study groups, and making professional presentations. She has not had any experience at all with co-teaching and conducting demonstration lessons. To gain credibility with her teachers, she knows that she must engage in her own professional development to further develop her coaching experiences by observing and working with more experienced leaders. Engaging in your own professional development communicates interest in self-growth and serves as an important message for teachers about the importance of self-reflection.

Figure 1.2. Self-Assessment Checklist of Coaching Competencies

	Strong	Developing	Not Yet Developing
Teacher observation			
Co-planning and co-teaching			
Demonstration lessons			
Locating resources			
Providing supportive feedback			
Facilitating team meetings			
Conducting study groups			
Making professional presentations			

DISPOSITION FOR LEADERSHIP

Even with knowledge of literacy and competencies with coaching, a leader will not be effective without the appropriate disposition for the job. Think about it. Effective literacy leaders are supposed to be able to facilitate collaborative dialogue with teachers, work alongside teachers to help them increase their capacity to meet students' needs, and be supportive rather than evaluative (Shanklin, 2006). Effective literacy leaders are expected to create trusting relationships, encourage multiple perspectives, be flexible, and foster learning communities that help teachers feel safe in exposing their concerns, challenges, and anxieties with their own teaching skills and abilities (Coskie, Robinson, Riddle Buly, & Egawa, 2005). They need to know how to communicate with teachers that it is okay to experiment, even if it does not work out exactly as planned, so that teachers have a growth mindset, rather than a fixed mindset, when it comes to changing the way they teach (Dweck, 2006; Kelly, 2013). Effective literacy leaders also must work closely and collaboratively with their principals, vice principals, and other school-based teacher leaders to build a culture of literacy within the school and the community. It is important for the literacy leader to work with the principal, who sets the tone for the school, to contribute to the type of message about literacy that is being communicated.

A literacy leader's disposition comprises his or her professional attitudes, values, and the beliefs that he or she demonstrates through both verbal and nonverbal behaviors, which define his or her character and orientation toward working with others. Research on effective leaders makes reference to disposition and an ability to work well with others. One study, for example, found that interpersonal/negotiating skills were the most frequently used skills in day-to-day interactions with others, especially the ability to work closely with others (Wepner, Clark Johnson, Henk, & Lovell, 2013).

Leadership Inventories

Some believe that one's ability to work well with others is inborn, while others believe that it can be developed. Leadership inventories exist to measure whether someone has the right disposition, temperament, or emotional acumen to be in a job that requires interpersonal interaction or work in team settings.

The Myers-Briggs Type Indicator® (MBTI) is one type of inventory designed to measure psychological preferences in how people perceive the world and make decisions. It is based on the work of Jung (1971), a Swiss psychiatrist and psychotherapist, who theorized about the principal psychological functions by which we experience the world (Myers, McCaulley, Quenk, & Hammer, 1998). The questionnaire includes 93 forced-choice questions that require an individual to choose one of two possible answers. The choices are a mixture of word pairs and short statements that reflect opposite preferences on the same dichotomy. Examples of questions include:

Are you usually:
  □ a "good mixer," or □ rather quiet and reserved?

Do you more often let:
  □ your heart rule your head, or
  □ your head rule your heart?

Examples of word pairs include:

| □ private | □ orderly | □ make | □ strong-willed |
| □ open | □ easygoing | □ create | □ tenderhearted |

Results indicate a person's preference for how one focuses on the world—Extraversion (E) or Introversion (I); how one focuses on basic information—Sensing (S) or Intuition (N); how one makes decisions—Thinking (T) or Feeling (F); and how one deals with the outside world—Judging (J) or Perceiving (P). A person is identified with one of 16 personality types that use the eight possible preferences (Briggs & Myers, 1998).

When Morgan took the questionnaire, she found that her preferred choices reflected an ENTJ (Extroversion Intuition Thinking Judging). In other words, she sees herself as decisive and able to assume leadership readily. She is quick to see illogical and inefficient procedures and policies, and is oriented to developing and implementing comprehensive systems to solve organizational problems. She enjoys long-term planning and goal setting, is usually well informed, and enjoys expanding her knowledge and passing it on to others (Myers & Briggs Foundation, n.d.).

Emotional Intelligence Inventories

Morgan also took a very short emotional intelligence inventory that has been adapted from a number of sources (e.g., Sterrett, 2001; Wilkins-Fontenot, n.d.) to engage in a thinking exercise with six main constructs of emotional intelligence (EI): self-awareness, self-confidence, self-control, empathy, motivation, and social competency. Morgan's score indicated that she has high emotional intelligence. However, she did discover that she could strengthen her social competency a bit by practicing making presentations in front of groups, conducting meetings, and figuring out ways to persuade others to adopt her point of view. She also found that, though she was able to engage with others, she was not sure whether she could read how others perceive her.

Much of the work on EI was popularized by Goleman (1995, 2004), who identified a wide array of competencies and skills that drive leadership performance. Although other theories exist (see, for example, Petrides, 2010), Goleman defines emotional intelligence as a combination of self-management and relationship skills. Self-management skills refer to self-awareness, self-regulation, and motivation. Relationship skills refer to empathy and social skill. Goleman believes these emotional competencies are not innate talents, but rather learned capabilities that can be developed. He and his colleagues (Goleman, Boyatzis, & McKee, 2004; Goleman, McKee, & Boyatzis, 2002; McKee, Boyatzis, & Johnston, 2008) have shown that leaders can develop emotional intelligence and serve as resonant leaders who are attuned to the needs of the people they lead, and able to create conditions where their people can excel. This is especially important for leaders in education whose success in classrooms, schools, and communities depends on their ability to inspire and motivate others (Mitch, 2014).

Morgan used these self-assessments to identify terms and descriptions about her own unique leadership approaches, strengths, and needed improvements. For example, she became aware that she is oriented toward solving organizational problems through planning and goal setting, yet she needs to take a step back to figure out ways to get others on board through team meetings and presentations so that they too embrace such changes. She found that these inventories served as the impetus for self-reflection.

STRATEGIES FOR USING LEADERSHIP ABILITIES TO PROMOTE TEACHERS' PROFESSIONAL DEVELOPMENT

Initial self-assessments of knowledge, skills, and disposition help to determine realistic expectations for leadership potential. Follow-up self-assessments, which take into account changes in abilities, beliefs, and experiences, help gauge current and future expectations. Morgan learned there is a lot that she needs to do before she is ready to walk into a classroom to do a demonstration lesson or help her colleagues with technology. She also came to realize that she is able to home in on the school's needs, yet must work on her ability to persuade others to do what she believes is the right thing for the school. Her self-assessment prompted her to communicate to her principal the areas in which she could help immediately, which contributed to her credibility with both him and the teachers.

Along with knowledge of self, literacy leaders need knowledge of the school and community. Leaders' ability to become successful change agents emanates from their recognition that leadership does not happen in a vacuum. Rather, leaders seek to know and understand their school in relation to the community. They use this knowledge to provide differentiated direction for their stakeholders and monitor progress frequently and comprehensively. Leaders can use six strategies to promote teachers' professional development, including environmental scans; collaborative goals and objectives; manageable plans; differentiated leadership; incentives and opportunities; and progress monitoring and self-reflection.

Engage in Environmental Scans to Understand the School

Environmental scans can help literacy leaders determine the direction and goals of a school's literacy program by gathering and analyzing both factual and subjective information about the internal and external environment. (Pashiardis, 1996; Popovics, 1990; Wepner et al., 2012). One type of scan is a SWOT (Strengths, Weaknesses, Opportunities, Threats) analysis, which is a framework for analyzing a community's strengths, weaknesses, opportunities, and threats. Developed by Albert Humphrey, SWOT analysis enables a leader to use a readily available inventory of contextually based needs to plan strategically for an organization. Figure 1.3 identifies questions typically asked during a SWOT analysis (Immigrate to Manitoba, Canada, n.d.; Wepner, 2011; Wepner et al., 2012).

A SWOT analysis for a changing suburban school could reveal the perceived strengths and weaknesses of a school and, more important, what is helping and holding back teachers from helping all their students achieve at acceptable levels. An example of a SWOT analysis that Morgan and her principal conducted with the teaching staff appears in Figure 1.4. This SWOT helped the staff see clearly that they work with dedicated colleagues, have help from a local university, and have put into practice certain programs that are beginning to succeed. They also came to realize that, with increasing numbers of diverse students, they need to better understand how to reach out to more students and their parents; otherwise, they face the possibility of seeing their colleagues fired because of unacceptable achievement gains. This analysis helped the staff better understand what needed to be done in relation to what already had been accomplished. This analysis also helped Morgan begin to have a big picture of the school from the teachers' perspectives.

Use Environmental Scans as a Springboard for Collaborative Goals and Objectives

Teachers' perceptions of their school can provide the impetus for further planning that capitalizes on strengths and opportunities while addressing weaknesses and threats. The SWOT example from Figure 1.4 reveals that even with the many interesting opportunities in the school for students' literacy development, the teachers do not necessarily work together within or across grade levels, have not had sufficient professional development on the Common Core State Standards

Figure 1.3. Questions for a SWOT Analysis

Strengths	Weaknesses
• What does your school do well? • What unique resources do you have? • What do others see as your strengths?	• What could you improve? • Where do you have fewer resources than other schools? • What do others see as your weaknesses?
Opportunities	Threats
• What good opportunities are available to you? • What trends would you take advantage of? • How can you turn your strengths into opportunities?	• What trends could affect you negatively? • What are other schools doing? • How would a weakness be a potential threat?

(CCSS), are not certain how to help their diverse student population, and are threatened by the new statewide teacher evaluation system. In a sense, they continue to do what they had been doing when the school had less diversity and fewer challenges. They need to figure out a way to align their instructional patterns with current expectations for a changing student population.

You can use the SWOT as a springboard for collaborative goal setting, whether for the school, grade level, or discipline. One collaborative technique for goal setting that can be used is *storyboarding.* Borrowed from business, storyboarding is a visual and participatory outlining technique in which key ideas or chunks of information about a topic are physically arranged so they can be reorganized. Storyboarding is essentially a three-step procedure: (1) brainstorming ideas, (2) organizing these ideas, and (3) developing an outline from the ideas. Index cards of different colors and sizes, moved about on a bulletin board or a wall surface, are used to display participants' ideas (Bunch, 1991; Wepner & Seminoff, 1993).

One or two facilitators (the literacy leader, principal, vice principal, teacher leader, or other building or district leader) create three to five questions to guide teachers' brainstorming. The first question can be used to break the ice and the remaining questions form broad topics for discussion and eventual outlining. For example, a first question might be a noted strength from the SWOT. Morgan and her principal used "What qualities make us a dedicated teaching staff?" The remaining questions might come from identified weaknesses, opportunities,

Figure 1.4. Example of a SWOT Analysis in a Changing Suburban K–6 Elementary School

Strengths	Weaknesses
• Dedicated teaching staff • Strong leadership team • Schoolwide incentives to read • After-school tutoring program • Students come from the local university to help with tutoring, small-group instruction, and after-school tutoring program • Part of strong school district with resources for special education and ELs	• ELs' standardized test scores in reading • Lack of knowledge about culturally sensitive curriculum and instruction • Collaborative work across grade levels • Lack of professional development on new standards • Technology • Lack of parent involvement is contributing to achievement gap
Opportunities	Threats
• Phonics-based, multisensory program in K–2 is showing promise • New community outreach coordinator with Hispanic background can help promote parent involvement • New reading program is aligned with the Common Core State Standards • New partnership with local university • Districtwide incentives for professional development	• New statewide teacher evaluation system based on students' standardized reading scores is putting teachers on warning • New principal evaluation system could affect principal's status • Immigrants continue to move into the neighborhood without legal status, knowledge of English, or gainful employment

and threats from the SWOT: "What needs to be done with diverse students' standardized test scores in reading?" "What kinds of professional development do you need to help you implement the Common Core State Standards?" "What kinds of professional development do you need to help you provide culturally sensitive curriculum and instruction?" and "What kind of help do you need with the new statewide teacher evaluation?" See **Online Figure A** for specific information on how to use the storyboarding procedure. [*Editor's note:* The online figures accompanying this book can be found at http://tcpress.com/free_downloads.html]

Consider electronic and web-based tools. Web-based and electronic tools can facilitate the storyboarding technique or a variation of this technique. Two examples of open-ended, web-based brainstorming tools are Bubbl.us (bubbl.us/) and *Gliffy* (www.gliffy.com). Two examples of web-based libraries of ready-made templates for brainstorming are *Exploratree* (www.exploratree.org.uk/) and *Freeology* (freeology.com/graphicorgs/). Additionally, literacy leaders can create templates from open-ended software programs such as PowerPoint.

Determine context for gathering information. The context for conducting environmental scans and engaging in collaborative goal setting will depend on the size and culture of the school, the quality of administrative leadership, and teachers' level of receptivity to participation. Some K–6 schools are small enough for the entire staff to participate together, especially when there is overall teacher support for and interest in collaborative planning. Other schools simply are too big or disparate in viewpoints to participate as a whole group. In such cases, different groups can be brought together at different times to engage in brainstorming. Morgan was fortunate to be able to work with her principal, a highly respected and energetic administrator, to co-facilitate the storyboarding technique with the entire teaching staff because her school is the smallest in the district, with only three teachers per grade level. Her colleague in another school in the district had to do it in clusters (K–2, 3–6, special education) because of the school's size.

Develop Manageable Plans for Professional Development

You can use information from environmental scans and collaborative goal setting to develop an annual plan that is manageable and doable. The key is to start small. Acknowledge that you simply cannot accomplish the many goals and objectives that teachers and administrators have for themselves, their classrooms, and the school all at once. Success with a select group and project helps set the tone for future endeavors. For instance, you can start by helping one 3rd-grade teacher learn how to use flexible grouping patterns with students or assisting the 1st-grade teachers in using a multisensory phonics-based reading program that was purchased for the school. You can then, for instance, work with the 2nd-grade teachers the following year to use the multisensory phonics reading program so that there is continuity with students' instruction.

Morgan and her principal determined from their school's SWOT and storyboarding that her first steps should be working with the

three 5th-grade teachers because of students' below-average standardized test scores, challenges in preparing students for the middle
school, and teachers' issues with working with their increased EL population. Their willingness to be coached on ways to learn how to use
the school's new reading program to help with student achievement
was an important finding for her. Morgan worked with the teachers as
a group and individually to develop a grade-level and individualized
coaching plan that could be accomplished during the year. See Chapter 5 for a description of different types of professional development
opportunities that could work for you as a literacy leader.

Practice Differentiated Leadership

Differences in teachers' strengths and weaknesses must be taken into
account in developing and implementing a professional development
plan. Such differences might be obvious immediately or may become
apparent with time. Differentiated leadership is similar to differentiated instruction in that the literacy leader is able to *scaffold* assistance
so that it is offered where that teacher is functioning and adjusted
accordingly to help reach learning milestones. For example, Morgan's
5th-grade teachers have the same issues in their classrooms because
the students are assigned heterogeneously; however, they are functioning at different levels with the new reading program, from serious
confusion with the menu-like options to full use with fidelity. Their
response to ELs also is very different, from resistance to the changes in
their classroom to an appreciation of a diverse student body. Differentiated leadership in the form of coaching must use multiple strategies
and approaches to accommodate individual needs so that the teachers
can make progress with their development (Nichols, 2010).

Approach Professional Development as an Incentive
and Opportunity

Work with your principal to help him or her recognize that teachers, as professionals, should be compensated for expending additional
time and energy to acquire new knowledge and skills. Such incentives
might include financial rewards; compensation time; opportunities
to attend conferences, symposia, and workshops; visitations to other
classrooms in others schools and districts; coursework covered by the
district; additional assistants for the classroom; or funds to purchase
resources for the classroom. These incentives communicate that professional development is not just additional work, but rather a highly

regarded chance to take advantage of a school's or district's resources to develop on behalf of students.

As expressed earlier, leaders need to demonstrate that they are willing to engage in different types of professional development opportunities (e.g., coaching, conference attendance, classroom visitations, and coursework) to function as effectively as possible. Morgan made arrangements with her principal to work with two 5th-grade teachers in another building who believe that students should read and learn through the Internet to develop "new literacies" (Leu, Forzani, & Kennedy, 2014). Morgan learned how to create a classroom wiki, which is a collaboratively developed and updated website. (Go to evansgradefive.wicomico.wikispaces.net/ for an example.) She also learned how to create a classroom blog, which is a discussion or informational site published on the web that includes discrete entries or posts. (Go to mesmrswhitesclass.blogspot.com/ for an example.) Morgan also observed how these teachers are using the SMART Board to teach literacy skills and iPads to develop specific skills with individual students. These professional development opportunities enabled Morgan to speak intelligently about ways that her 5th-grade teachers could use technology in their classrooms.

Monitor Progress and Self-Reflect

As you help teachers help their students achieve, become familiar with and document teachers' efforts, progress, and frustrations to understand teachers' frame of mind and possible next steps. One of Morgan's 5th-grade teachers, Mr. Hilon, is now fully comfortable working jointly with the push-in teacher for ELs, and engaging ELs in follow-up instruction. However, he continues to struggle with his grouping patterns for his ELs and non-ELs. On the other hand, after 4 months of individual coaching sessions, Mrs. Theo, another 5th-grade teacher, still does not want to be responsible for teaching ELs because she is concerned that the majority of students in her classroom will suffer as she takes time away from them to focus on engaging her ELs. She still believes that she is not responsible for children who cannot speak English. Each teacher needs something different, and Morgan needs to figure out how to work with each of them.

Documentation through notebooks or journaling on a daily, weekly, biweekly, or monthly basis captures the actions taken, teachers' responses to such actions, and your own responses to such actions. A careful analysis of the patterns revealed through documentation can indicate the degree to which changes can be made with professional development. For example, Morgan can have some impact on Mr. Hilon because his challenge is more organizational than attitudinal. On the other hand, Mrs. Theo's belief system is interfering with her ability to take responsibility for her entire class of students. Share your documentation with your principal and administrative team to engage in collaborative problem solving on behalf of teachers who are having difficulty in making essential instructional shifts.

Take the time to document your own progress as a leader. Self-reflection, or careful thought about your behaviors and beliefs, helps enlighten you about what you do and why you do it. It helps you take a step back from the daily routine to study what you are doing well and what you need to change or improve. Self-reflection enables you to analyze your successes or failures in relation to your context. There are many ways to engage in self-reflection: journals, blogs, chat rooms, peer discussions and feedback, videotaping, performance evaluations, questionnaires, focus groups, think-alouds, and self-charting. Figure 1.5 offers a charting exercise that Morgan used to record what transpired during a small-group meeting with Mrs. Theo and her principal. This self-charting tool documents solved and unsolved issues, lessons learned, and recommendations for the future (Wepner, Henk, & Lovell, 2015).

DOS AND DON'TS OF LEADERSHIP

As you provide professional development for your teachers, there are some leadership tips that can help you thrive in your role. The dos and don'ts below come from our own experiences in schools and school districts.

The Dos

Do analyze your leadership behaviors in relation to the context. Use findings from your leadership inventories and self-reflective exercises to determine when you use different leadership styles for providing direction, implementing plans, and motivating those in your building or district. While in the classroom, your style could have been more authoritarian in order to keep close control over students' behaviors and achievements. As you work with teachers, you probably vary your leadership style in different situations. While working with individual and small groups of teachers, you might use a coaching

Figure 1.5. Example of Chart to Use for Self-Reflection

Purpose and Date	People Involved	Resolved Issues/ Accomplishments	Unresolved Issues	Lessons Learned	Recommendations for Future
Help Mrs. Theo change her attitude about working with ELs November 16	Mrs. Theo, Principal Morgan	Recognized the legitimacy of Mrs. Theo's concerns, given her history in the school and her previous success with students

Helped Mrs. Theo understand how the principal made class assignments, and how he gave her the fewest numbers of ELS in the 5th grade because of his concern for her resistance

Helped Mrs. Theo understand the additional services provided to her students and her responsibilities in relation to these services

Provided Mrs. Theo with a list of expectations on behalf of the students

Explained ways in which Morgan can offer assistance | Concerned that Mrs. Theo simply gave lip service to the principal

Uncertain whether Mrs. Theo will change her attitude or will take advantage of my offer for professional development

Uncertain how Mrs. Theo will respond to me now that I have involved the principal | Cannot assume that my once-friendly colleague will be responsive to my suggested professional development offerings

Need to be more open-minded and understanding of my colleague teachers who resist change because they have their reasons

Cannot impose my beliefs onto other teachers, and must meet them where they are

Need to listen to what my colleagues are saying so that I can figure out how to meet them where they are | Need to figure out ways in the future to handle these types of situations without involving the principal

Will offer to work with her group of ELs to show her how doable it is for her to work with them in conjunction with the EL teacher who pushes into her classroom

Will offer to sit with her to adapt her lessons so that they can work with her ELs

Will make arrangements for her to visit other 5th-grade classrooms with similar student configurations, and will make arrangements to take her to a conference to help get ideas |

style to help your colleagues build lasting pedagogical strengths or an affiliative style to create bonds with the teachers to build trust. As you lead meetings, you might use a democratic style to build consensus and teacher ownership, a pacesetting style to get teachers to act quickly on ideas that already have been vetted and agreed upon, or a coercive style that demands compliance because all else has failed (Goleman, 2000). Acknowledge and capitalize on leadership styles that work in relation to the climate, outcome expectations, opportunities for interactions (e.g., one-on-one, teams, small groups, or large groups), and frequency of interactions (e.g., daily, biweekly, weekly, bimonthly, or monthly).

Do have the courage to keep leading. Once you are in a leadership position, be prepared for criticism. Having a thick skin is critical for survival in leadership positions. Although it can be difficult to not take things personally, which others will admonish you to do, try to figure out ways to help yourself understand that you simply are a scapegoat for others' frustrations. When you can maintain your own level of professionalism and stand up for what you know is right, you can transcend the most frustrating and hurtful moments. The owner of the Brooklyn Dodgers, Branch Rickey, had the right idea when he said to Jackie Robinson, the first-ever African American baseball player of the mid-20th century, that he wanted a player who had the guts *not* to fight back, and to turn the other cheek to racist comments on the field and in the country (Helgeland, 2013). This is what leadership is all about: the ability to keep moving in the face of the mightiest challenges.

Do recognize individuals' potential for growth. If leadership is about bringing out the best in others, it means you need to see others' potential for growth. If you focus on others' deficiencies ("She is not organized" or "He is too harsh with his low achievers"), you will not be able to see the good ("She has wonderful rapport with her students" or "He is helping his students achieve"). Teachers want to succeed with their students. Some may communicate otherwise or behave differently, but that is probably for reasons beyond your control. If you decide to use your discoveries about your teachers to identify and take advantage of their good qualities, chances are you will eventually meet with success.

Do be open-minded and communicative. The ability to see the good in others stems from an open-mindedness toward diverse viewpoints, attitudes, and behaviors. You need a willingness to listen to, observe, and accept different ways in which teachers and administrators interpret their situations and responsibilities. Similarly, you want others to be open to what you bring to your leadership role so they are willing to be responsive to your suggestions. When you communicate frequently, clearly, and convincingly about pertinent topics for the teachers and the school—from the most mundane scheduling issue to interesting new sources of funding for classrooms—you are reminding them that (1) you exist, and (2) you are there to help make their lives easier and better. Use a mix of methods such as email, texting, face-to-face exchanges and meetings, telephone conversations, websites, and written notes to ensure that information is shared and dialogues take place regularly about challenges, possibilities, and accomplishments. The more you communicate, the easier it will be to convince your colleagues to move toward common goals that help the students and the school.

The Don'ts

Don't display favoritism. Those being led naturally have their antenna up for disparities in treatment. They know when one of their peers is getting more resources, assistance, and attention. Resentments build and spread against those favored and the leader who is showing favoritism. Those favored also can end up at odds with peers, which can impede progress. Leaders naturally gravitate toward people who share similar beliefs, approaches, likes, and dislikes. However, as a leader, it is important to do your best not to play favorites. Look for traits in others that are appealing so that you communicate to them and others the many ways in which you value their existence and contributions to the school's vitality.

Don't let others dictate your roles and responsibilities. Even with a job description that includes explicit roles and responsibilities, leaders often have a good deal of wiggle room in how they spend their time and energy. Teachers, administrative staff, and parents will have views on what should be accomplished, how something should be accomplished, and when it should be accomplished. Accompanying these views are directives, declarations, and invitations to respond to their views. Stay focused on and balanced with what you believe must be done, based on the information you have gathered from your environmental scans and collaboratively established goals and objectives. Otherwise, you are bound to be disappointed with the outcomes.

Don't stop gathering data. Making assumptions is something we all do in many areas of our lives. An assumption is something taken for granted or accepted as true without proof. A principal tells us that one of the teachers teaches without reference to students' achievement, and we assume that the principal is correct. A teacher tells us that a student's misbehavior stems from his dysfunctional family, and we believe it. Although it is difficult to question others' claims, promises, and declarations, sometimes it is important to do just that in order to have accurate information for responding appropriately to a situation. Otherwise, you are the one who can get into trouble with teachers, the administration, and parents. Don't even assume what appear to be the most trivial assertions such as "The books were ordered" or "The faculty meeting will be canceled next week" without checking into the facts and with sources that can confirm or deny such statements.

Don't allow disappointments to affect your sense of purpose. Successful leaders do not give up. Regardless of obstacles along the way, they persist with what they need to do. They have a mindset that change is constant: What might seem impossible one day may become highly probable days, months, or even years later. Successful leaders abide by the essence of a quote attributed to Calvin Coolidge (1872–1933), the 30th president of the United States, that nothing in the world—not even talent, genius, or education—can take the place of persistence. The idea to "press on" has solved and will solve whatever problems exist.

ENVISION THE POSSIBILITIES

Fast-forward 5 years. Morgan epitomizes someone who has persisted. She continues to be the school's literacy leader, and has grown beyond her own expectations in truly being able to help her teachers. She has managed to get invited by the teachers into every classroom. As a result, Morgan has expanded her understanding of teachers' responsibilities at each grade level, and has had opportunities to co-teach and conduct demonstration lessons in many of these classrooms. All but two teachers have been receptive to her help. Mrs. Theo still refuses to change the way she teaches, and still harbors resentment toward the changing student population. The principal is working with the district to help her take an early retirement package. The other teacher has resisted any help and, among other areas, is having trouble with flexible grouping strategies to differentiate instruction. Morgan is working with the principal to bring in a literacy leader from a different school to work with the second resistant teacher for about a month. In exchange, Morgan will spend time at the other school to help with one of their projects.

Otherwise, Morgan is pleased with the teachers' growth. They are working much more collaboratively across grade levels on developing culturally sensitive instructional plans for ELs. They are using new communication strategies to engage parents of ELs, and are helping with workshops and programs for these parents. Morgan appreciates the ways in which the teachers have addressed some of the weaknesses identified in the original SWOT, yet she is acutely aware that the same threats related to students' standardized test scores and teachers' evaluations remain. The teachers continue to inch their way to higher pass rates, but they get discouraged when they see so many low scores, which they did not see a decade ago.

Morgan still struggles with her roles and responsibilities almost daily. She struggles with the disparity between what the state expects and what can be realistically delivered with students' achievement. She struggles with the differences between her own expectations for her teachers and what they can realistically deliver. She also struggles to balance what she wishes she could be as a leader with what she can realistically provide. Even with Morgan's perceived struggles, she has come to appreciate that the essence of her job is to constantly figure out how to keep up with and help others with changing conditions, opportunities, and expectations. Morgan also recognizes that an important part of her job is to envision the possibilities for creating optimum conditions in the school for teachers' professional development and students' achievement. She works daily to address existing challenges as she strives for possible opportunities that will ultimately improve the school.

As was the case with Morgan, your vigilance in identifying and realizing possibilities as you address challenges is your ticket to a successful leadership journey. Although it is not easy to be a literacy leader at the school or district level, it is remarkably rewarding when you have the wherewithal to be honest with yourself about what you can and cannot accomplish in relation to your colleagues, students, and community.

KNOW YOUR IMPACT ON TEACHERS

An effective literacy leader has the intellectual, social, and psychological capital to help teachers believe in and act on principles that contribute to students' success. Effective leadership is not about magic or magnetism, but rather about the way you give daily, positive, and caring attention to those you lead. As with effective teaching, there is no formula for effective leadership. It is about the interaction of the leader and the teacher in relation to the school environment. The most important step for becoming an effective leader is to have the courage to take a good hard look at your knowledge, skills, and disposition. This self-assessment provides an important anchor for making decisions about realistic and potential strategies that you can pursue within the context of your school environment. It also serves as an important modeling tool for teachers so that they too are willing to assess their own instructional strengths and weaknesses in relation to students' achievement. If you as a literacy leader are effective with teachers, chances are your teachers will be effective with their students. This chapter has provided different ideas and strategies for helping bring this to fruition.

LITERACY LEADERSHIP TOOLKIT

The three exercises below help you assess yourself as a leader by determining what you like and do not like, identifying ways to change, and demonstrating ways in which you have indeed changed. Take your time in realizing the kinds of changes that you want to make.

Exercise 1.1: Mirror, Mirror

Look at yourself in the mirror. What do you see? Use the items below to determine your leadership potential or create your own list of items to reflect on your leadership abilities.

Know my stuff	Most of the Time	Sometimes	Rarely
Like what I do	Most of the Time	Sometimes	Rarely
Enjoy people	Most of the Time	Sometimes	Rarely
Confident to make a difference	Most of the Time	Sometimes	Rarely
Have the right personality for the job	Most of the Time	Sometimes	Rarely
Good at negotiating with others	Most of the Time	Sometimes	Rarely
Know what I'm supposed to do	Most of the Time	Sometimes	Rarely

Willing to take risks	Most of the Time	Sometimes	Rarely
Willing to change the way I do things	Most of the Time	Sometimes	Rarely

Exercise 1.2: "I CAN"

Identify the items from Mirror, Mirror for which you circled "Rarely." Generate three "I CAN" (Au, Raphael, & Mooney, 2008) statements that will enable you to change. For example, if you circled that you are rarely willing to take risks, you might write:

- "I CAN" take risks with the kinds of comments that I make to teachers about their teaching to help them improve.
- "I CAN" take risks by pushing myself to speak in front of the whole school about new literacy goals.
- "I CAN" take risks by encouraging the principal to buy more technology for the school.

Exercise 1.3: "I DID" Challenge

Create an "I DID" chart that addresses your "I CAN" statements, as shown below. Return to your Mirror, Mirror exercise to change your "Rarely" to a "Sometimes" or "Most of the Time." Repeat this cycle of three exercises as often as needed until you are satisfied with what you see in yourself as a leader.

Challenge	Target	Activities
Take Risks	Teachers	• Collected comparison data of students' test scores for teachers • Made simple suggestions after every lesson • Videotaped teachers so that they could see for themselves their teaching practices
	Public Speaking	• Created monthly schedule to speak • Practiced speaking in front of a mirror • Created notecards with big print to help jog my memory
	Principal and Technology	• Demonstrated new technologies to principal • Showed principal students' responses • Prepared 3-year technology budget plan

CHAPTER 2

Know Your Community and Your School

- Literacy leaders need to know the community of their school in order to provide appropriate literacy instruction.
- Collaboration and partnerships with the community foster literacy within and outside the school walls.
- Successful community partnerships for literacy develop through data collection and collaborative planning.

Amy, a classroom teacher, and Suzanne, their suburban district's coordinator for English learners, pored over the DIAL-3 scores used to screen the literacy readiness skills of the incoming kindergarten class. The pattern they had seen in the past was occurring again. A gap persisted between the scores of English-speaking students who attended a prekindergarten program and those whose first language is not English, but Spanish, who did not attend a pre-K program. Embracing the concept that all parents want the best for their children, Amy and Suzanne developed a plan, the Kindergarten-Providing Academic Skills and Strategies (K-PASS) program. They received a mini-grant of $1,500 from their district's Staff Development Center to offer three parent workshops on family literacy strategies and three workshops for students, and to purchase bilingual academic supplies and materials. They invited the Hispanic parents whose children scored below the 30th percentile on the DIAL-3 subtest when screened at kindergarten registration in the spring to a series of workshops in June on literacy. Amy and Suzanne gave the workshops in Spanish, and encouraged the parents to use specific reading readiness strategies during the summer, and in the language they felt most comfortable. When the students entered kindergarten that September, the DIAL-3 scores of the children who participated in the K-PASS program improved 67% (Gómez, Lang, & Lasser, 2010).

This vignette indicates that Amy and Suzanne intuitively and intellectually understood the needs of their school's community. They knew that the lower scores of Spanish-speaking incoming kindergartners had little to do with intelligence or lack of native language skills. They realized that the discrepancy had to do with knowledge and use of their second language, English. In a grassroots effort to diminish the gap between native speakers of English and those for whom English is a second or third language, they invited Hispanic parents to collaborate with them in developing their children's literacy skills.

CHANGING SCHOOLS AND CHANGING STUDENT POPULATIONS

Today's educational climate is changing on several fronts, from curricular mandates to student demographics. Our schools must keep abreast of these changes in order to serve our students well.

Amy and Suzanne were experiencing a changing student population in their district. The number of states reporting that at least 20% of their kindergarten population is Latino has risen from eight states in 2000 to 17 states in 2012. Additionally, it is projected that by 2060 Hispanics will make up 31% of the overall U.S. population (Korgstad, 2014). Student demographics are changing across our nation regardless of locale—north, east, south, west, urban, suburban, or rural. Our nation has had to address the complications associated with a unique immigrant population of undocumented and unaccompanied children from Central America who are crossing the U.S.-Mexican border (Korgstad, 2014; Korgstad, Gonzalez-Barrera, & Lopez, 2014). The state of Ohio exemplifies trends occurring nationally. The state's economy depends on rural farming communities and large manufacturing cities. To remain stable as the global economy changes, Ohio's schools must develop a highly educated workforce. With the changing demographics of a 10% decline in Caucasian students and a corresponding 9% increase in Hispanic and Asian students, Ohio's schools are suddenly confronted with a highly diverse student population (Robison, 2014). Historically, the students who belong to the newest demographic groups experience educational achievement gaps and employment inequalities. They are less likely to complete high school, receive a college degree, or be employed in a professional field. School leaders can respond to the rich, multilingual, and multicultural diversity change in their schools by aligning teaching methodology to the students' changing assets and needs (Keller, 2012).

As a literacy leader, you and your teachers are coming face-to-face with the challenges, both internal and external, of our changing schools and changing students. Internal pressures are those encountered within the school district: district curriculum, district programming, district scheduling, district and school leaders, teachers, support staff, and students. External pressures come from outside the school district: parents and the community, local budgets, and state and national standards and educational mandates. As school and district leaders, you must comply with legal, union, and budgetary regulations as well as encourage collaboration among all other members of the school community.

TAKING STOCK OF YOUR CHANGING COMMUNITY AND SCHOOL

To face the challenges you encounter inside and outside the school walls, it is critical to take stock of the literacy resources your school and community have to offer. However, you can save valuable time and energy by first completing Exercise 2.1 in the Literacy Leadership Toolkit at the end of this chapter. This community needs assessment can be used in conjunction with the SWOT analysis discussed in Chapter 1. A community needs assessment of literacy is a systematic study of what your community knows about literacy, its attitudes toward literacy, its opinions about literacy, and its interest in literacy. A needs assessment can be direct and formal, or indirect and informal in design (McCawley, 2009). The assessment helps pinpoint areas of concern about literacy, not only for those working in the school, but also for other members of the community such as parents, business leaders, and taxpayers. These literacy needs could be related to a variety of areas such as student and/or teacher skill sets, curriculum mandates, and budgetary constraints. Although Suzanne and Amy did not conduct a formal needs assessment, they identified the needs of the students in their community. They used students' screening test scores as data, and developed a plan for their success in school. They searched for funding for their project, and found it through the Staff Resource Center, which operates with funds from local and state organizations. Often, partnerships with constituents of the school's community help solve some of the challenges. The potential partnerships are endless.

Teachers

Your teachers are crucial allies in the promotion of literacy skills for your school's students. Teachers serve as the direct link between the students and the literacy curriculum. There are three major considerations when taking stock of your teachers: (1) their knowledge of literacy, (2) their disposition toward literacy, and (3) their literacy pedagogy. Do not assume you know what your teachers know or do not know. Begin by asking yourself: What is their knowledge of literacy, literacy instruction, and literacy material? How do they respond to changes in curriculum, students whose first language is not English, or peers and others observing their teaching? What does literacy "look like" in their classrooms? Chapter 3 explores ways to get to know your teachers in greater detail.

Students

To provide appropriate literacy instruction, as literacy leaders you need to know the students well. Begin looking at your students' literacy strengths. As Genishi (2002) states, "Children who are learning English begin their school lives with their 'language glass' half full, not half empty" (p. 66). Amy and Suzanne realized that their students' strengths were much more than a number on the DIAL-3. All the children in the K-PASS study were developing language and literacy skills, but in Spanish rather than English. Some questions to ask are: Who are your students? What assets do they bring to literacy instruction? What is the language of their literacy assets? It is essential to determine which literacy skills the students already have before planning literacy instruction. Figure 2.1 provides a Student Demographics Chart that can assist in documenting students' characteristics. Chapter 4 offers an in-depth discussion about strategies to use to get to know your students.

Families

The concept and image of what constitutes a family has changed over time. We have moved from the 1960 definition of family as "parents and their children as a group" (Guralnik, 1960, p. 271) to a much broader definition that includes single parents, parents of blended families, same-sex parents, as well as caretakers and guardians in the role of parents. There is no one combination of individuals, language, or

Figure 2.1. Student Demographics Chart

School:

Teacher:

Grade:

Class:

Stu-dent Name	Age	Ethnicity	Lunch	English Profi-ciency	Language Spoken at Home	Read-ing Level	Distance Between Home & School	Main Trans-porta-tion

Source: Adapted from Edwards, 2008

culture that constitutes a family. Thus, in order to guide your teachers to make appropriate decisions about literacy instruction, you want to know the characteristics of your school's families. The Family Demographics Chart (Figure 2.2) is similar to the Student Demographics Chart (Figure 2.1), but with a focus on the family. The information from a completed Family Demographics Chart yields some basic data about the families in the school. Merging student demographics with family demographics develops a demographic school profile, and provides a useful overview of the students and their families (Edwards, 2008).

The Family and Community Engagement (FACE) framework uses knowledge about students and their families to promote family–community relationships. FACE outlines four components of family involvement: (1) student performance, (2) cultural considerations, (3) family beliefs about academic success, and (4) strategies to promote success (Bridges, 2013). Each component warrants careful consideration for literacy leaders as they reach out to their students' families.

Student performance. The first school for young children is family, and parents are powerful models for their children (Honig, 1994). Research shows that when parents are involved in the education of their children, the children do well in school (Fan & Chen, 2001; Lee & Bowen, 2006; LeFevre & Shaw, 2012; Thelamour & Jacobs, 2014). Additionally, parental involvement has been found to be a greater predictor of literacy achievement and development than student ethnicity, family income level, and mother's level of education (Dearing,

Figure 2.2. Family Demographics Chart

School:

Teacher:

Grade:

Class:

Stu- dent Name	Parent/ Care- giver Name(s)	Num- ber of Family Mem- bers	Siblings' Name/ Age/ School	Parent/ Care- giver Level of Education	Lan- guage(s) Spoken by Parent(s)/ Caregiv- er(s)	Parent(s)/ Caregiv- er(s) Em- ployment
			/ /			
			/ /			
			/ /			
			/ /			

Source: Adapted from Edwards, 2008

Kreider, Simpkins & Weiss, 2006; International Reading Association, 2002). Given the impact that families have on the education of their children, it behooves you as a literacy leader to develop a trusting relationship with your students' families to work as partners in the students' education. In fact, literacy leaders in the field strongly endorse the use of parents as partners in the literacy instruction of their child (Allyn, 2012).

The International Reading Association (IRA) developed a position statement to recognize the importance of family–school partnerships (International Reading Association, 2002). The statement emphasizes the need for collaboration between school and family. A first step is for you to assess which of the following four levels of family–school partnership currently exists at your school (Henderson, Mapp, Johnson, & Davies, 2007):

1. ***Partnership school***—We are all-inclusive with families and the community. Everyone works together so all students are successful.

2. ***Open-door school***—Parents have many options for involvement, the community usually responds to our needs, and we are working on even greater participation.

3. **Come-if-we-call school**—Parents can offer little at school, and should come to school only when asked. The parents' role is to work with their children at home.

4. **Fortress school**—Keep the community and parents out of the school. We know what we are doing and it is not the place for others to come in.

What level is your school? Are you content with that level? Do you want to make another level your goal?

Next, you can use a series of critical questions to evaluate the school's polices, practices, and approaches to collaborating with families, with the understanding that one formula does not exist for family involvement. School-level questions relate to the following:

- The school's definition of parental involvement
- The policies related to the roles parents assume
- The perception of parent involvement in policymaking
- The impact of parental involvement on achievement
- The effects of parental involvement on parent and student attitudes
- The most effective characteristics of parental involvement
- The most effective types of parental involvement for your families' ethnic, socioeconomic, and cultural backgrounds (International Reading Association, 2002)

Cultural considerations. There are several considerations to review before reaching out to parents and families, particularly if the families' culture and languages differ from those of the majority of the school population or the teachers of the school. Schools in the United States expect parents to be involved in their children's education. Depending on the culture of the school, this might mean parents are expected to fundraise and compete for prizes, attend parent–teacher organizations, review and help with homework, inform teachers of issues happening at home, bring in cupcakes for birthday parties, respond to calls from the school regarding their child's behavior, and read with their child every night. Such parents often advocate for their children in terms of curriculum, achievement, and behaviors. We have even coined the term *helicopter parents* for those who appear to be overinvolved in their children's education. These are not the expectations or culture of education for many other cultures. For example, in Spanish the expression *bien educado*, which literally translates into English as *well educated*, connotes a different meaning in Spanish. The message is that the person is well mannered and has nothing to do with formal education. Hispanic parents take great pride in raising their children to be *bien educado* (McKeon, 2004; Wepner et al., 2012). Students from the Chinese culture are expected to listen, rather than actively participate and ask questions. While education in the United States is somewhat competitive and individualistic in nature, education in other cultures is collective in nature or, as a result of the political climate, does not foster competition.

During an English language placement test, newly immigrated Russian cousins conferred with one another and shared answers in Russian. The parents were called in and chastised because of their children's "cheating." The parents responded by offering some cash to the principal. In the former Soviet Union, giving money for favors or to resolve problems was often a common solution. The parents did not understand the culture of American education, and tried to resolve the situation as they would have in their native country. If the literacy leader administering the placement test had an awareness of this collective perspective, the cousins' interaction might not have been identified as cheating. The literacy leader could have simply put his or her index finger on his or her lips and separated the cousins for the remainder of the test. Understanding cultural differences can resolve school culture conflicts by ameliorating potential school–home–community tensions, empowering parents with knowledge of school values and rules, and respecting the students' culture.

Well-intended groups, such as parent–teacher organizations, send home school flyers and other written communication in the languages of their student population. Although this acknowledges multilingualism and demonstrates a willingness to include all language groups, it might not meet the goal of communication. The translation is often achieved by asking a native speaker of the language to translate or by using web-based translators. By doing this, there are the assumptions that the translation is accurate and professional, and the parents/families are literate in their native language. Often, the intent of the message is lost in translation. Some cultures, such as many indigenous cultures, do not have a written language, or the family may speak a dialect of the first language. Other means of communication such as face-to-face conversations, open forums with translators, or language-specific parent mentors might be more effective to engage a culturally diverse community.

A new approach to engaging families in South Texas is PTA Comunitarios. Funded through a U.S. Department of Education's Investing in Innovation (I3) grant, PTA Comunitarios represent a shift in PTA's traditional role of holding parent meetings once a month for the basic purpose of fundraising. The Comunitarios are a new model of family leadership to enhance authentic outreach to the community in order to engage parents to explore important academic issues at the grassroots level. Authentic outreach is not a once-a-month meeting with one person speaking to an audience. It is face-to-face, regular, and consistent communication where partners listen to concerns of the community, identify needs, and collaborate on solutions. The focus is how we—family, school, and community—work together for academic success. In the Comunitarios model, meetings are:

- conducted in the language of the families—in this case, Spanish;
- attended by all those who have a stake in the students' education—parents, siblings, relatives, neighbors;
- participatory in nature, with group projects such as going to school board's open meeting; and
- led through shared leadership among members.

Additionally, projects do not involve fundraising. Transportation networks are developed, and engagement is fostered by home visitors called *promotoras* (Intercultural Development Research Association, 2014; Montemayor, 2013).

Amy and Suzanne's K-PASS program at the beginning of the chapter has many of the same elements as Comunitarios. Parents are brought together because of a school issue, given training in their native language on how to promote literacy skills at home, and encouraged to use Spanish as a literacy tool. A collaborative spirit emerged between the school and the parents and an increase in participation in school events occurred during their children's years in the school (Gómez, Lang, & Lasser, 2010). Your literacy leadership can use the characteristics of PTA Comunitarios when attempting to engage multilingual families in literacy-related issues.

Family beliefs about academic success. Success and how it is measured varies from family to family, culture to culture. Academic success may be valued by some while social or economic success is valued by others. The meaning of academic success can vary in each family and within each culture. Edwards (2009, 2011) asserts that we should apply the principles of differentiation to our work of partnering with parents in promoting their children's academic success. We must move away from the standard literacy night for parents and "tailor what we do for the unique cultural and linguistic needs and strengths of the communities in which we are working" (Bridges, 2013, p. 42). In order to differentiate, you must know your community, parents, and students well. Completing the activities in this chapter's Literacy Leadership Toolkit will provide data for developing a plan for community and parent engagement in literacy.

Strategies to promote success. Different regions in the United States have used different strategies to successfully engage families in their children's education. In Chicago, the Chicago Child-Parent Centers serve the needs of early childhood students by fostering parent involvement in school and at home (Dearing, Kreider, Simpkins, & Weiss, 2006). The Houston Independent School district partnered with the Houston Area Urban League to implement Scholastic's *Read and Rise* program. Houston further developed partnerships for literacy with Wal-Mart, grocery stores, and State Farm insurance. As a result, parent participation in literacy nights has increased dramatically (Bridges, 2013). Although there are many strategies and elements that are successful in engaging families in their children's education, the fundamental element is relationship. Families participate in their child's education when they feel welcome, valued, and respected.

"A third (33 percent) of America's youngest children live in households where English is not the only language spoken—a circumstance that implies both risk and promise for their development" (Murphey, Cooper, & Forry, 2013, p. 3). It is your responsibility as a literacy leader to embrace the promise and nurture it to literacy success. This can be achieved by developing partnerships with your school's community members and those who have a stake in the children's education.

External Mandates

In addition to internal school pressures, there are external mandates from the federal government and state education departments. Mandates encompass many aspects of school life beyond education. For instance, there are state, local, and federal mandates that relate to the health and safety of faculty, students, and their families. The purpose of mandates is usually to provide equity, transparency, and account-ability; there is considerable debate about their effectiveness, feasibil-ity of implementation, and equity. Some examples of such mandates are the Annual Professional Performance Review (APPR) of teachers and administrators, Individualized Education Plans (IEPs) for students with special needs, internal and external audits of business offices, col-lection and reporting of students' Body Mass Indexes, and transpor-tation of students with special needs. In addition to mandates, there are laws, rules, and regulations that must be followed in particular situations—for example, private and charter schools, and educating students who are homeless. The implementation of federal mandates is usually left to the states. As a result, state and district mandates and standards vary from state to state, and from district to district. A comparison of four states' (South Dakota, North Carolina, Michigan, and Illinois) response to the federal mandate of No Child Left Behind (TeamWeek3, n.d.) revealed that different standards, identification criteria, and assessment tools are used to comply with mandates re-lated to the literacy instruction of English learners. As a literacy leader, you may feel conflicted about following external mandates and pro-viding the literacy instruction that students need.

Tatum (2012) documents one example of the conflict between compliance with mandates and its effectiveness. He states, "Federal policies and mandates, while warranted, can unintentionally make it more difficult to provide high-quality literacy instruction to young African-American males" (p. 1). He proposes a student-centered approach that considers instructional, sociocultural, and personal factors, rather than the data-based accountability assessments that often place these young men in remedial classes where they "com-monly receive less demanding and/or poorly conceptualized reading instruction"(p. 2).

When obligated to comply with external mandates, you can seek answers to the following questions: What are the local/district literacy mandates? What are the state mandates? Federal mandates? What is the student population? Who are the students? Are they English learners? Are there students with special needs? What are the spe-cial needs of the students? How will the implementation of the man-dates affect literacy instruction and students? What assessments are required? How frequently are they administered? What do parents believe literacy means? What are the school's, parents', students', and teachers' expectations for literacy instruction?

You need to be well versed in local, state, and federal mandates and regulations for literacy instruction. You must also have in-depth knowledge of your students and school community. When literacy leaders are empowered with knowledge about mandates, the school community, literacy pedagogy, and students' needs, they are equipped to make instructional decisions that balance the needs of all stakeholders.

Budget

Directly related to mandates and resources is the school district's budget and the portion of the budget that is allocated to literacy and all other areas. Mandates will affect how your school district spends its school budget and possibly limit flexibility in how the money is spent. As a literacy leader, you want to be able to balance the needs of students and teachers with the confines and restrictions of the district's budget. Though the overall budget might be large and may seem sufficient to meet the needs of the school and community, the individual budgetary lines related to literacy might be inadequate for purchasing an online literacy assessment or software focused on particular literacy skills, hiring a specialized teacher, or adding books to classroom libraries. Unfortunately, monies often cannot move from one budgetary line to another. Mandates can pile up and budgets often are not increased to comply with them. The concept of unfunded mandates becomes a real issue with which all literacy leaders must contend.

When the school's budget does not provide the financial support necessary to support literacy programs and instruction, seek out other resources to provide high-quality literacy instruction for your students.

Resources

Your school's community is brimming with potential resources for literacy instruction. Such resources can often fill in the budgetary gaps, and offer support that school budgets cannot provide. Amy and Suzanne of our vignette went to their district's Teacher Center, wrote a proposal, and received a mini-grant to implement their vision of the K-PASS program. There also are people within the community who might be willing to participate to support the power of literacy development. Ask yourself the following questions: Are there parents and family members who can share a folktale or story that affirms their cultural heritage? Are there people within the community whom students can interview for a student newspaper? Can local experts share their expertise to strengthen a how-to writing unit? Do community members have opposing views on local issues to help make the craft of argument more accessible and meaningful for students?

Begin by speaking with parents and community members to find out what matters to them and how they can become a part of the literacy life of your school. Work with your literacy team to complete the Community Investigation activity in the Literacy Leadership Toolkit to document and analyze the assets and issues of living in your school's community. This activity will help you notice the many types of buildings and activities that make up the community, the nature of the community, and the variety of experiences community members have. The information you glean will enable you to help teachers better connect lessons to the lives of students they teach.

Use the information from your parent/community conversations, the Community Investigation activity and the Community Needs Assessment activity in the Literacy Leadership Toolkit to consider the ways in which the community can support the literacy lives of students. Does your community have a public/local library? Can you collaborate with the library to purchase and feature bilingual and multilingual books? Sponsor a book fair? Program a read-aloud? What other agencies are in the community? Can they donate time, goods, or money to sponsor a literacy-related activity? Use the chart of community resources in Figure 2.3 to help you determine the usefulness of such resources for your students.

One of our Changing Suburbs Institute® (CSI) professional development schools recently hosted a World Read Aloud Day (WRAD) event to engage with the annual LitWorld global event dedicated to read-alouds. They invited local police officers, restaurant owners, bodega owners, parents, the district superintendent, and the mayor to read aloud either a favorite book or one that was chosen for them. They read in English and Spanish. They had their pictures taken with classes, and they signed certificates for every child.

In Ossining, New York, a CSI district, an anonymous benefactor has made provisions for a book to be given to every baby born in local hospitals whose home address is in the town. A representative from the school district presents that book to the baby's mother before she leaves the hospital. The school system takes this opportunity to develop a culture of literacy at birth, and continues to foster it from pre-K through high school.

Figure 2.3. Evaluating Community Resources

Purpose	• Do the goals and purposes of the community resources enhance student learning and engagement? • Can the resources be shared across grade levels? • Is the community connection a one-time event or a repeated engagement over time?
Accessibility	• Are the resources accessible on-site? • Will additional resources be needed for the school to access the community resources?
Shared Evaluation	• In what ways will the community resources be discussed and evaluated by all constituents to enhance student experiences long-term?

Source: Adapted from Cunningham & Enriquez, 2013

An educational publishing company and warehouse is located in the community of one of our professional development schools. The principal arranged for her faculty to go to the warehouse and select "seconds" at a reduced price or free. Barnes & Noble sponsors a summer reading program. If students read eight books, complete their summer reading form, and come into the store, these students receive a free book at their reading level. In another of our professional development schools, the local movie theater shows child-appropriate movies on Wednesdays at 10:00 A.M. in the summer. Any child who brings a book report about a book he or she has read during the summer to the theater is admitted free.

In order to provide the best experiences in literacy, look at each community member, business, and agency as a potential resource in the literacy education of your school's children.

CONNECTING TO AND WORKING WITH THE COMMUNITY

In order to make literacy a community goal, make connections with your surrounding community. Connections are made through face-to-face conversations that allow for questioning, listening, clarifying, and finding mutual understandings. Each community is different, with its own history and resources. Treadway (2000) suggests that schools incorporate the community in building the knowledge, skills and values that could enhance learning. The relationship between a community and a school should be a two-way street since both have something to offer each other, but making that a reality requires that teachers know both what is available and how to make use of that knowledge. And most significantly, they must develop the disposition that experimental learning is possible, interesting, and important. (p. 2)

The Community Investigation activity from the Literacy Leadership Toolkit discussed previously gets school faculty outside of the school's walls and into the community. Connections are made by walking the streets, speaking with community members, and viewing the community as a resource for literacy education. A useful source for working with the community is the local Chamber of Commerce. Look to this organization for partnerships that can be formed to address the needs and goals of both businesses and schools. The Coca-Cola Company founded the Council for Corporate & School Partnerships in 2001 to address the workforce needs that businesses will require in the future. Businesses find that partnering with schools increases employee morale; schools find academic improvement for their students; and the community encounters a healthy economy (Sloan, 2008).

COLLABORATING WITH COMMUNITY PARTNERS: A TALE OF TWO SCHOOLS

Two of our CSI professional development schools, Thomas Edison Elementary and Park Avenue Elementary, are examples of how collaborating with community partners, albeit with different pathways, affects literacy instruction positively.

Thomas Edison Elementary School

When a new principal arrived in 1996 at Thomas Edison Elementary School, a suburban school outside of New York City, she found the unexpected: a Title I school with a student population of children of immigrants who were relatively poor and struggling with the basic needs of clothing, shelter, nutrition, and health care. Approximately 50% of the students were second-language learners of English with weak literacy skills. Fewer than 20% of the 4th-grade students reached benchmark on the annual state assessment in 1999. Teachers were frustrated with trying to educate students whose life circumstances inhibited their learning. Parents were struggling with their daily life as immigrants. Students were trying to make sense of a new language and a strange educational system. Their poor nutrition, limited health care, and emotional and social stressors were affecting their ability to learn. Likewise, social and emotional problems at home affected students during the school day. The principal reached out to faculty, parents, students, and community-based organizations to collaboratively explore the conditions, needs, and resources of the school community (Gómez, Ferrara, Santiago, Fanelli, & Taylor, 2012; Santiago, Ferrara & Blank, 2008; Santiago, Ferrara, & Quinn, 2012).

Embracing the philosophy of educating the whole child, the principal developed partnerships with community agencies and thus created a full-service community school. Whole child education considers the child's intellectual and ethical competencies, social and emotional development, physical development, and educational development (Santiago, Ferrara, & Quinn, 2012). Blank, Melaville, and Shah (2003) define a community school as "both a place and a set of partnerships between the school and other community resources. Its integrated focus on academics, services, supports and opportunities leads to improved student learning, stronger families and healthier communities" (p. 2). In a full-service community school, the partnership services are provided within the school's walls. By 2008, Edison's full-service community had partnerships in six areas: (1) school-based health center, (2) therapy and family casework agency, (3) parent education and capacity building groups, (4) after-school enrichment program, (5) Manhattanville College–Thomas Edison Professional Development School, and (6) adult education classes. The partnership of these groups has benefited children, families, and the community in many ways. Parents feel they have a voice in their children's education. They attend classes to become citizens and learn English. Some students are learning how to self-manage their asthma, and are getting flu shots and medical care in school. Teachers receive professional development in pedagogy and have access to tutors and student teachers for their students (Gómez et al., 2012; Santiago, Ferrara, & Blank, 2008). Although the school now has a new principal, many of the services are still in place because of the strength of the community's involvement with the school.

Park Avenue Elementary School

Park Avenue Elementary School, also a full-service community school, took on a different partnership: a partnership with the school's parents. Like Edison, Park Avenue's demographics have changed. Historically, the students were predominantly White with English as their first language. The school's population now is about 65% Hispanic, and for most of that 65%, Spanish is their first language or the first language of their parents. There is an increasing number of businesses owned or run by Spanish-speaking Hispanics in the community. The Spanish language now has a significant presence in the community and on the school's playground.

During an open school night, one English-speaking parent rose and stated that he wanted equity for his child when it came to language. Perplexed, the principal asked him to explain. He went on to say that the children who speak Spanish at home enter school with one language, and graduate from school proficient in two languages. He wanted his child to be bilingual too. The principal, a former bilingual teacher, seized the moment. She opened up a dialogue about second-language instruction. She polled the group present that night and found interest in Spanish instruction for their children. She explored the notion with other stakeholders in the school and the community. She also examined teachers' and parents' philosophies about teaching a second language to children and parents' expectations for their children's learning a second language. After about a year of researching the topic, speaking with experts in the field, forming parent–teacher committees, visiting local schools offering bilingual and/or dual-language instruction, and conferring with us as her college partner, the Dual Language Academy began in kindergarten. Subsequently, the principal added one grade each year to the Academy.

Park Avenue decided to implement the 50-50 model of dual-language instruction, in which classes are comprised of an equal balance of English-speaking and Spanish-speaking children. Details of dual-language programs are in Chapter 8. The dual-language model was selected over other bilingual models because it best fit the desires and needs of the community. The goal is multilingualism and equity in language instruction. All students receive curricular instruction in their first and second languages. All students are second-language learners (Calderon & Minaya-Rowe, 2003; Collier & Thomas, 2009).

These two schools serve as examples of how you and your principal can collaborate with your community to provide literacy instruction. The leaders in both schools listened to and evaluated the needs and desires of their communities. They then partnered with members of the community to develop an action plan and enlisted the expertise that existed in the community to accomplish their mutual goals. Give voice to your community and listen to their ideas to create a collaborative spirit.

CREATING A PLAN

Collaboration and partnerships with the community do not usually happen serendipitously. Successful partnerships require the creation of a plan. Literacy leaders are not the sole creators of literacy action plans. A variety of constituents can develop the plan through committee work that is based on data from a variety of sources. All stakeholders in the community can offer valuable information to you and your literacy team. The Community Needs Assessment and Community Investigation exercises in the Literacy Leadership Toolkit can guide you with the steps and data needed to develop an action plan. The action plan needs to include federal, state, and local mandates as well as the resources available for addressing students' literacy needs.

REFLECTING AND RESPONDING TO CHANGING COMMUNITIES AND SCHOOLS

With many schools across the United States experiencing a demographic shift in the student population that might not look like, act like, or sound like the student population of a few years ago, we often need to break away from traditional literacy approaches in order to help teachers best meet the literacy needs of their students. Tried and true strategies might not be as effective as they were in the past, as our school population is different from those of the past. Today's students and their families represent a variety of different languages and cultures. When confronted with a population that is different, we often recognize the need to change, but might be uncertain as to how or what to change. After some reflection about your own literacy leadership knowledge, skills, and dispositions (Chapter 1), explore your school's community. Look beyond the school walls and engage with the members of the community. Gather data about the community in relation to literacy. Use such data to work collaboratively with all stakeholders to create a literacy action plan that will best serve the students and community. Be creative in capitalizing on the school's community resources and developing partnerships. Balance external mandates with budgetary realities to provide the best literacy instruction for your students.

LITERACY LEADERSHIP TOOLKIT

The exercises below help you take a look at the community in which your students live. An analysis of the findings provides areas of needs and information about resources for your school's community.

Exercise 2.1: Conduct a Community Needs Assessment
(Adapted from McCawley, 2009)

Use the following structure and guiding questions to plan for a community literacy needs assessment.

1. ***Objectives:*** What do you want to know about literacy and your community?

2. ***Audience:*** Which members of your community are you targeting? Whose needs, opinions, and attitudes do you want to explore?

3. ***Data collection:*** What data will give you the information you are seeking about your community and literacy? How will the data be collected? Directly or indirectly?

4. ***Assessment instruments:*** What will you use to collect the data? Interviews? Surveys? Focus groups of parents and/or community members? Working groups of teachers? Student data?

5. ***Data analysis:*** How will you go about analyzing the data collected?

6. ***Action plan:*** What will you do with the data? What changes in literacy instruction are indicated from the data? How do you implement the literacy changes?

Exercise 2.2: Community Investigation
(Adapted from O'Sullivan, 2001; Remillard, 2001; University of Tennessee, 2001)

"Investigating" the school's neighborhood by taking photos or video clips, observing the buildings and activities that make up the community, and interacting with the people who work and live in the neighborhood should allow you to "see" the needs of your community with a new lens, especially the community's literacy interests. You and your literacy team will learn more about the following:

- Organizations that exist in the community (churches and businesses)
- Geography and architecture of the community (flat, renewal, rural)
- Types of housing available (single-family, apartment)
- Different kinds of employment (government, industry, farming, construction)

During this community investigation, you and your team should do the following:

- Explore a 3-mile (minimum) radius in each direction from your school
- Gather artifacts and photos (flyers, information packets, and so on)
- Analyze your findings as a group
- Use your findings to inform your literacy instruction

Suggested roles. These do not have to be separate tasks completed by particular individuals; however, each should be done during the investigation. A clipboard is useful.

1. ***Scout:*** Reads the directions on a map, and leads the group around the area; needs a map.

2. ***Note-taker:*** Records where you go and what you see; records the photographs/videos taken and places and people of interest; charts the journey of the group.

3. ***Photographer:*** Takes 15–20 photos/video clips of the buildings, historical places, and other things of interest (if they are allowed).

4. **Tabulator:** Administers any surveys and analyzes data about housing, business, churches, recreation agencies, and so on; should be a person who is detailed.

5. **Collector:** Collects objects, brochures, community newspapers, biological, and environmental evidence (for example, leaves and flora); tells note-taker what is collected and why; needs a collection bag.

Observing school's community. Mark a slash mark for each item you observe:

Type of Building	Mark a slash (/) for every example
Single-Family Dwellings	
Multifamily Housing	
Apartment Building(s)	
Farming Structures	
Churches/Buildings of Worship	
Schools	
Municipal Buildings	
Business/Commercial Buildings	
Parks/Green Spaces	
Other	

Photos. Consider the following when preparing your investigation:

- Types of housing you see in the neighborhood. What kind is most common?
- Issues that you observe (trash, graffiti, potholes, parks, and so forth) and location.
- Evidence of construction/reconstruction/renovation/repair.

Take 15–20 photos/video clips that best represent the characteristics of the neighborhood. Use a chart, as follows (on the next page), to keep a record of the photos that you take.

Photograph/Clip	Subject/Concern	Location
1.		
2.		
3....		
15.		

Questions. Consider using the following questions for each area of the investigation:

For a predominantly business area

1. What do you notice about the retail center?
2. What can you find out about the history of this location?
3. Who are the people you notice around the retail center?
4. What do you notice about the mix of tenants in this area (in different part of the area)?
5. What services are provided in this neighborhood (check out government and social service agencies)?
6. Are there any historic plaques in the area? Should there be?

For a predominantly residential area

1. What services are available for youth and families in this area?
2. What goods and services are *not* available in "the neighborhood"? Where do people go to buy these?
3. What type of park space is available? Consider the use of open space in this district (safety issues for children and youth).
4. What kinds of retail options are available?
5. What is the most common way for people from this neighborhood to "make it" economically?
6. What is the racial mix of the community?
7. Has this changed over time, if at all? In what ways?
8. What is the economic mix of the community? What housing has been improved, or not?
9. What community groups are in the neighborhood?

For safe spaces for children to play and get to school

1. What are safe ways for students to get to school?

2. What are the differences in housing?

3. What are the traffic patterns?

4. What kind of open spaces are there for physical recreation? Where do children and youths congregate and play?

5. What are the positive places for children and youths to go (Community centers, recreation centers, and so on)?

Final analysis and debrief. The team needs to address the following questions.

1. What did you and your team find
    - Interesting about the process?
    - Helpful about the process?
    - Difficult about the process?
    - Enjoyable about the process?

2. How does this process and information relate to "anchoring learning in students' diverse life contexts"?

3. What did you learn about the community history, geography, culture, and so forth that you did not know before?

4. What issues related to the community emerged from your investigation? What might be some next steps regarding these issues?

5. How would you apply this experience to your literacy instruction?

6. In what ways, if any, were your perceptions changed or enhanced by this experience?

CHAPTER 3

Know Your Teachers

- Literacy leaders know how to assess teachers' content knowledge, skills, and dispositions in order to work with them effectively.
- Literacy leaders use their knowledge about their teachers to communicate and foster literacy achievement for students.
- Literacy leaders lead by modeling problem solving, using data, providing support, and allocating time and space for teacher collaboration and inquiry.

Marcus, literacy leader for his building in a rural school district, reviews Javier's portfolio and reading assessment scores at the request of his classroom teacher Mara. Mara is a mid-career teacher who has been in the district for 5 years. She is known to run a "tight ship," and has experienced good results in teaching literacy to her 2nd-graders. She has been a vocal and active supporter of teachers' rights as her district moved to a new Annual Professional Performance Review (APPR) process that uses students' performance on annual state assessments as a measure of teacher effectiveness and reappointment. Mara approached Marcus because she is concerned about Javier and his lack of progress in reading. Javier's latest Developmental Reading Assessment (DRA) score as a 2nd-grader was 2, equivalent to reading English at a kindergarten level. Mara cannot figure out how to help Javier, and she is concerned that his test scores could affect her APPR rating.

Marcus carefully reviews the documents he has on Javier. He notes that Spanish is spoken at home and, although Javier's parents are currently working on a local farm, both received their bachilleratos *(equivalent to a high school diploma) in their home country of Costa Rica. Javier is receiving some support services in English because it is his second language. However, there are too few ELs in the school to require a designated English as a Second Language class. Marcus feels he needs more information about Javier and goes into Mara's class to observe Javier's language and literacy skills. From his classroom observation, Marcus discovers that Javier is a very active, inquisitive, and social 2nd-grader. He communicates effectively in English with Mara and his peers. Marcus realizes that there must be a mismatch between Javier's current DRA score in English (2) and his ability to think, problem-solve, and verbally express his ideas. Marcus has experience working with English learners. He knows that second-language acquisition takes approximately 5 years or more and a well-developed first language promotes the acquisition of a second language. He decides to assess Javier's Spanish language skills. His DRA score in Spanish is 18: on grade level! Ecstatic, Marcus immediately runs to tell Mara the great news. Mara's response is, "So? It won't count because it's in Spanish. The school only considers English scores."*

GETTING TO KNOW TEACHERS

Marcus and Mara have very different reactions to Javier's DRA score in Spanish. Marcus is delighted because he views the Spanish score as an asset and knows how to use Javier's reading skills in Spanish to develop his reading in English. Mara's reaction appears to represent her frustration at not being able to help improve Javier's reading in English and her anxiety about being evaluated on her students' performance on standardized tests in English. What does Mara's remark reveal to Marcus about ways to help Mara? How does he move forward to help Mara understand the significance of Javier's DRA score in Spanish? How does he guide Mara and her instruction to support the strong literacy skills Javier possesses? The first step is to know your teachers as both educators and as people.

Teachers as Educators

Literacy leaders who know their teachers as educators have assessed their teachers' knowledge base, teaching skills, and dispositions. They focus on these three main areas because these three key teacher qualities greatly affect student learning (Jadama, 2014).

Teacher knowledge. Teacher knowledge encompasses content, methodologies, and curriculum. Teachers with strong content knowledge know and understand the facts, concepts, and structure of a content area (Burgess, 2006). The knowledge base for literacy is vast. The foundation of literacy instruction consists of the psychology of reading and reading development, which includes reading, writing, and spelling. Teachers of literacy need to have knowledge of the English language structure such as phonetics, phonology, morphology, orthography, semantics, syntax, and text structure, as well as how to assess reading and writing in the classroom (Moats, 1999). They also need to know about, for example, children's literature and narrative, phonemic awareness, phonics, fluency, vocabulary, decoding, reading comprehension, and composition (Cunningham, Perry, Stanovich, & Stanovich, 2004; Learning Point Associates, 2004; Moats, 1999). As a literacy leader, you need to know the extent of your teachers' knowledge base. When gathering information about your teachers' knowledge base, remember that all teachers have strengths as well as areas to develop. As with your own professional development, gaining knowledge about literacy is a lifelong process of growing and learning.

Teachers with strong knowledge of methodologies know how to impart or teach their knowledge about literacy to their students. Some examples of methodologies for teaching literacy include reading and writing workshop, guided reading, multisensory instruction, word study sorts, and close reading.

Connected to knowledge of subject matter and methodologies is curricular knowledge. Teachers with strong knowledge of curriculum select and adapt materials and programs that are best suited for the population they are teaching. These teachers know what is expected of students within their own grade level as well as below and above their grade level. They are aware of the scope and sequence of the curriculum, and know how to adjust the curriculum so that it is culturally responsive for all students.

These teachers also know how to select literacy materials and programs that match the needs for students' literacy instruction. Likewise, these teachers know the best means of instruction for the particular literacy skill, materials, and students. Some informative questions you can ask about your teachers' literacy curricular knowledge are: Which diagnostic assessments do my teachers know how to implement? Are my teachers aware of literacy assessments in languages other than English? Has the teacher selected the best leveled book for his or her class? What does he or she know about the word study materials that accompany the literacy program? Are the texts selected for guided reading appropriate for the children? Has the literacy or grade-level team included titles that represent the multiculturalism of the students? How do the literacy materials align with the students' social studies curriculum? Is technology infused appropriately to enhance the lesson and provide access to literacy curriculum for all students? Teachers need to have knowledge of literacy, know how to impart that knowledge to their students, and select materials that best meet the needs of their students when providing literacy instruction. Use the Checklist of Teacher Knowledge exercise in the Literacy Leadership Toolkit to determine your teachers' knowledge base. The information gained from the checklist provides you with data to prepare and provide support to teachers in needed literacy areas.

Clearly, Mara's response to Marcus's exciting news about Javier's reading level in Spanish reveals that Mara would benefit from additional knowledge about teaching reading to second-language students and the facility to help Javier transfer his reading skills from his native language to a new language. Part of Marcus's role as a literacy leader is to help Mara build her own knowledge in this area. Marcus can provide Mara with some professional development opportunities to increase her knowledge about teaching students from different language and cultural backgrounds.

Teaching skills. Teaching skills are the practical and effective application of teacher knowledge. When a teacher has developed teaching skills, he or she has the ability to move teacher knowledge into practice in diverse classroom settings so that all students learn (National Council for the Accreditation of Teacher Education [NCATE], 2010–2014; Uppsala University, n.d.) In broad legal terms, teaching skills encompass the abilities to: "(a) increase student learning, achievement, and the ability to apply knowledge; (b) effectively convey and explain academic subject matter; (c) effectively teach higher-order analytical, evaluation, problem-solving, and communication skills; and (d) employ strategies grounded in the disciplines of teaching and learning" (USLegal, 2001–2015). In the classroom, teaching skills present a myriad of actions and behaviors as teachers apply the knowledge they have acquired. As a literacy leader, you can ask the following questions that pertain to your particular educational context:

- Do my teachers effectively adapt and differentiate literacy instruction to meet the needs of students? Students with disabilities? English learners? Gifted and talented students? Students with low literacy levels? Those with high literacy levels?

- Do my teachers assess student learning in literacy in an ongoing fashion with a variety of assessment types? Does literacy assessment include measures of higher-order thinking skills?
- Do my teachers teach literacy strategies that are research-based? At the students' appropriate reading level? Do they include comprehension as well as phonics?
- Do my teachers provide appropriate and timely corrective feedback to students?
- Do my teachers manage their classrooms effectively in terms of physical environment, materials, students' behaviors, and literacy instruction?
- Do my teachers communicate effectively with students, parents, and colleagues?
- Do my teachers reflect on their teaching and teaching practices? (Moats, 1999; Rush, 2015; Uppsala University, n.d.; USLegal, 2001–2015)

Marcus asks himself these questions about Mara. He discovers that Mara possesses most of the knowledge and skills of an effective literacy teacher, except for one basic area: teaching literacy to ELs. Marcus also realizes that, in addition to knowledge and skills, Mara will also need the disposition to work with students who are culturally and linguistically diverse to effectively teach literacy to ELs.

Teacher dispositions. According to Dewey (1910/1933), along with knowledge and skills, teachers need to possess three other characteristics in order to be effective: open-mindedness, wholeheartedness, and intellectual reasonability. Dewey's terms characterize teacher dispositions of empathy, caring, reflection, and willingness to adjust (Talbert-Johnson, 2006; Taylor & Wasicsko, 2000). Schön (1983, 1987) explored the ideas of teacher reflection and willingness to adjust. Teachers draw on their past experiences and professional knowledge to reframe new situations and solve problems through reflection. Schön's (1983) model of reflection separates thinking from doing by creating two categories of reflection: reflection-in-action and reflection-on-action. The first takes place automatically and unconsciously in the teaching moment, while the second occurs after instruction and is a conscious action. Reflection-in-action aligns with the definition of teacher dispositions as trends in behavior or "habits of mind" (Katz & Raths, 1985). The behaviors, verbal and nonverbal, demonstrate a teacher's attitudes, values, and beliefs through interactions "with students, families, colleagues, and communities" (National Council for the Accreditation of Teacher Education, 2010–2014). The value of fairness and the belief that all students can learn are paramount dispositions for teachers in culturally and linguistically diverse contexts. You will probably find it difficult to identify the relationship between teachers' dispositions and effective teaching because, despite years of research, clear definitions and means for assessing teacher dispositions have been elusive. This is especially true with ethnically, culturally, and linguistically diverse student populations in urban and rural settings (Talbert-Johnson, 2006; Taylor & Wasicsko, 2000; Thornton, 2006). Observe keenly, listen carefully, and model fairness, caring, and empathy as well as any other dispositions deemed important by your school and district. The criteria used for evaluating teacher candidates' dispositions can serve as a guide in determining teachers' dispositions. Some characteristics noted by the Council of Chief State School Officers (2011) worth exploring include whether teachers are:

- respectful of all students regardless of their background, language, skills, abilities, and talents;
- confident that all students can learn;
- thoughtful about the use of instructional resources and their effect on students;
- supportive and positive in learning environments;
- communicative and respectful with students, families, colleagues, and community members;
- reflective and observant of students, their families, colleagues, and self; and
- flexible and open to new ideas, thoughts, comments, and the suggestions of others.

In communities where the student population is culturally and linguistically diverse, it is also important to discern whether or not teachers demonstrate positive dispositions when working with students whose cultures and languages are not in the majority or not the same as those of the teachers who teach them. It is not so much what they say as how they relate to diverse students. How do they view a child whose first, second, or third language is not English? Do they consider the student's native language an asset? Is the teacher respectful of the languages and cultures? Does the teacher know something about those languages? If not, does he or she consider investigating the fundamentals of those languages such as the alphabets or directionality? Of the cultures related to the languages? About the cultures of his or her students that differ from their own? The answers to such questions help guide you in mentoring and coaching your teachers. The Teacher Knowledge About Language and Culture exercise in the Literacy Leadership Toolkit has questions that can help you gather information about teachers' knowledge and dispositions related to culturally and linguistically diverse students.

In addition to reviewing teaching knowledge, skills, and dispositions, you must also consider teachers' professional careers because the amount and type of professional development and coaching required to help particular teachers will differ, depending on their prior experiences. Is the teacher a first-year teacher? A career changer? Relatively new to the school and its environment? Is the teacher probationary? Tenured? Mid-career? Close to retirement? Did the teacher have previous experience with culturally and linguistically diverse populations in a prior career? Take these types of questions into consideration to differentiate and foster relationships that will help your teachers develop their professional knowledge, skills, and dispositions and, at the same time, increase their students' literacy skills and achievement.

Teachers as Individuals

Teachers are not only educators, but also individuals with their own assets, needs, interests, and personalities. They, too, enter the classroom with their own set of personal, cultural, and linguistic backgrounds and needs related to their profession. Teachers have multiple identities and view themselves through the *looking glass self* (Cooley, 1902). Because teaching is a social activity, teachers see themselves through the lenses of others: colleagues, students, parents, the government, and the media. The images others have of them can be in direct conflict with how they see themselves (Harrison, 2013). Get to know your teachers, not only as educators, but also as individuals. Teachers differentiate their instruction for their students according to their readiness, needs, interests, learning styles, skills, and personality.

Similarly, differentiate how to relate to your teachers as you guide them through a new literacy curriculum mandate, a difficult encounter with a parent, or the implementation of a new literacy strategy. A new teacher has a different set of skills from a mid-career educator; therefore, your plans for each will differ in the type, length, and frequency of support.

If a teacher's culture is different from the majority of his or her colleagues, students, or literacy leader, he or she might experience internal tensions. DuBois (1953) characterized this as a struggle of "two-ness"; the struggle between school culture and climate that is historically based on White middle-class values and the cultural norms of what may not be middle-class or White (Anderson, 2008). As a literacy leader, you need to learn about teachers' cultures and backgrounds, value them, and use them as assets in their work relationships. By being a people watcher and having candid conversations, you can gather information that will support the professional development of individual teachers and align it to the literacy needs of the students.

One way to get to know teachers as people is to observe them when they are asked to change from something they are very comfortable doing to a process, curriculum, or methodology that is new and different for them. There are four types of initial reactions to the ideas of change: hostile, experimenters, yes-buts, and go-alongs (Farrell, 1983; Rusbult & Zembrodt, 1983; Tjemkes & Furrer, 2011). Figure 3.1 presents a graph of these reactions on a continuum ranging from being cooperative to uncooperative and reacting in an active to passive manner.

The experimenters and go-alongs are generally cooperative during the process of change. The experimenters' active nature often leads them to be the first to support the change. They enjoy the challenge and adventure of implementing something new. The go-alongs also are agreeable to the change suggested, even though they react passively to whatever is recommended. They do not usually present a problem for you when you are trying to implement a change. As a literacy leader, you can quickly identify both experimenters and go-alongs, and use their cooperative nature to help implement a change in process, curriculum, or methodology.

The hostile and the yes-buts demonstrate a more uncooperative reaction to change. The reaction of the hostile teacher is active and often vocal, whereas the reaction of the yes-buts is initially

Figure 3.1. Teachers' Reaction to Change

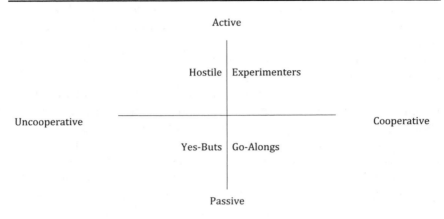

agreement (yes) to the change and then a roadblock (but) as to why it will not work. Reeves's (2006) study of more than 2,000 teachers' and administrators' reactions to change indicated that 53% were willing to model changes (experimenters), 28% were fence-sitters with no action on the initiative (yes-buts), 17% of the teachers and administrators were willing to assist and share the new initiative (go-alongs), and 2% were toxic, vocal, and actively opposed to the initiative (hostile). Reeves (2009) advised leaders to put their energy, appreciation, and support with the 70% (experimenters and go-alongs) on board with the proposed change "rather than continue to engage in ineffective and emotionally draining combat with the Toxic 2" (p. 54). Though Reeves recommends not engaging with the hostile teacher who reacts to your suggestions and coaching negatively and actively, working with him or her can be productive. The initially hostile reactors can actually become enthusiastic supporters as they gain knowledge and skills about the change proposed. This group is worth focusing on in intentional and concrete ways. Usually the last to support change is the yes-but teacher because it is his or her nature to be passive.

As individuals, teachers react differently to comments, recommendations, and criticism. Whether a teacher reacts to change as an experimenter, go-along, hostile, or yes-but is usually related to personality and his or her personal and professional identities. Does the teacher see the cup as half full or half empty? Does the teacher have high or low self-esteem? Is the teacher a risk taker or risk averse? Is the teacher teachable? It is important to know about your teachers' personal traits and characteristics in order to help them work effectively with all students.

Marcus sees Mara as a yes-but teacher who is experiencing conflict with both her professional and personal identities. Yes, she knows how to teach literacy and has used those strategies to teach Javier. Yes, Javier scored on grade level in reading Spanish. But, the strategies are not working for him in reading English. But, only English reading scores count. Through her looking glass self, Mara sees herself as a competent teacher who has been successful in teaching literacy, but in Javier's case, she is beginning to question her teaching ability or professional identity. She is also worried about how Javier's scores will affect her APPR and her ability to provide for her family, which is an important part of her personal identity. Marcus begins to develop a plan to help Mara with Javier. He will use Mara's strengths to develop knowledge, skills, and dispositions to help Javier learn to read in English. Mara's success with improving Javier's reading scores will in turn help her feel less anxious and more confident.

Capitalizing on Their Strengths

Effective literacy leaders gather both professional and personal information about their teachers in order to know as much as possible about their knowledge, skills, and dispositions as well as their personal, cultural, and linguistic traits, and characteristics. They use this information to develop plans and strategies to work effectively with their teachers, and to help students receive appropriate literacy instruction.

Mara's "yes-but" reaction to Marcus's news about Javier is the most difficult kind of reaction to change. Marcus sets out to gather as much information as possible about Mara so he can devise a plan to help Mara understand the asset Javier possesses by being able to read on grade level in his native language. His first inquiry is about Mara's assets as a teacher. Mara has the teacher knowledge required to teach literacy at her grade level. She is well versed in a balanced literacy instructional framework. Her selection of texts in English is appropriate for her English-speaking students, and she is well acquainted with the scope and sequence of her 2nd-grade curriculum, as well as the 1st and 3rd grades' curricular expectations.

Next, Marcus explores Mara's experiences as an individual. She has little experience working with second-language learners. She is a third-generation American. She is overwhelmed with the new curriculum mandates and APPR formula that includes her students' state test scores. She needs her job because her husband was recently laid off. And although she has been tenured, she is one of the newest teachers in her building. Marcus has observed that Mara is strong-willed and hardworking.

Armed with this information, Marcus is ready to create a plan to help Mara understand Javier's assets, use them to improve her literacy instruction in English, and alleviate her fears of APPR. He wants to capitalize on Mara's strengths. Marcus also wants to help Mara acknowledge and address her needs. Even what appear to be attitudinal issues and instructional shortcomings can be used as assets to benefit the teacher's professional development and teaching. Mara's pessimism about Javier's scores stems from her need to succeed in her job. Likewise, her "instructional shortcoming" reveals a lack of knowledge in the specific area of teaching ELs proficient in their native language, not her overall teaching ability. We often do not see ourselves as others see us. In order to improve our teaching, there must be an acknowledgment of a need. Price explains (2006) that "we need to be ever mindful of the multi-dimensional nature of teaching skill and of our weaknesses as well as our strengths. For purposes of becoming better teachers, awareness of our weaknesses is probably more important because there's so much more room for improvement" (p. 9).

Marcus leverages Mara's intelligence and literacy knowledge to develop her knowledge about second-language acquisition and its relationship with reading in one's native language. Marcus will prove to Mara that Javier's DRA score in Spanish *does* count. Mara needs to acquire knowledge about language and language acquisition in order to help Javier read in English. If she can give Javier appropriate literacy instruction that improves his reading, she will also alleviate her anxiety about how his test score will affect her APPR score. Marcus begins his conversation with Mara by asking her to respond in writing to the prompts from the Teacher Knowledge About Language and Culture exercise in the Literacy Leadership Toolkit. This exercise requires Mara to reflect on her cultural and linguistic knowledge and dispositions toward Spanish and second-language acquisition. They then discuss the prompts. Marcus encourages Mara to be reflective in order to build capacity as a teacher of culturally and linguistically diverse learners.

COMMUNICATING WITH TEACHERS

Communication between you and your teachers is the glue that will support literacy instruction. Like teachers, we have our own styles, knowledge, skills, and dispositions (see Chapter 1). We need to recognize this with the various modes of communication that we use because of their potential impact on the message delivered. In some cases, an email or memo is a sufficient means of communication. Sometimes, dropping into a teacher's classroom to speak face-to-face is preferable so that the message is not misunderstood, and questions can be asked for clarification. Effective leaders know to use the mode of communication that fits the situation, topic, and needs of their teachers. They understand the importance of nonverbal communication with verbal messages. They are careful that their verbal messages match their nonverbal cues. Clear communication is direct and explicit, and helps create a trusting, collaborative environment. Clear communication incorporates data or facts with an opening for finding solutions; it helps avoid a "blame game" and "it's not possible" mindset. Often, the best communication skill is listening. When we listen, we provide teachers with an opportunity to find their voice.

Leading as a Learner

To lead as a learner means that you have information, in the form of data, about what is happening in your school. You have analyzed the data, developed goals in relation to the data, and strategically planned to implement any changes necessary. Reeves (2006) offers the Leadership for Learning framework to facilitate school change and improvement. You can plot your understanding of student achievement results in relation to the educational antecedents (see Figure 3.2).

The vertical axis displays student work, and the horizontal axis indicates what teachers have done. The left side of the graph, whether "Lucky" or "Losing," indicates that it is difficult to determine reasons for students' achievement results. The right side of the graph, whether "Leading" or "Learning," indicates that you can dig into the data to understand reasons for students' achievement results, whether high or low.

In addition to using student achievement data, look to teachers to learn about the ways to best serve them. Leadership approaches range from being consultative to confrontational. The consultant style

Figure 3.2. Leadership for Learning

	Lucky	Leading
Achievement of Results	High results, low understanding of antecedents	High results, high understanding of antecedents
	Replication of success unlikely	Replication of success likely
	Losing	**Learning**
	Low results, low understanding of antecedents	Low results, high understanding of antecedents
	Replication of failure likely	Replication of success likely
	Antecedents of Excellence	

Source: Reeves, 2006

works in collaboration with teachers, learning along with them, modeling, and co-teaching at their elbow. Marcus implemented this style by modeling and co-teaching a literacy lesson on academic language using cognates with Javier's reading group. Mara was able to see how using the group's first language provided a bridge to developing reading skills in English. The confrontational approach is more prescriptive in nature, telling teachers what should be done, and perhaps, modeling a particular approach or program in isolation (Steiner & Kowal, 2007). If Marcus were to tell Mara to read an article about linguistically diverse students and follow the principles found in the article, he would be demonstrating a confrontational approach. Which is your particular style? If "we envision a teaching profession that embraces collective accountability for student learning balanced with collaborative autonomy that allows educators to do what is best for students" (Commission on Effective Teachers and Teaching, 2011, p. 1), then the consultant style that encourages teacher voice is preferable.

Giving teachers a voice contributes to a collaborative environment. DeWitt (2014) provides five reasons why giving teachers a voice results in positive outcomes for teachers and their students. When you listen to your teachers you are (1) tapping into teachers' expertise, (2) living a democratic process, (3) providing a positive school environment, (4) maximizing the outcome of any school initiative, and (5) listening to students' voices. When teachers express their thoughts, ideas, and opinions, they reveal their knowledge, skills, and dispositions, which can help literacy leaders better understand their strengths and needs. Listening to teachers' voices validates them as participants in decisionmaking. When you model the process of listening to your teachers, it is likely they will follow your example and listen to their own students' voices. In both cases, providing an opportunity for teachers and students to use their voices is the "recognition of different voices, voices traditionally silenced or marginalized" (Llorens, 1994, p. 8). Although some teacher voices "may threaten or challenge your own" (Hargreaves, 1996, p. 17), it actually helps to learn about the individuals and reasons for the different and dissonant voices.

Teachers' challenging voices can serve as a means to build their capacity to respond as creative problem-solvers and collaborators (Moran, 2007). Any information gained from listening to teachers' voices can and should be used to plan and develop their ongoing professional development. When Marcus listened to Mara's dissonant voice about Javier's DRA scores in Spanish, he discovered an opportunity to collaborate with Mara and create solutions to what Mara viewed as a problem.

Balancing Individual and Collective Goals

As a literacy leader you find yourself in a perpetual balancing act. You are obligated to follow and enforce the mandates and directives from the state, the district, and your supervisors. You must consider what is fair to ask of teachers, given their individual strengths and weaknesses. Most of all, you must lead with the conviction to provide the best literacy instruction possible for the students in your school. The need to meet the goals of all the constituents can be overwhelming. To steady the pushes and pulls between individual and collective goals, start with the teachers. They are the ones who have daily and direct contact with students. It is up to teachers to implement the literacy strategies, programs, and curriculum in the classroom. Leverage teachers' individual strengths and professional goals as contributions to the collective goal. Balance can be achieved through a continuum of learning opportunities that range from workshops on broad topics to direct coaching in the classroom. Work with teachers to use a collaborative resource management format to determine where on a continuum to begin their own professional development. Progressing through the continuum from least to most collaborative formats are literacy presentations, classroom visitations, collaborative planning, literacy study groups, peer or coach demonstration lessons, peer coaching, and co-teaching (Moran, 2007). Co-teaching positions the teacher's professional learning with the literacy leader in the teacher's classroom so that both share the responsibility for instruction. Learning opportunities can be differentiated and scaffolded for individual teachers and their students. Additionally, learning opportunities should be offered in an ongoing manner.

If teachers have the professional capacity to meet students' needs, then the teachers' personal needs are also met (Moran, 2007). The continuum of professional learning opportunities provides options that literacy leaders can use to serve individual teachers' goals, which in turn provides the means to accomplish collective goals. Marcus begins with a literacy study group on second-language acquisition and the cognitive processes of being bilingual to address Mara's need to understand the connection between reading in one's native language and learning to read in a second language. He then moves to some coaching demonstrations and ultimately co-teaches a literacy lesson with Mara to help her reach her goal of improving Javier's reading scores. Javier's need to learn to read in English will be facilitated, Mara's need for her students to perform well on the state reading examination will be met, and her anxiety about losing her job because of her APPR rating will be diminished.

MENTORING, SUPERVISING, AND EVALUATING TEACHERS

Literacy leaders play multiple roles in their interactions and relationships with teachers. There are several important behaviors that characterize effective interaction with teachers. Eight of these behaviors are (1) demonstrate respect for teachers; (2) listen to what all teachers have to say, regardless of knowledge or experience; (3) challenge teachers to continue to develop knowledge, skills, and dispositions; (4) collaborate with teachers, administrators, parents, and community members; (5) be truthful with teachers; (6) provide a safe environment for teachers to voice concerns, try out new techniques, and collaborate with others; (7) show empathy for teachers as individuals and professionals; and (8) celebrate teachers' successes and risk taking (L'Allier, Elish-Piper, & Bean, 2010; Long, K., 2014; Shanklin, 2006).

Mentorship and Supervision

Mentor and supervise teachers with a clear purpose derived from concrete data. Use numerous data sources. Gather data at many levels: district, school, classrooms by grade level, individual teacher, and individual student. What are your district's literacy goals? How do the district's goals subscribe to state and local regulations and mandates for literacy? What are the school's literacy goals? What is required of 2nd-graders? Sixth-graders? What are the 3rd-grade teacher's knowledge, skills, and dispositions? What is Javier's reading profile? What are his assets and needs in reading? All these data are used to develop learning opportunities for teachers and instruction delivery to students (Shanklin, 2006). The type of learning opportunities match the needs discovered through a thorough analysis of data (see Chapter 5 for a discussion of different professional development opportunities).

Literacy supervision implies being present to oversee or observe what is happening in the classroom. Teachers need their literacy leaders to "be there" with direct interactions that offer support, instruction, time, confidentiality, and empathy. Supervision should be collaborative, with the ultimate goal of meeting the students' literacy needs. This requires a balance of managing time, developing trust, and knowing what type of support best fits the teachers. Supportive supervision requires allocating time for classroom observations, conversations, co-planning, demonstrations, co-teaching, and peer observations, inside and outside classrooms.

Evaluation

The focus of teacher evaluation is shifting. Depending on the position you hold, you may be required to assess teachers' performances by completing a rubric mandated by your district and in accordance with law and union regulations. Or you may be a peer coach required to do informal evaluations in order to provide appropriate support. You may have limited control over which observational rubric or framework is used. Such decisions are often made at the district level, and as a literacy leader, you must comply. However, you can control the conversations before, during, and after teacher evaluations. A collaborative evaluation experience helps keep all stakeholders' goals and objectives present as everyone works toward student learning and instructional improvement.

According to Danielson (2011), there are two main purposes for teacher evaluation: to ensure quality teaching and to promote professional development. There are three essential criteria for evaluating the quality of teaching. The first is a clear definition of quality, or good teaching. What is it? What does it look like? What are the components of high-quality teaching? Once quality is defined, the second criterion is the development of valid assessment systems for teacher evaluation that emanates from teacher conversations about good teaching. Specific language about teaching helps teachers evaluate their own teaching practices and prepare instruction. The third criterion is skillful evaluation of high-quality teaching. Evaluators, whether serving as mentors, supervisors, or coaches, must be proficient and skillful in recognizing high-quality teaching characteristics. Danielson (2011) contends that the teaching profession is well served when both quality assurance (specific evaluation criteria and trained evaluators) and professional learning (the result of teacher evaluations) are embedded in the evaluation system's design. This represents a shift from traditional teacher evaluation where the administrator observes and provides critiques of the lesson without specific evaluation criteria. Providing specific criteria that delineate the characteristics and qualities of "good teaching" to the teacher, as in the form of a rubric, allows the teacher to reflect and compare the lesson against the evaluation criteria. You and the teacher have reason to discuss and collaborate about the lesson. The teacher has the opportunity to tell you what happened the day before and the special challenges that might have occurred, and to self-assess and reflect. Such collaboration can lead to shared conclusions and decisions rather than a single, isolated view of a single lesson by an administrator that can potentially trigger teachers' defensive responses to comments and suggestions.

The instruments used to evaluate teachers and their literacy teaching can take many forms and can cover a multitude of teaching areas, including teacher knowledge, skills, and dispositions. They should also provide specific feedback about teachers' use of methods and strategies so that teachers know how to improve instruction. We have moved away from the ubiquitous "good job" that provides no guidelines or support for teacher improvement. Teacher evaluations should be multidimensional and should offer specific guidelines for teachers to use to improve their craft. Hanover Research (2012) has identified multiple measures by which to evaluate teachers. This multiple-measure approach increases validity and reliability of teacher evaluations, decreases subjectivity, and requires multiple and diverse data sources. Some possible data sources beyond traditional supervisory classroom observations and students' test scores include reports and surveys from students and parents, peer and self-evaluations, teacher portfolios, and professional development. Multiple data sources provide a full picture of the teacher's ability; however, more data are not necessarily better. Do not place too much weight on potentially unreliable data, such as self-evaluations and testimonials, yet be aware that such information can contribute to an overall assessment of teachers' performance (Hanover Research, 2012).

The evaluation process should provide teachers with feedback and a means to improve literacy instruction and practice. When you schedule time to conference with teachers about their teaching, rather than hand them observational checklists or evaluation forms, a collaborative relationship can be developed. Both you and the teacher have the opportunity to listen, speak, and problem-solve to ultimately better serve the children. The mutual exchange of ideas goes a long way in helping to build a collaborative environment focused on improved teacher performance.

CREATING A TRUE LEARNING COMMUNITY

By knowing your teachers well, you can use their assets and needs as a catalyst for creating collaborative inquiry groups to help improve student achievement and skills in literacy. Teachers possess assets that can enhance a leader's ability to promote literacy across the school. Teachers' inclinations to build relationships, maintain a sense of purpose, and improve their own professional practice can encourage their colleagues to improve their own practices (Donaldson, 2007). Fostering a professional learning environment for all members of the school community values and empowers teachers, which, in turn, can improve school climate and student success. Collaborative inquiry that supports teachers requires certain conditions and practices: (1) ownership that is shared, (2) effective use of data, (3) a culture of collaboration, (4) inquiry as a stance, (5) creation of a shared purpose, and (6) a system of support (Nelson, 2012). One successful teacher-driven type of collaborative learning is a professional learning community (PLC).

DuFour (2004) defines a professional learning community as an approach in which educators work together to achieve their collective learning goals through processes of inquiry, problem solving, and reflection upon practice. The objective is student learning. PLCs differ from committee work or teamwork for a specific time-sensitive issue. There are two foundational assumptions that ground PLC work for literacy improvement: first, that teachers who are living the daily experiences in the literacy classrooms have knowledge that can be best understood by colleagues who are also experiencing similar conditions in their classroom; and second, that participation in a PLC increases teachers' educational knowledge and this knowledge contributes to student learning (Center for Comprehensive School Reform and Improvement, 2009).

The focus of a PLC is developed collaboratively by you and your teachers as you respond to three basic questions: "What is it we want each student to learn? How will we know when each student has learned it? How will we respond when a student experiences difficulty in learning?" (DuFour, 2004, p. 8). The school needs to provide time and space for teachers to collaborate, share experiences, analyze student data, and discuss solutions so they have shared responsibility for the common goal of student learning (Center for Comprehensive School Reform and Improvement, 2009). PLCs are successful and effective when you know and value teachers' knowledge, skills, and dispositions, and provide frequent and consistent opportunities for teachers to work together (Jesse, 2007; Mindich & Lieberman, 2012).

Marcus thinks Mara would benefit from a PLC focused on the literacy development of ELs. He gathers other teachers who are teaching ELs to read in English. He poses the questions: What is it we want our ELs to learn? How will we know when they have learned it? What will we do when a student experiences difficulty in learning? He provides the teachers with research articles on reading in a second language. Mara's knowledge of first-language literacy and its relationship to second-language literacy begins to develop as she discusses these articles with her peers. Marcus leads the group to apply the research to the classroom. He allocates time and space for them to meet and discuss strategies. Using the recursive inquiry process, Mara tries new strategies with Javier using his first language to develop his reading skills in English, analyzes new outcomes data, and brainstorms next steps with her PLC. Mara experiences the elements of a true PLC: collaboration with peers, shared ownership of the process and purpose, data-based inquiry, empowerment through building professional knowledge and skills, and a support system. She ends up learning new ways to work more effectively with Javier.

LEAD YOUR TEACHERS TO LEAD

Teachers bring numerous assets to classrooms. They possess knowledge, skills, and dispositions about literacy, their classrooms, their schools, and their communities. You can tap into their wealth of knowledge and resources, and engage teachers to work collaboratively to better serve the students they teach. Effective literacy leaders understand that "complexities of change leadership require not the perfect composite of every trait, but rather a team that exhibits leadership traits and exercises leadership responsibilities in a way that no individual leader, past or present, possibly could" (Reeves, 2009, p. 54). You need to know and value your teachers' assets. Engage them in self-reflective and collaborative inquiry, and challenge them to grow professionally in their knowledge, skills, and dispositions. Allocate frequent and consistent time to work with teachers to analyze student data, problem-solve, and create plans and opportunities for their students to develop as literacy learners.

LITERACY LEADERSHIP TOOLKIT

The two exercises below help you gain information about your teachers' knowledge of literacy, language, and culture. Use the information you gather from them to provide opportunities to increase their literacy knowledge, skills, and dispositions.

Exercise 3.1: Checklist of Teacher Knowledge

Use the checklist to become acquainted with your teachers' knowledge of subject-matter content, methodologies, and curriculum (Burgess, 2006). Adapt the chart to fit your school and district's expectations for teacher knowledge.

Literacy Knowledge Basis	Level of Knowledge H—high, M—mid, L—low	Comments/ Observations
Literacy Content		
Children's literature and narrative		
Phonemic awareness		
Phonics		
Comprehension		
English syntax		
English morphology		
Second-language acquisition		
Semantics		

Literacy Knowledge Basis	Level of Knowledge H—high, M—mid, L—low	Comments/ Observations
Literacy Methodologies		
Guided reading		
Reading workshop		
Multisensory techniques		
Think-alouds		
Use of Big Books		
Modeling		
Book clubs		
Assessment strategies		
Feedback techniques		
Literacy Curriculum		
Grade-level literacy curriculum		
Scope		
Sequence		
Below-grade-level literacy curricular expectations		
Above-grade-level literacy curricular expectations		
Alignment of Materials with Content Areas		
Social studies		
Mathematics		
Science		

Exercise 3.2: Teacher Knowledge About Language and Culture

Use the questions below as prompts to an open discussion with teachers about their knowledge and dispositions related to language and culture. The questions can be asked orally, or you can request that the teacher respond in writing. Once completed, review the responses in one-on-one conferences, in small groups, or anonymously through tools such as Google Docs (online text document for collaborating with other people in real time) or Google Forms (online form for collecting information on spreadsheet). The prompts below are designed for Spanish. Modify the questions to reflect the languages and cultures of your student population.

Prompt	Response
How are English and Spanish the same? How are they different?	
How is learning to read English similar to learning to read Spanish?	
If a child can speak English, why would it be reasonable to think that he or she can read English? Why not?	
What do you do if a student speaks Spanish in your class?	
Why would a student speak or want to speak Spanish in your English-speaking literacy class?	
How do you communicate with the parents of your students who do not speak English?	
How do you teach reading to a child whose first language is not English?	
What is the sequence of reading skills you would teach to a child whose first language is not English? How is the sequence the same and different for English-speaking students?	
What instructional strategies have you used to teach Spanish-speaking students to read in English? Were they successful? What is your evidence? If not, what are your next steps?	
What information, guidance, or resources would you find helpful as you teach your Spanish-speaking students to read in English?	

CHAPTER 4

Know Your Students

- Literacy leaders can help teachers become familiar with the meaning of different labels associated with linguistic diversity, and take the time to understand how a student's cultural and linguistic background might impact his or her learning.
- Literacy leaders can help teachers collect data about culturally and linguistically diverse students' reading, writing, speaking, and listening as well as their social behaviors by adapting commonly used data collection tools.
- Literacy leaders can help teachers use their knowledge of students' language, culture, and learning strengths and needs to make instructional decisions that go beyond ability grouping and other traditional practices.

It is the second day of school for Juan, who recently arrived from Honduras. He is seated on the rug listening and watching as Mrs. Gold engages students in the morning ritual of discussing the date and the weather.

"Criss, Cross Applesauce, Juan," intones the teacher, noticing that he is not seated like the other children.

Juan is looking down at the carpet and he doesn't move.

"Juan, please sit like the other friends," explains Mrs. Gold. He doesn't stir until María, a Mexican American classmate, whispers to him in Spanish.

"María, Juan is here at school to learn English, so please don't speak to him in Spanish," admonishes Mrs. Gold.

Later in the teachers' lounge, she tells the story to Mr. Varani, the literacy coach. She concludes by stating, "And the whole time he kept looking at the floor instead of looking me in the eye. I don't know what I should do with him. Maybe I should move his desk to the side of the room until he learns a little English."

Mr. Varani pauses to consider how he can diplomatically help his colleague correct her misconceptions before they impact Juan's 1st-grade experience in his new school.

Few educators would argue with the premise that teachers and leaders must know their students. Indeed, many teachers dedicate a significant portion of the opening days of school to activities designed to learn about the students who share their classroom. Learning about the needs, resources, and interests of culturally and linguistically diverse students is particularly important, but linguistic and cultural barriers complicate the process. It takes time to learn about an individual student and, in the meantime, teachers must be careful about the assumptions that they are making. Because of her limited experience with language learners, Mrs. Gold does not understand why Juan does not make eye contact or follow basic directions. She views his first language as an impediment to learning a second. Someone more familiar with the Latino culture would see that Juan is adhering to a cultural expectation that a respectful boy does not look directly at an adult authority figure. For teachers with more knowledge about second-language acquisition, Juan's Spanish is a bridge toward his acquisition of English as well as an innate part of his identity. Juan's teacher needs to take the time to get to know him as an individual, in addition to getting to know the community and culture from which he comes, including his family. She needs to learn how his first language interacts with English and how his developing language proficiency can positively impact his learning.

Mrs. Gold can use that knowledge of Juan's cultural and linguistic background to integrate him into the classroom community through meaningful social and academic interactions. Culturally and linguistically diverse students belong at the center of the classroom, not on the periphery.

UNDERSTANDING LANGUAGE LEARNERS

If asked to describe an English learner, many mainstream citizens may picture a Spanish speaker from a large family of lower socioeconomic status who recently arrived in the United States. Although some ELs do fit this profile, many others do not. Some students come to the United States because their university-educated parents' international companies transferred them here. There are also students who were born in the United States, but who speak a language other than English (or Spanish) at home. Cultural and linguistic diversity also encompasses students who speak nonstandard varieties of English such as African American Vernacular English (AAVE). Gere et al. (2008) published a policy brief through the National Council of Teachers of English (NCTE) that outlines the heterogeneity among students learning English. More than half the students labeled as ELs were born within the United States. They come from families of varied levels of educational attainment and socioeconomic status and they speak a variety of languages outside of school.

A first step in understanding students is learning how they are labeled within your district. Literacy leaders should be familiar with the terminology used to describe language learners to be able to share this knowledge with their colleagues, and help them understand the impact of these labels on students' lives. Some districts continue to use the term *Limited English Proficient* (LEP) to describe students who have not mastered their new language, despite its implicit deficit message. The neutral terms *English language learner* (ELL) and *English learner* (EL) are more widespread in recent years. As educators deepen their understanding of the importance of students' home languages, *multilingual learner* (Mitchell, 2012) has become more prevalent because it emphasizes that English should not supplant another language.

There are also descriptors that reflect students' background beyond their relative language proficiency. *Newcomer* refers to young people who have recently arrived from another country. *1.5 generation* describes students who graduated from a U.S. high school and continued to college, but who still require additional support in the acquisition of academic language. *Emergent bilingual* refers to people who are learning two languages, a process that occurs gradually and not within a set time frame. *Sojourners* or *transnationals* (Skerrett, 2012) are students who come over with their families for a few years, often because of their parents' employment. Another useful term is *Language Minority Student* (LMS), a more inclusive label for young people because it includes those who speak nonstandard dialects of English in the home as well as those who speak additional languages. Teachers are also likely to encounter *students with little or interrupted formal education*, generally abbreviated as *SLIFE* or *SIFE*. These young people often come from rural areas or regions affected by war, natural disaster, and other cataclysmic events. They may have reached an advanced age without regularly attending school. Even the most common classroom procedures will seem foreign to these young adults. All of these terms are accurate in certain contexts, but some of them also reflect the politics beneath the surface of the teaching and learning of language. It is important to avoid labels of language learners, such as LEP, that reflect a deficit perspective.

Other useful terms refer to the languages themselves and how they are being used rather than to the students learning with and through them. *Cognates* are words that look and sound similar across different languages, and share the same meaning. *Code-switching* or *code meshing* (Michael-Luna & Canagarajah, 2008) is the act of purposively using two or more languages in the same sentence or conversation. More recently, linguists have also adopted the term *translanguaging* to describe how bilinguals move fluidly back and forth between languages. Calling language learners' attention to the existence of cognates as well as to their practices speaking two languages can help promote metalinguistic awareness. Although culturally and linguistically diverse students can struggle with the acquisition of English, multilingualism has been proven to have cognitive and neurological benefits (Bialystok, 2011), and should not be treated by teachers as a problem to be solved but rather a strength to be harnessed.

As a literacy leader, help teachers learn about the languages spoken by their students. How does the first or heritage language interact with English? A plethora of information is available on the Internet at sites such as the Frankfurt International School's page (Shoebottom, 1996) on language difference (http://esl.fis.edu/grammar/langdiff/) as well is in print texts such as McWhorter's (2000) book *Spreading the Word: Language and Dialect in America*. Being aware of the key features of the languages spoken in their classroom can help teachers better interpret the data they collect about their students, as will be discussed in greater detail in later sections.

UNDERSTANDING BACKGROUND AND EXPERIENCES

As described in Chapter 2, in order for teachers to be able to connect with culturally and linguistically diverse students, they need to have knowledge about their students' lives outside of school, particularly their families and their cultural norms. With whom is the child living?

What is his or her experience, if any, with formal education? When, why, and how did his or her family come to the United States? In addition to general information, teachers need specific data about their students' language and literacy practices so that these culturally and linguistically diverse learners are better integrated into the classroom and school community.

Respecting Cultural Differences

At the beginning of the chapter we saw how Mrs. Gold viewed Juan through her own cultural lens, evaluating his academic potential as well as his dispositions based on the codes that guide mainstream U.S. adult–child conversations. An understanding of what Philips (1992) calls invisible culture would help her bridge the cultural differences that caused her misunderstanding with Juan. In schools, culture is often viewed as the visible markers of an individual's identity. What does he wear to school? What does he eat for lunch? What holidays does he celebrate? Although this information is helpful when planning an international fair, other questions will be more useful in the classroom setting. What rules govern conversations between children and adults? Who can initiate a conversation? How do speakers take turns within a conversation? Where does a child look when speaking to an adult authority figure? What topics are appropriate to be discussed publicly? These invisible aspects of culture typically have a substantial impact on a student's social and academic success in the classroom.

Language is at the center of schooling, and understanding that students arrive to school with different experiences with language socialization is crucial when considering how to help students participate in instructional and social conversations. Lovelace and Wheeler (2006) offer an informative overview of common problems that arise from a mismatch between language socialization patterns in the home and school, and teachers' expectations. They cite research on potential conflict between the passive-receptive interaction patterns seen in the dominant culture in Western society and the participatory-interactive patterns seen in many African American families and other linguistically and culturally diverse groups. These two researchers recommend that teachers serve as cultural mediators, or members of the mainstream culture who can serve as cultural guides for outsiders. Literacy leaders can help teachers assume this role by introducing them to culturally responsive teaching that sets high expectations, values student voices, and uses varied instructional formats based on data about individual students that are interpreted in the context of their cultural and linguistic backgrounds.

Capitalizing on Experience

No young person, even one who has never entered a classroom, arrives at school as a blank slate. Even the most economically disadvantaged students come armed with experiences that can contribute to their social and academic success. Moll, Amanti, Neff, and Gonzalez (1992) used the term *funds of knowledge* to describe the "historically developed and accumulated bodies of knowledge and skills that are essential to household or individual well-being" (p. 133). These social and cultural resources include the mathematical knowledge embedded in construction work and the chemistry of cooking as well as many other forms of practical expertise. Although the concept originally applied to professional and domestic knowledge gained in family and community networks, it has been expanded to include peer-based expertise as well. The funds develop in apprentice-like relationships with experts, and are exchanged within the community through reciprocal relationships. Literacy leaders can help teachers and principals capitalize on students' social and cultural resources by creating curriculum that takes them into account and can help culturally and linguistically diverse families feel more welcome at their school to share their expertise or funds of knowledge (Quiroz, Greenfiled, & Altchech, 1999).

STRATEGIES FOR GETTING TO KNOW STUDENTS

Teachers are aware of the need to get to know their students. As a literacy leader, you can help them by reminding them of the potential impact of both classic strategies and newer approaches for learning about their students. At a fundamental level, teachers should be kid-watchers, conducting informal observations of all of their students, particularly those who are socially and academically vulnerable. At the next level, teachers can compile data about their students using simple tools such as anecdotal records and interest inventories that have been adapted to better serve culturally and linguistically diverse students. Much of this information can be collected without significantly altering classroom routines.

Informal Observation

In the opening vignette, Mrs. Gold's incomplete understanding of Juan's cultural background caused her to misinterpret his behavior. All teachers must pay attention to their students' actions and interactions across the course of a typical day; however, those working with culturally and linguistically diverse students must do so with an extra level of awareness of how these students' language proficiency and social and cultural practices impact their classroom lives.

Genishi and Dyson (2009) found that literacy leaders can help teachers recognize that they need to pay particular attention to culturally and linguistically diverse students' social behaviors as well as their academic strengths and needs. Teachers' observations of students should be viewed as a means of learning about a child's knowledge and know-how, and not as surveillance or the mere completion of a checklist. Teachers such as Mrs. Gold can benefit from recording notes over time to gain an ongoing sense of progress made by students such as Juan.

Anecdotal Record-Keeping

Anecdotal records are an effective and adaptable tool for recording information about students. Simple graphic organizers can help teachers take stock of a child's progress with specific literacy skills such as letter recognition, phonemic awareness, decoding, and fluency.

They also provide more global views of students' academic and social identities within the classroom community. Generic tools are available through commercial publishers and school districts in electronic and paper formats. Google Docs can be used to create, update, and share charts about students' academic and social behaviors. Apps such as Evernote (Apple, 2015), One Note (Microsoft, 2015), and Google Keep (Google, 2015) allow teachers to record audio and digital images, providing a more comprehensive portrait of a student's development.

Though the tools mentioned above are useful for all students, culturally and linguistically diverse learners typically require an extra layer of analysis, particularly in the beginning of the year or when they first enter the classroom. A basic literacy checklist can be easily adapted to pair crucial information about language differences with data about students' developing literacy skills in the areas of reading, writing, speaking, and listening. Similarly, some basic notes on culture can provide a context in which to interpret general observations about student interactions during instructional time, in the hallway, on the playground, or in other social spaces in the school. Examples of adapted charts are provided in the Literacy Leadership Toolkit at the end of this chapter.

Interest and Experience Inventories

Answers to many questions about students lie in the young people themselves. Work with teachers at the beginning of each year to ensure that they have access to one or more interest inventories that are developmentally and culturally appropriate for their students. Many interest inventories are available through commercial publishers such as Scholastic or online through sites such as Pinterest, but teachers can also design their own to better meet their students' needs. Insights into students' interests outside of school can provide the foundation for relevant and engaging instruction. For younger students or beginning ELs, these interest inventories can feature images as well as text. Students can respond to graphic representations of options on a Likert scale, or they can draw in response to more open-ended questions.

Twenty-first-century literacy is multimodal as children across different ages and from varied backgrounds are increasingly exposed to texts that include still and moving images, audio, and print. Multimodal texts are especially effective for culturally and linguistically diverse students because they can provide information in more than one medium by blending print or spoken text with images, which makes the information more comprehensible. Classroom teachers can learn a great deal by asking their students to compose simple and complex multimodal texts. Low-tech options can include a paper coat of arms in which students decorate a shield with images that reflect their interests and experience, while more technologically advanced assignments can include digital stories. Cummins et al. (2005) share the successful use of dual-language identity texts at a diverse urban elementary school. Culturally and linguistically diverse upper elementary students in Toronto collaborated to create multilingual and multimodal texts about the migrant experience for an interdisciplinary unit within the English language arts (ELA) and social studies classes. Van Sluys and Reinier (2006) document the use of multimodal and multilingual literacy projects with culturally and linguistically diverse elementary students, explaining how four newcomer students used journals, drawings, and other texts to learn language and form a community. Both of these projects use technology to engage and empower students by tapping into funds of knowledge from their experiences as immigrant youth, while also providing teachers with a window into students' lives and interests outside of the classroom.

One element that connects these two projects beyond their multimodality is their acceptance, and even celebration, of the students' home languages, whether Spanish, Mandarin, Arabic, or a nonstandard dialect of English such as AAVE. A student's home language is one of his or her most fundamental funds of knowledge, providing both a potential bridge to the acquisition of Standard English and a lifeline to family and a wider community. Literacy leaders must explain to teachers that they should allow and encourage the use of home language (Thomas & Collier, 2003) in order to build on that fund of knowledge. In turn, they must help teachers incorporate those languages into the classroom in meaningful ways. Howard's (2001) case study of four teachers who worked effectively with African American students stresses the confluence of culture and communication by relying on strong oracy to strengthen written communication. Schwarzer, Haywood, and Lorenzen (2003) offer practical pointers for monolingual teachers who want to create multilingual learning communities for ELs: offering books in home languages, including the languages in class environmental print, and asking students to serve as language experts. Native language assessments can also provide information about students' needs and capacities, especially in the beginning of their acquisition of English.

USING DATA TO UNDERSTAND STUDENTS

In the course of a typical day, a teacher makes hundreds of conscious and unconscious decisions. Which book should be read during read-aloud? What prompt should be used for the informational text writing exercise? What reading group would be best for the new student? Some of these decisions have serious and possibly immediate consequences for students. Historically, culturally, and linguistically diverse students have been placed in special education programs in disproportionate numbers because of teachers' incomplete understanding of both language socialization and language acquisition (Cummins, 1979). The section that follows outlines some key tools that teachers can use to collect data about students' language proficiency and cultural background.

TYPES OF ASSESSMENTS AND TOOLS

Carefully crafted literacy standards such as the Common Core State Standards (National Governors Association Center for Best Practices & Council of Chief State School Officers, 2010) highlight the distinct but reciprocal nature of speaking and listening and reading and writing. These language arts areas reflect a range of interrelated skills, and as a literacy leader, you can help teachers collect data about their students' strengths and needs in each. Two useful tools teachers can use to frame simple classroom assessments for culturally and linguistically diverse students are the WIDA CAN DO Descriptors (Wisconsin Center for Education Research, 2014a, b) and the NCSSFL-ACTFL Can Do Statements (American Council on the Teaching of Foreign Languages, 2013) for different levels of English proficiency, which outline different literacy tasks that ELs can typically complete across different levels of development. Teachers can use these guidelines to plan simple but effective assessment tools to collect data about language learners.

Speaking

Oral language is the foundation of reading and writing, and it is a fundamental mode of communication in classrooms of all levels. Oracy is especially important for ELs because they are often learning to read and write while they are learning to speak and comprehend aurally. Although culturally and linguistically diverse students may initially be reluctant to communicate orally, their conversational skills will typically develop more rapidly than their academic literacy skills. Cummins (1980) developed the distinction between Basic Interpersonal Communication Skills (BICS) and Cognitive Academic Language Proficiency (CALP) in response to the high percentage of culturally and linguistically diverse students referred to special education classes. While a young person might learn the English spoken in the cafeteria in 2 to 3 years, often without an identifiable accent, the same student might require as long as 10 years (Collier, 1995) to perform to his or her full academic potential in a science class or on a high-stakes test if he or she received no formal instruction in his or her first language. Proficiency in conversational English is not an indicator of readiness to take a state exam. Students need basic conversational skills to participate in the classroom community, and they need academic language skills to be successful in the Common Core era.

ELs often pass through a silent period (Krashen, 1981), or a time when they choose not to speak but rather focus their energy on absorbing the sights and sounds of an unfamiliar environment. Teachers should respect this time period, not forcing students to speak before they are ready. This phase can last 6 months or longer, but concerned teachers can request hearing tests. Once students are ready to produce verbal output, teachers should remember that listening is not a passive act, and should be practiced in the context of meaningful interactions with peers as well as with the teacher.

Listening

In a typical school day, students spend a great deal of time listening to peers as well as to the teacher, a process that is quite cognitively demanding for language learners, especially in the earlier stages of proficiency. As a literacy leader, help teachers make themselves understood by monitoring the rate, complexity, and clarity of their speech. They can also provide visual support to make the input more comprehensible. One popular method for making auditory input more comprehensible for students with basic language skills is the Total Physical Response (TPR) method (Asher, 1969). In TPR, the teacher introduces key words and phrases by accompanying them with a meaningful gesture. Students then use these gestures when they hear the words and phrases they signal. According to Asher, this mixture of oral, aural, and kinesthetic input provides a more authentic approximation of the conditions under which children acquire their first language. The TPR method was originally intended to teach vocabulary, typically at the beginning level of proficiency, but it has also been used in conjunction with storytelling (TPRS) (Ray & Seely, 1998) to make the method more versatile and relevant to more advanced learners.

Data collection tools for speaking and listening. Data about speaking and listening proficiency are crucial when planning and delivering instruction. These two skills are closely related, and can be difficult to separate, but different tools can help teachers focus on one or the other, or both. Help teachers be aware of the area they wish to target and the current proficiency level of the learner in question. Figure 4.1 describes five proficiency levels, and provides appropriate teacher prompts to engage students in dialogue.

When a new student such as Juan arrives at school, your teachers can gather data about his speaking proficiency by asking him to describe pictures or narrate the action in a brief visual story. The pictures make the questions more comprehensible because they reduce the frequency of interaction between listening and speaking. Wordless picture books can provide an excellent starting point for such oral descriptions. Options range from accessible early childhood texts such as Crews's (1991) *Truck* to more complex texts such as Tan's (2007) *The Arrival*. This book is appropriate for older, more advanced learners. Once students are in the beginning stage, the teacher can ask questions of varied complexity levels to prompt speech, beginning with basic yes or no questions: "Is this a truck?" or "Is it red?" The interview should continue with questions that require more open-ended responses such as "What do you see?" or "What is happening here?" For more advanced students in the developing, expanding, and bridging stages, these questions can also elicit responses that are not directly in the text, such as "How do you think this person is feeling?" or "What do you think will happen next?" Another useful question in the era of the CCSS is "How do you know that?"—a basic inquiry that reinforces the use of evidence when making a claim or building an argument. It is worth noting that in the entering stage (also known as the silent period) this activity can gauge basic listening skills by asking students to nonverbally indicate where something is on the page.

As a literacy leader, help teachers be aware of the complexity of the language being produced and the comfort level of the student. Teachers should begin with a question that is easily comprehensible and noninvasive, setting the student at ease. Subsequent questions should reflect whether the student answered easily and can handle a more demanding question, or struggled and thus needs a more accessible prompt. When a young person volunteers information, such as "My papi has a truck" after being asked to point to a truck, the teacher should ask appropriate questions to extend the output produced. For less advanced students like Juan, she might ask "What color is his truck?" while more advanced students like his classmate María could respond to the question "How does he use his truck?"

Literacy leaders can also encourage teachers to assess their students' listening proficiency by asking them to respond to video or audio clips of different lengths and language complexity. Students at the lower end of the proficiency spectrum will require the support provided by video clips, while older or more advanced learners can handle the cognitive demand of audio clips. Teachers must remember that the responses they require to the listening texts will measure another skill such as speaking or writing unless they ask

Figure 4.1. Speaking and Listening Assessment Activities Using Picture Books

Proficiency Level	WIDA CAN DO Descriptors (Listening (L) & Speaking (S))	Appropriate Textual Features	Suggested Texts and Teaching Points
Entering	• Point to stated pictures, words, phrases **L** • Follow one-step oral directions **L** • Match oral statements to objects, figures or illustrations **L** • Name objects, people, pictures **S** • Answer WH- (who, what, when, where, which) questions **S**	• Familiar story or topic • Typical story structure • Illustrations for each page • Illustrations that support the storyline or text • Illustrations that contextualize the story • Simple language	Tyler (2007), *First Day of School* Families, cultural diversity, school Diaz-Strom (2000), *Carmen's Colors* Colors, weather, sharing Figueredo (2011), *What Can Fly?* Comparing/classifying/measuring, nature/science, vehicles in motion, nonfiction
Beginning	• Sort pictures, objects according to oral instructions **L** • Follow two-step oral directions **L** • Match information from oral descriptions to objects, illustrations **L** • Ask WH- questions **S** • Describe pictures, events, objects, people **S** • Restate facts **S**	• Little text per page • Predictable and repetitive text structures	Lee (1996), *I Had a Hippopotamus* Animals, imagination Suen (2000), *100 Days* Counting, cultural diversity, classroom experiences O'Brien (2003), *A Special Day* Time/days of the week, holidays/traditions, families, cultural diversity
Developing	• Locate, select, order information from oral descriptions **L** • Follow multistep oral directions **L** • Categorize or sequence oral information using pictures, objects **L** • Formulate hypotheses, make predictions **S** • Describe processes **S** • Retell stories or events **S**	With a familiar story or topic: • Less dependence on illustrations • More text per page • Slightly more complex text With an unfamiliar text or story: • Illustrations that support the story line or topic • Typical story structure • Simple language • Little text per page • Predictable and repetitive text	Sneed & Fonseca (2005), *Punched Paper* Imagination, holidays/traditions, games/toys, friendship, cultural diversity Lake (2005), *Pop Pop and Grandpa* Immigration, home, grandparents, families, cultural diversity, childhood experiences Reynolds (2004), *Living in an Igloo* Weather/seasons/clothing, families, environment/nature, cultural diversity

Figure 4.1. Speaking and Listening Assessment Activities Using Picture Books (continued)

Proficiency Level	WIDA CAN DO Descriptors (Listening (L) & Speaking (S))	Appropriate Textual Features	Suggested Texts and Teaching Points
Expanding	• Compare/contrast functions, relationships from oral information **L** • Analyze and apply oral information **L** • Identify cause and effect from oral discourse **L** • Discuss stories, issues, concepts **S** • Offer creative solutions to issues, problems **S** • Offer creative solutions to issues, problems **S**	• Fewer illustrations • More complex text	Pérez (2013), *My Very Own Room* Siblings, sharing and giving, immigration Elya (2006), *Home at Last* Overcoming obstacles, families, education, dreams, aspirations
Bridging	• Draw conclusions from oral information **L** • Construct models based on oral discourse **L** • Make connections from oral discourse **L** • Engage in debates **S** • Explain phenomena, give examples, and justify responses **S** • Express and defend points of view **S**		Armand (2011), *Love Twelve Miles Long* U.S. history, slavery, responsibility, heroism, families, dreams and aspirations, discrimination Nelson (2009), *Quiet Hero: The Ira Hayes Story* Conflict resolution, biography/memoir, empathy/compassion, leadership Atkins (2008), *Get Set! Swim!* Sports, identity/self-esteem/confidence, responsibility, overcoming obstacles

Adapted from the WIDA Can DO descriptors for the levels of English language proficiency, PK–12, speaking and listening

The WIDA CAN DO Descriptors work in conjunction with the WIDA Performance Definitions of the English language proficiency standards. The Performance Definitions use three criteria: (1) linguistic complexity, (2) vocabulary usage, and (3) language control, to describe the increasing quality and quantity of students' language processing and use across the levels of language proficiency.

for nonverbal responses such as drawings or gestures with a nod or a thumbs-up.

Speaking and listening are an integral part of the classroom routine, and teachers must monitor their students' progress closely. There are numerous readily available technologies such as the aforementioned apps Evernote (Apple, 2015) One Note (Microsoft, 2015), and Google Keep (Google, 2015) that allow teachers to record students' verbal output over time to reveal progress as well as areas that need reinforcement.

Reading

Reading is fundamental to academic success, and culturally and linguistically diverse students face special challenges when mastering this skill. Students typically learn to read in their first language after they have gained oral fluency, whereas many language learners learn to read their new language while they are learning to speak it. In this situation, students do not have a tacit knowledge of how the new language works, which makes reading a laborious process. However, once a language learner gains some proficiency in the target language, he or she often develops an increased degree of metalinguistic awareness as he or she moves back and forth between two languages. Vocabulary and its connection to word recognition also impacts reading proficiency in a new language. Although a small working vocabulary makes reading challenging, reading itself is an excellent source of comprehensible input, providing repeated access to unfamiliar words at a pace more easily controlled by the learner.

A crucial element for assessing students' reading proficiency is the text used. Choosing a text for a reading assessment involves careful consideration of its language demands and its content. Figure 4.1 also provides a description of learner behaviors for different language proficiency levels adapted from WIDA CAN DO Descriptors (Wisconsin Center for Education Research, 2014a, 2014b), alongside information on textual features to target at each level and suggestions for authentic texts. This information can help teachers strategically choose print texts of assessments of reading alone and in conjunction with other areas of literacy. The texts chosen for Figure 4.1 were published by Lee & Low Books, an independent publisher dedicated to culturally and linguistically diverse books. Though text selection is important for all readers, it is especially important for language learners. When faced with a passage beyond their proficiency level, these young readers will often shut down. The text's topic is another key consideration; beginning readers are more likely to persevere if the topic is interesting or familiar. Many educational publishers offer leveled books across different genres. Children's and adolescent literature from popular publishers can also work in many contexts. The Common Core State Standards Appendix B (National Governors Association Center for Best Practices & Council of Chief State School Officers, 2010) offers a list of excellent texts organized by grade, but the level of these texts should be viewed cautiously when working with language learners. Asking a 6-year-old such as Juan who recently arrived to the United States to make sense of *Frog and Toad Together* (Lobel, 1972) is unreasonable, exemplary though the text may be. The Lee & Low website (https://www.leeandlow.com/) contains search functions that allow educators to make selections not only by grade level, but also by reading level and theme. Each book description features a description of its language features and themes as well as a teacher's guide. Many texts are published in Spanish as well as in other common languages. Chapter 9 offers further insight into the process of creating a classroom library that meets the needs and piques the interest of culturally and linguistically diverse students.

After choosing an assessment text, a teacher's next step is to determine how readers will respond to the text in meaningful ways. As a literacy leader, you can help teachers make an appropriate choice. When working with students who are learning language, literacy leaders should encourage teachers to move beyond the traditional measure of written responses to written comprehension questions. This variety is useful on two basic levels: It can help teachers use methods appropriate to students' levels and make responses more engaging. For a student in the beginning levels of language proficiency, making a drawing is an appropriate reading comprehension exercise. For more proficient students, written responses ranging from text-based comprehension questions to extensions of the story are developmentally appropriate and more authentic, given the demands of the literacy curriculum they are expected to master. Of course, writing is another key academic skill, which needs to be assessed both in connection to reading and on its own.

Writing

Writing is a crucial academic skill, and one that is cognitively demanding for culturally and linguistically diverse students. Many students suffer from writing anxiety, and this insecurity exists for language learners as well. Silva's (1993) review of research on the differences between second- and first-language writing reveals that second-language writers typically spend less time planning, composing, and reviewing their writing. Language learners are often concerned with surface level errors—at times, to a degree that is almost paralyzing. Teachers must help culturally and linguistically diverse students move past this paralysis.

Although ELs might struggle to compose text, they should be given the opportunity to do so. This writing should also be assessed for its content, or its message, rather than merely for its grammar and mechanics (Hudelson, 1989). Culturally and linguistically diverse students at the expanding level and above can be encouraged to take control of their own error correction through the use of both general and targeted writing checklists. These lists can be designed according to students' age and proficiency levels and to reflect targeted linguistic structures, such as pronouns or specific verb tenses (see Figure 4.2 for an example of a checklist). Teachers can create a basic template, and modify it to focus on specific learner needs.

Writing is a skill that develops over time; so teachers should document their students' progress at regular intervals. Apps such as Evernote (Apple, 2015), One Note (Microsoft, 2015), and Google Keep (Google, 2015) can be used to create multimodal records of students' writing, complete with images of their work. Of course, teachers can maintain paper portfolios of student work, along with hard copies of anecdotal records and other data tools. Teachers can also use document cameras to project an image of annotated student work onto a screen or whiteboard, using this technology to provide feedback in real time.

Writing assessments for culturally and linguistically diverse students vary widely, depending on the students' age and language proficiency. As with speaking assessments, younger students and those with lower levels of English proficiency can respond to pictures or other visual stimuli such as pages from a wordless picture book. More advanced students can write in response to written prompts of varying levels of complexity, producing texts of developmentally appropriate length and complexity. Classroom-based research with multilingual students reveals the affective and cognitive benefits of multilingual writing on topics that resonate with their interests and experiences (Coady & Escamilla, 2005; Laman & Van Sluys, 2008). ELs can feel

Figure 4.2. Writing Behaviors Checklist

Writing Behaviors	Yes, I Did
Did you remember to start every sentence with a capital letter? *Sentences start with capital letters.*	
Did you remember to use capital letters for names and proper nouns? *Names of people and places like Juan and Honduras start with capital letters.*	
Did you remember to end every sentence with punctuation such as a period, question mark, or exclamation point? *Sentences end with a . an ! or a ?*	
Did you remember to check your: Past-Tense Verbs *Many past-tense verbs end with –ed (walked, talked) but lots of others don't follow this rule (sang, read, drew, gave).*	

empowered when they are not only allowed but encouraged to use their first language, and that language can form a bridge to new learning.

Bilingual/Native Language Assessments

Many teachers may not be aware that common literacy assessments such as the Developmental Reading Assessment (DRA) are available in Spanish, and the results of an assessment given in a students' stronger language actually provide more accurate information about his or her proficiency. Chapter 3 began with a vignette in which a young boy's DRA score jumped close to 20 points when he was tested in Spanish. Unfortunately, his classroom teacher did not appreciate the implications of these results, probably because her job security depends on her students' scores in English, not Spanish. Literacy leaders should help teachers understand that higher-order thinking skills are transferable across languages once a student acquires a certain level of proficiency in each (Cummins, 1979). Data about languages other than English are relevant when considering a young person's capacity.

Native language can be used in less formal contexts to obtain more precise results about students' specific skills. For example, when proficient speakers of students' dominant language are available, allowing an EL to respond to questions in his or her dominant language after reading a text in the target language can offer a more accurate assessment of his second-language reading proficiency. Of course, those responses can be oral or written, based on the student's age, first-language writing proficiency, and the teacher's reason for collecting student data.

CONSIDERATIONS FOR ASSESSMENTS

The word *assessment* often conjures up images of high-stakes tests, an unfortunate reality that impacts many educators' interpretation of the term. In actuality, assessment serves many purposes; it can be used to help students learn as well as to document their current level of proficiency in the key literacy skills. Both summative and formative assessments are important for different reasons. Summative assessments are high-stakes measurements given by the teacher at the end of a unit or periodically to determine student placements, or administered by the state annually to measure school and district performance. Formative assessments, or assignments, provide data about students' needs and strengths on a regular basis to help students with their learning. Assessments can be analyzed along two distinct but connected axes: formal and informal, and annual and ongoing. Literacy leaders need to ensure that teachers understand the differences between them and the distinct purposes they serve.

Formal Versus Informal

Formal assessments are typically summative measures that are given at the end of a lesson sequence or unit, and they are designed to measure student mastery of content or skills, often indicated by a grade or rating. Most districts require the regular administration of formal assessments because they provide valuable information about students' achievements. For example, students' scores on the DRA reveal reading proficiency across crucial subskills such as decoding and fluency. Increasingly, districts expect teachers to apply the data collected from formal assessments to their teaching through targeted instruction. Though these measures of student progress are important, so are the less formal observations made by teachers when they see a student reading, writing, speaking, and listening during their daily classroom routines. Discrepancies often exist between formal and informal assessments, especially for culturally and linguistically diverse students.

At times, teachers can learn as much about a student such as Juan from watching him read a book with a peer as they can through his DRA results. Literacy leaders should encourage teachers to trust their instincts about the students who share their classroom, even when formal assessments tell a different story than informal assessments. They should use the information from both formal and informal assessments to plan instruction that captures student interests and builds on their strengths as it addresses student needs.

Annual Versus Ongoing

High-stakes tests that are given once a year by outside entities provide a useful snapshot of student proficiency levels at the time of the test, but they can also burden students with labels that follow them for 12 months, if not their entire education—a circumstance that implies assessment involves the intermittent measure of a set of static abilities. In reality, assessment is an ongoing and dynamic process that helps teachers identify student assets and needs while tracking student growth. Literacy leaders should help teachers recognize the importance of assessment for this purpose. Chapter 7 provides information about different types of assessment instruments.

All students are more than the labels assigned to them by standardized assessments, especially culturally and linguistically diverse students whose developing language proficiency may lead teachers to view them as less capable. Reading assessment data should be used for more than assigning a student such as Juan to a reading group or directing him to choose a book from a particular bin in the classroom library. Student writing should not be dissected with a red pen to reveal every grammatical and mechanical error. Assessment data should be used to target linguistic and content-based support that is grounded in students' experiences.

USING INFORMATION TO
MAKE SOUND INSTRUCTIONAL DECISIONS

The previous sections outlined some tools for collecting meaningful data about culturally and linguistically diverse students by acknowledging not only their cultural backgrounds and their proficiency levels in English but also how their home language interacts with their new language. The next step in the process involves knowing how to use this information to plan targeted instruction across the different literacy skills.

Planning Speaking and Listening Instruction

Students will feel more comfortable speaking up if they have the tools needed to sustain a conversation when there is a breakdown in communication. Even students at the beginning proficiency level can participate in basic conversations with the proper scaffolding. For example, students could use sentence starters for science that begin with phrases such as "I observed that . . ." or they could make a comparison in various content areas by using a frame such as "_____ are similar because _____, but different in that _____." A modified method for younger or less proficient students involves using printed or visual signs that signal their agreement, disagreement, or confusion about the topic being discussed. For example, students can hold up or display cards with visuals such as question marks to signal confusion, thumbs-up to indicate agreement, and thumbs-down to show disagreement. Both mainstream students and their culturally and linguistically diverse peers should be taught and evaluated on their use of clarification formulae such as "I don't understand" or "Can you repeat that?" so they can sustain a conversation past the inevitable confusions and miscommunications (Dooley, 2009). Literacy leaders need to help teachers and building leaders understand the importance of providing culturally and linguistically diverse students with the opportunity to engage in meaningful discussions with their peers.

Informal speaking and listening activities should be integrated into the daily practices of a classroom. Remind teachers to make use of established strategies such as Turn & Talk, Think-Pair-Share (Lyman, 1987), and other techniques that provide both peer-to-peer dialogues for all students and a safe rehearsal space for language learners to practice speaking.

Students can engage in a variety of formal speaking activities, making presentations and performing skits in live formats with video and audio recordings. These projects can cover language as well as content by focusing on particular grammatical and rhetorical structures. Sentence frames, or sentences that contain blanks for the students to complete (for example, "___ and ___ are similar because they are _____."), can help culturally and linguistically diverse students produce academic discourse. These tools will help teachers get richer data when they assess individual participation in the instructional conversations embedded in activities such as book clubs and reading and writing workshop.

Planning Reading Instruction

Imagine a scenario in which literacy coach Mr. Varani is helping his colleague understand that there is no one-size-fits-all approach to choosing classroom texts for culturally and linguistically diverse students because newcomer Juan's needs are quite different, even from his classmate Maria's. Once Mrs. Gold has chosen a text from her carefully cultivated classroom library, she needs to take the time to assess the language demands of the text, taking note of the unfamiliar words and language structures. Juan might need support to understand even common words. Simple bilingual picture books, such as *Mouse Paint/ Pintura de Ratón* (Walsh, 2010), offer engaging multimodal and multilingual comprehensible input. At other times, a book can serve to teach a specific grammatical or rhetorical structure. Older, more proficient students might be ready to work on complex grammatical structures such as the conditional clauses introduced in a book such as *If You Give a Mouse a Cookie* (Numeroff, 1985). Mentor texts, or texts that serve as models or exemplars, can thus serve as models of language structures (for example, complex verbs) in different genres.

Planning Writing Instruction

Above all, writing is a means of communication, and literacy leaders should encourage teachers to ask students to write to an authentic audience about topics that matter to them. Even prompts from high-stakes texts can be adjusted to reflect students' interests and funds of knowledge. Coady and Escamilla (2005) documented the work produced by Latino students when they responded to the prompt "What would you do if you were principal for the day?" The responses reflected the experiences and the collectivist values of the students as they constructed an argument about how to be an effective school leader. The researchers also noted the potential social and academic impact of allowing native language responses when appropriate.

Moving Beyond Ability Grouping

Many teachers use the default method of grouping by ability. The term *ability* itself is problematic when describing any student because it implies an innate and fixed quality rather than a developing capacity. Ability is an especially challenging term for culturally and linguistically diverse students because of the history of their misclassification into special education. Literacy leaders like Mr. Varani must help teachers like Mrs. Gold learn to distinguish the language proficiency of students like Juan from their capacity to learn and grow. Consciously substituting the term *proficiency* for *ability* can help educators begin to make that shift.

Young people are social by nature. Inasmuch as 21st-century workplaces are becoming increasingly collaborative, group-work is an effective learning strategy, although it should not be used exclusively. Literacy leaders can help teachers move beyond grouping by general proficiency to using pairs and small groups. Particularly at the beginning levels of proficiency, language learners benefit from being paired or grouped by language. Ideally, a student at the bridging level should be paired to support a classmate at the entering level. In the opening vignette, rather than silencing the exchange between Juan and his classmate María, Mrs. Gold could have encouraged this useful partnership by seating the two students close together and encouraging María to act as Juan's guide to the social and academic practices of their classroom. Spanish-speaking, Chinese-speaking pairs, or Korean-speaking pairs should also form larger groups with English dominant students and other language learners, but teachers must provide additional support to promote cross-cultural collaborations. Dooley (2009) affirms the importance of teaching students the tools to both sustain and deepen peer dialogue across different languages and cultures.

Although culturally and linguistically diverse students should often be clustered by home language when working in larger mixed-language groups, heterogeneity and not homogeneity promotes the acquisition of literacy skills. Teachers should create groups with varied proficiency levels so the striving students can benefit from more advanced peers, a practice in keeping with Vygotsky's (1980) principle of the zone of proximal development. Strong students deepen their understanding by helping their less proficient classmates. Data from anecdotal records can help teachers create both balanced groups and targeted instruction groups. The latter are not based on a static measure of student performance, but rather an identified need for support in a specific area, often for a brief period of time.

Heterogeneous groups can be a powerful tool for building classroom community. Teachers must take students' social needs into account when creating groups, balancing introverts and extroverts, and detail-oriented learners with big-picture thinkers. Teachers can also use the data collected about students' interactions in social spaces to plan teams with complementary personalities.

Differentiation

As with many trendy terms in education, the word *differentiation* has been overused to the point that it has become almost meaningless. Teacher candidates are often asked to include a section on differentiation toward the end of their lesson plan, as if it were something that can be easily added in the final stages of the planning process. Differentiation starts at the beginning of the planning process, and continues throughout, impacting what is taught, and how it is taught and to whom. Tomlinson and Imbeau (2010) outline distinct aspects of differentiation and the relationship between them: the content, process, product, and effect of the curriculum and readiness, interest, and learner profile of the students. They also explain the importance of the classroom system, which consists of the learning environment, curriculum, assessment, and instruction. Teachers should consider each of these variables when planning instruction, making differentiation a complex and comprehensive process.

When it comes to differentiating materials, text selection is an art as well as a science. Literacy leaders can help classroom teachers use data from interest and experience inventories to choose high-interest texts for both whole-class and small-group instruction. Of course, students with different proficiency levels might share a fascination with the same topic; teachers can collect texts of varied complexity on popular subjects such as sports and animals to address different levels of readiness. Students can also respond to texts in particular ways, based on their proficiency levels, interests, and strengths. Students themselves can play a role in the differentiation process when they are allowed to select their mode of response to a reading by acting out a key scene, writing a new ending, or making a collage of important themes and ideas.

The flexible grouping practices discussed above also promote differentiated instruction. Students can be clustered for targeted instruction, particularly within the framework of reading and writing workshop, as will be discussed in greater detail in Chapter 7. The data collection tools discussed previously make visible students who share the same need, whether it is practice with phonemic awareness or support in mastering irregular past-tense verbs. Adaptations to these tools that account for students' backgrounds represent another layer of differentiation that allows teachers to recognize the impact of language and culture on students' learning. Targeted instruction based on differences between Spanish and English will allow a student such as Juan to master a skill (for example, making a proper noun possessive) with greater ease and a stronger sense of the benefits of being bilingual. When done well, differentiation is a means of empowering students by helping them recognize their own potential for growth.

DATA-DRIVEN AND STUDENT-CENTERED INSTRUCTION

Relationships are at the center of teaching and learning, and knowing their students helps educators strengthen those bonds. Understanding culturally and linguistically diverse students involves recognizing their individual attributes, needs and interests, and cultural backgrounds as language learners. With the right tools and the proper attitude about students' capacities, teachers can adjust their practices and their thinking in small but meaningful ways. Literacy leaders can help teachers look beyond standardized test scores to recognize the social and cultural resources these students possess that help with their instructional needs.

LITERACY LEADERSHIP TOOLKIT

Use the two exercises below to help teachers systematically collect data on students' individual strengths and needs without losing sight of their linguistic and cultural backgrounds. These anecdotal charts can be adapted to record important information about the difference between English and students' other languages.

Exercise 4.1: Language Difference and Skill Charts

Use the customized anecdotal chart to record students' behaviors in relation to their home language. Place a summary of distinct language features at the top of a chart with space to take notes on students' speaking, listening, reading, and writing.

Classroom Languages Compared With English				
Spanish		Arabic		
Informal and formal registers; a highly phonetic language with a similar alphabet but distinct phonology; typical word order Subj-Verb-Obj; adjectives typically come after nouns; speakers can leave out the subject in a sentence because it is implied by the verb; five fixed vowel sounds		Different alphabet; text is read from right to left; fewer vowel sounds; considerably different verb tenses (e.g., no *to be* in present tense; adjectives follow nouns; no indefinite articles (*a, an*); few cognates with English		
Student	Reading	Writing	Speaking	Listening
Name: Juan Mendez Home Language(s): Spanish spoken exclusively in the home				
Name: Fatima Abdullah Home Language(s): Arabic spoken in the home; father and older siblings speak Intermediate English				
Name: Home Language(s):				

Exercise 4.2: Student Background and Social Interactions

Use this anecdotal chart to highlight the interplay between students' interactions in the social spaces in the school and their cultural backgrounds. Include information about students' collaboration with peers and their behaviors in key spaces such as the playground and the lunchroom. Include notes on students' family situations and key features of their culture in General Observations.

	Collaborating/ Peer Relations	General Observations
Name: Juan Mendez Cultural/Family Notes: Newcomer from Honduras (2 months in United States); father is a landscaper and mother cleans offices; lives with parents, two siblings and maternal grandparents; collectivist orientation; concern with respectful behavior, especially with elders		
Name: Fatima Abdullah Cultural/Family Notes: Arrived from Morocco a year ago; father is a carpenter; mother stays home; Muslim; collectivist orientation; respect for elders		

CHAPTER 5

Know Professional Development Options

- Literacy leaders create collaborative learning communities to empower teachers and build leadership.
- Literacy leaders design professional development experiences to strengthen and refine the everyday practices of teachers and impact student learning.
- Literacy leaders engage teachers as active partners in determining the content of their learning and the methods by which they engage in learning.

Caroline, a literacy specialist in a culturally, linguistically, and economically diverse school, was facilitating a grade-level meeting in grade 3. Together, the three 3rd-grade teachers and Caroline were discussing their past experiences with professional learning, how they each learn best, and ideas for designing their future individual and collective professional learning opportunities. Yasmin, the grade-level leader at the Franklin School, had come prepared; she had compiled a list of certificates she had received from attending 1-day and multiday workshops sponsored by the district and outside providers. Kelly, a 3rd-grade teacher, began to talk about the book her grade-level teachers had jointly decided to read last year in response to questions the group had about new teaching strategies that the teachers wanted to try. Caroline noticed the puzzled look on Yasmin's face. As Kelly continued to talk about how reading and discussing the book together impacted her thinking and her teaching practices, Yasmin's intense look changed from confused to thoughtful; she was obviously thinking about what Kelly was saying. After Kelly described some of the ways in which her teaching had shifted, Caroline said, "Yasmin, I noticed your interest in what Kelly was describing. Would you care to share what you are thinking?" Yasmin replied, "I guess I never really thought about our work together as professional learning. I only thought about the workshops that I have attended." Kelly responded, "When I thought about the professional learning I had been involved in, the first thing that came to mind was the work we do as a grade-level team. Not only have we read and discussed books and tried out the strategies we read about, but we also continually analyze student work and discuss ways in which we can best meet their needs. I counted that too." Mike, another member of the 3rd-grade team, chimed in: "Absolutely, I agree. I also thought about the monthly meetings with Caroline. Those meetings are curriculum meetings. We design, refine, and reflect on our curriculum during those meetings, and I counted that as professional learning as well." "Wow," Yasmin replied. "I never thought of those things as professional learning. It was just a part of what we do as teachers."

Yasmin's response to the idea that professional learning extends beyond district-sponsored workshops is not uncommon. As an experienced teacher of more than 15 years, Yasmin had been told, year after year, what workshops she would attend and what days of the school's calendar were "professional development days." These three teachers' reflections and open discussion about the value of their professional learning experiences signaled a hopeful shift to Caroline that professional learning can be planned with teachers and can take into account their past experiences as both learners and teachers.

As a literacy leader, one of your responsibilities is to support, plan, and lead the professional learning experiences of the teachers in your building or district. It is imperative to understand the needs of the teachers with whom you work, and to meet those needs through a variety of different approaches.

WORKING WITH YOUR TEACHERS TO MAKE DECISIONS

The Twitter feed "Children are the priority. Change is the reality. Collaboration is the strategy" (Judith Billings, as cited by School Improvement Network, 2014) probably resonates with literacy leaders. Literacy leaders understand that professional development must be tied to student learning, especially as teachers grapple with the challenges of working with a changing student population and a changing parent community. Literacy leaders understand the importance of positioning themselves as lifelong learners so that they in turn can help their teachers appreciate the need for professional development to make sound decisions that are grounded in research and practice. Literacy leaders also know that they need to help their school communities collaborate to meet short-term and long-term student needs.

With so much pressure on today's teachers because of changing standards, increased teacher accountability, and high-stakes testing, literacy leaders often hear "Just tell me what to do and I will do it" from both new and experienced teachers. New teachers, eager to please, are unsure of their skills and need to build their teaching knowledge. Very experienced teachers feel weary and discouraged from the constant blame they receive for their students' lack of achievement. Professional learning that encourages reflection and collaboration rather than prescription and compliance is a key to empowering teachers as decisionmakers and building a community of learners.

OUTSIDE THE SCHOOL DISTRICT

There are many opportunities for you and your teachers to engage in professional learning outside of the school district. Continuing education courses, graduate programs, teacher inquiry groups, and professional association conferences are some of the most common forms of professional development.

Continuing Education and Graduate Coursework

Many independent consulting firms (e.g., LitLife), state-affiliated centers (e.g., New York Boards of Cooperative Educational Services, or BOCES), and nonprofit agencies (e.g., West Ed) offer continuing education courses and professional development opportunities for teachers. These offerings usually respond to needs in schools and classrooms as a result of new state mandates. Because many of the centers and nonprofit agencies are partially, if not fully, state-funded, their leaders attend statewide meetings and are knowledgeable about decisions that impact teachers and leaders. For example, many teacher centers offered workshops on the Common Core State Standards (National Governors Association Center for Best Practices & Council of Chief State School Officers, 2010) while the standards were being adopted and revised at the state level. Knowing change was taking place, leaders became steeped in the standards and their potential impact on classroom practices.

Many states require that teachers obtain a master's degree either to qualify for or continue certification. Some states require a master's degree for permanent certification, or require completion of a master's degree within a specified amount of time to keep certification. Formal learning in graduate classes can be a powerful source of professional development. We have seen our literacy specialist students change their teaching practices as a result of their coursework. They began the program by examining theories focused on the impact of culture on language and literacy, and then worked with diverse students in field-based courses. This opportunity to apply theory to practice helped them shift their perspectives and transform their teaching practices.

Teacher Inquiry Groups and Conferences

Teacher inquiry groups are usually voluntary groups of educators who come together for a specific purpose. For example, the Literacy for Social Justice Teacher Researcher Group (renamed in 2013 Educators for Social Justice) in St. Louis, Missouri, began in 2001 so teachers could come together to study their own teaching practices and build socially just communities. This teacher inquiry group now offers many professional learning opportunities (e.g., book clubs, film discussions, and an annual conference) for educators throughout districts in St. Louis. Teacher inquiry groups are one model of professional development that accounts for the needs of individual teachers within a community of learners where peers serve as guides (Rogers et al., 2005).

Most professional associations hold annual conferences around a central theme. Professional development conferences provide you and your teachers with opportunities to expand and deepen your professional knowledge, become aware of innovative practices, network with fellow educators, and become rejuvenated and inspired. Literacy leaders should regularly attend and present at state, national, and even international conferences. At conferences you can share research and writing, and connect with and learn from colleagues whom you do not have the opportunity to see on a regular basis. You can listen to and engage with leaders in the field, and hear about innovative practices in schools. You can work together with colleagues to envision how such innovative practices would work in your classrooms and schools, and think about how students would benefit from the experiences. Finally, you can walk away a little more confident in yourself as a learner and leader. Professional association conferences can have an uplifting impact on you and your teachers.

Harnessing the Power of Outside Professional Development to Sustain Change

There has been growing criticism toward single-day workshops and professional association conference attendance (Ball & Cohen, 1999; Garet, Porter, Desimone, Birman, & Yoon, 2001; Joyce & Showers, 2002). This criticism is not so much about the workshops themselves, but about the challenges of sustaining professional learning over time and directly connecting the content and strategies to the classroom. As a literacy leader, think about ways in which workshops and conference attendance can become increasingly powerful learning experiences. This can be achieved by choosing conferences and sessions that are aligned with classroom and school goals and initiatives, creating a strategy for learning and reflecting while at the conference, and continuing the learning once teachers have returned to the classroom. See **Online Figure B** for guidelines for enhancing the value of conference attendance.

Teachers should be able to choose the conferences they attend. However, with budget constraints and competing goals, support for conference attendance has to be limited to those conferences that will further the work that literacy leaders are doing with their teachers in relation to the school's goals. Once you and your teachers determine that the conference connects to your defined goals, work with your teachers to identify individual sessions or strands that are relevant to the work being done in the school and note anticipated outcomes. This information can usually be found in the online program and session descriptions.

If possible, plan to bring a team of teachers to the conference so they can help bring back information and ideas to the school. In order to navigate large conferences, plan ahead. As a leader for the group, schedule time to meet in the morning to communicate individual plans for the day and meet at the end of the day to debrief about the sessions. Use this time to determine topics to explore further, materials to investigate purchasing, or ideas for next steps in your school and classrooms. Use this individual time to reflect on the many ways you can support individual teachers to shift their instructional practices.

Once your team of teachers has returned to school, bring them together to share individual plans for continuing to learn. Meet with the principal (if he or she did not attend) to share teachers' plans and seek approval for reaching out to those teachers who did not attend. The principal's awareness of the conference's benefits will help secure funding for future conferences.

AT THE SCHOOL DISTRICT LEVEL

In his study investigating organizations that made the leap from "good to great," Collins (2001) found that transformation is never the result of "a single defining action, no groundbreaking program, no one killer innovation, no miracle moment" (p. 14). Rather, improvements are the result of a "cumulative process, step by step, action by action, decision by decision" (p. 165) while moving in a consistent direction over an extended period of time. Literacy leaders can help schools transform their practices by working with school- and district-level leaders to align change initiatives across the schools and designing professional learning experiences for teachers that connect to the district-level initiatives.

Aligning Change Initiatives

Often, school and district leaders work tirelessly to craft a mission statement (i.e., a clear and distinctive view of the district's purpose) and goals for the district. It is not the words of these statements that create and sustain change. Rather, it is the actions of stakeholders and the alignment of those actions with the mission and goals that lead to change. The way each is incorporated into the curriculum, teaching practices and strategies, and professional development opportunities enables sustained change to occur. It is imperative that literacy leaders identify misalignments. This may mean talking to stakeholders and asking them the kind of questions listed in Figure 5.1. The answers to these questions allow literacy leaders to attend to misalignments and make adjustments so that alignment occurs.

Professional Development that Connects to District Initiatives

Most school districts continue to have districtwide professional development days designated on the school calendar. It is essential that these days not only connect to district initiatives, but also be valuable for *every educator* in the district. This can be achieved by carefully considering when it is most beneficial to hold districtwide professional development days versus school-based professional development opportunities. Literacy leaders should work with their district leaders to help them appreciate the benefits of each and determine ways to build different professional development calendars. Below

Figure 5.1. Aligning Mission and Goals with Actions

- If our mission and goals represent our core values, what obstacles get in the way of our meeting the district or school's mission and goals?

- Identify something in your daily work that is consistent with the district or school's mission and goals.

- Identify something in your daily work that is inconsistent with the district or school's mission and goals.

are some questions to help guide leaders in making decisions about districtwide professional development:

- What is the overall goal for the day?
- How would teachers from across the schools in the district benefit from coming together?
- How would professional development be supported?

AT THE SCHOOL BUILDING LEVEL

The term *professional learning communities* has become widespread in schools across the United States; however, its meaning changes in different contexts. Professional learning communities are meant to be communities of educators caring for and working together to improve student learning by engaging in continuous learning of their own (DuFour, 2004). It is with these intentions that literacy leaders must work to create spaces and structures for teachers to learn and grow together. Chapter 3 described how a professional learning community could be used to help teachers adjust to their changing student population.

As Collins (2001) explained, it is vital for a school to work together as a professional learning community to develop a shared mission for literacy teaching and learning that is based upon common ideals. This can be an energizing learning experience that leads to coherence in programs and a renewed commitment to the school (Wepner et al., 2012). This mission statement should include teachers' hopes and beliefs about what strong literacy instruction looks and sounds like in successful classrooms. It can then serve as the impetus for a professional development action plan that challenges and supports teachers' growth. The Literacy Leadership Toolkit at the end of this chapter provides a framework for developing such a plan.

Building Capacity

Lambert (1998) called for a broadening of the concept of leadership that suggests sharing the responsibility for learning and sharing decisionmaking when possible. The literacy leader or even the leadership team of the school cannot make all the decisions. In a review of literature on capacity building, Stoll, Bolam, McMahon, Wallace, and Thomas (2006) found that a focus on building collective capacity within schools is critical for sustainable improvement in student learning. They define capacity as "a complex blend of motivation, skill, positive learning, organizational conditions and culture, and infrastructure of support" (p. 221). Fullan (2010) gives two reasons why capacity building is effective: "One is that knowledge about effective practice becomes more widely available and accessible on a daily basis. The second reason is more powerful still—working together generates commitment" (p. 72). In order to inspire and sustain change, building capacity is essential to your work as a literacy leader.

Job-Embedded

Job-embedded professional development has become common language in federal legislation. For example, the Race to the Top grant application (U.S. Department of Education, 2010) makes reference to this type of professional development. In addition, guidance for using American Recovery and Reinvestment Act funds to support Individuals with Disabilities Education Act (IDEA) Part B and Title I activities promotes the enactment of job-embedded professional development in high-need schools (U.S. Department of Education, 2009a, b).

Job-embedded professional development is grounded in day-to-day teaching practice, and is intended to improve teachers' content-specific instructional practices with the goal of improving student learning (Darling-Hammond & McLaughlin, 1995; Hirsh, 2009). Most of the professional development structures described in this chapter are job-embedded. It is essential for a literacy leader to have job-embedded professional development as a primary goal.

Finding Out What Teachers Want and Need

Adults learn best when professional learning is self-directed and builds upon prior knowledge and experiences (Drago-Severson, 2004). One way to accomplish this is for literacy leaders to design and conduct a survey for teachers that can guide their work. This survey should prompt teachers to reflect on their own strengths and needs connected to the overall literacy goals of the school. For example, if the literacy goal for the school is to implement writing workshop, the survey should only include items around aspects of writing workshop, even though teachers may also need support in other areas. Figure 5.2 provides an example of a teacher survey to help guide in the planning of professional learning connected to teachers' needs.

OPTIONS FOR PROFESSIONAL DEVELOPMENT

When teachers participate in high-quality professional development directly focused on their curriculum and instructional techniques, they tend to use instructional practices connected to higher achievement (Darling-Hammond, Chung Wei, Andree, Richardson, & Orphanos, 2009). The following examples of job-embedded professional development can help achieve this goal.

Study Groups

Study groups are voluntary, participant-driven groups that have clear learning goals. Members are expected to explore new information, apply it, and discuss it in a risk-free environment over a specified period of time. Study groups focus on student work, response to professional literature, information from workshops or conferences, or school data analysis. Study groups have one facilitator or rotate the leadership. Although study groups are voluntary, they require a certain level of commitment by all members. Study groups are ineffective if members do not fulfill their commitment to read, supply student work, or attend on time. Study groups allow teachers to become "researchers" to promote their professional development. Teachers take charge of their own learning, and learn about research because they are involved in it (Rodgers & Pinnell, 2002).

Figure 5.2. Sample Professional Learning Survey for Teachers

Teacher's Name: _____   Grade Level: _____   Date: _____

Dear Teachers,

Welcome to the new school year! As we begin the school year, please remember that I am here to support you as we move toward our district and school goal to implement Writing Workshop K–5! To help me plan my coaching for the year, please complete the brief survey below and return it to me by September 15. This survey will help us as we work together to strengthen the writing of all our students by refining the teaching they receive. Thank you in advance for your time and collaboration!

Sincerely,

Part One: Please indicate how comfortable you feel with the following aspects of Writing Workshop (5 is the most comfortable and 1 is the least comfortable)

1. Mini-lesson (Planning)

    1   2   3   4   5

2. Mini-lesson (Teaching)

    1   2   3   4   5

3. Independent Writing

    1   2   3   4   5

4. Conferring 1:1

    1   2   3   4   5

5. Small Strategy Groups

    1   2   3   4   5

6. Guided Writing Groups

    1   2   3   4   5

7. Share/Debrief

    1   2   3   4   5

8. Unit Planning

    1   2   3   4   5

9. Assessing Student Writers

    1   2   3   4   5

Part Two: Please rank the following professional learning opportunities in order from 1 (most valuable) to 10 (least valuable) for your continued learning.

____ 1:1 Coaching by Literacy Coach   ____ Grade-Level Collaboration

____ Classroom Visits   ____ Book Clubs

____ Peer Coaching   ____ Mini-practice Highlights

____ Study Groups   ____ Demonstration Lessons

____ Collaborative Lessons   ____ Action Research

Collaborative Analysis of Student Work

Looking at student work collaboratively is a powerful practice. Collaboration with others can yield provocative ideas and multiple strategies from perspectives other than one's own. Collaborative analysis of student work can provide a course of action that includes changed perceptions of students, revised curricula and teaching strategies, and new goals. Such an analysis can also clarify expectations. For example, as a result of looking carefully at student writing, teachers might create a grade-level writing rubric and come to a shared understanding of what it means to reach each level on the rubric.

Collaborative professional learning centered around the development, collection, and analysis of student work allows educators to work together to learn about their students' strengths and needs, design small-group and whole-class teaching that is responsive to these needs, and deepen their knowledge and skills as they revise their curriculum (Wepner et al., 2012).

Franklin School's 3rd-grade team decided to collaboratively analyze their students' responses to nonfiction texts. Students were taught specific strategies to help them closely read the texts, take notes, and respond in their reader's notebooks. The group decided that investigating the students' work would allow them to (1) get to know the students as readers, (2) provide a place to start their teaching, and (3) collect data to monitor student growth in closely reading nonfiction texts.

The teachers developed a series of strategy lessons around a shared text to introduce to each class. Students read nonfiction texts during independent reading and tried out the strategies. They recorded their thinking directly on photocopied short texts, on sticky notes (if the text was a book, or an original copy), and wrote responses in their reader's notebooks. The teachers each brought a sampling of five students' work to analyze together during their next meeting. The teachers discussed their reflections on teaching the strategies and their anecdotal notes drawn from their observations of their conferences with students (e.g., what they saw the reader do, or not do; students' strengths and needs). Attention then turned to the student work they brought to share. Each teacher briefly introduced and discussed one of their students' work samples. The group discussed what they noticed about the student's work (both strengths and needs) and how the student's writing represented an understanding of the text (or not). These conversations helped the teachers create a shared mission for their students, develop a common language about close reading of nonfiction texts, and extend their knowledge about the reading process and writing in response to reading.

After analyzing all the students' work together, the teachers created a list of possible topics for mini-lessons based on similarities across students' work. Then, teachers worked alone and in pairs to develop mini-lessons to use for the whole class and in small groups. Teachers also continued to discuss individual students' strengths and needs, and role-played various possibilities when conferring with students one-on-one or in partnerships.

Teachers met together on a weekly basis throughout this unit of study to reflect on their teaching, discuss students' work, and develop lessons. They developed a comprehension rubric to quickly assess students' comprehension of texts and reading responses. At the end of the unit, teachers compared students' initial work in their reader's notebooks to their final work at the end of the unit.

This brief description of an intensive, unit-long, teacher-designed, professional learning experience demonstrates one literacy leader's efforts to promote his teachers' collaborative work. Literacy leaders can facilitate this process with small groups of teachers by guiding them as they select student work to analyze, posing questions to deepen the conversations (e.g., How do you know that? What evidence supports that statement?), gathering additional resources, and following up in classrooms to assist teachers as they revise their teaching in response to what they learned. Literacy leaders can support teachers as they develop ways to better understand their students' strengths and needs, refine their teaching to meet the needs of their diverse learners, and collaborate to foster meaningful change in their classrooms and for their students.

Topic-Specific Coaching

Topic-specific coaching is particularly useful for teachers when new curriculum, instructional, and assessment mandates arise. Literacy leaders are in a position to use coaching strategies to help their teachers have a better understanding of what they are supposed to do to create engaging learning for every student in their class. In her second year at the school, Caroline spent time in all the K–5 classrooms. The school adopted the Developmental Reading Assessment (DRA) (Beaver, 2012) several years before Caroline joined the faculty. Teachers were required to use this assessment three times per year (September,

January, and June). In September, Caroline had the opportunity to see several teachers administer the DRA, and she noticed that there were inconsistencies in the ways the teachers were administering the assessment. For example, one teacher would catch every word that a child said, another teacher would summarize what the child said, and another would not note much at all. After sensing that the training and support for these teachers must have been different, Caroline followed up with individual teachers to discover that many of the teachers simply saw the DRA as a mechanism for placing students in guided reading groups. Given this new knowledge, and the short timeline of 3 months before the next round of DRA assessments, Caroline met with the principal to get permission to focus the majority of her literacy coaching that fall on how to administer the DRA. Caroline planned large (whole-school) and small group (grade-level) meetings with new teachers and experienced teachers to reintroduce the DRA, model its administration, and analyze student data collected in the past. Caroline then worked in individual classrooms to model and support teachers as they started the next cycle of assessments. Caroline also scheduled time at grade-level meetings to discuss how student data from the DRA can directly inform instructional decisions.

Caroline's time in *every* classroom in the school across the school year helped her gather information about strengths and needs of every teacher's assessment practices. Caroline was able to identify the need to support teachers in the administration and use of the DRA and develop topic-specific coaching strategies on this schoolwide benchmark assessment.

Book Clubs

A Reading Recovery teacher at an elementary school in the Midwest became concerned that the group of teachers with whom she ate lunch daily had been complaining about feeling overwhelmed, increasingly tired, uninspired, and frustrated with district and state demands. She decided to ask her colleagues if they would join her in reading and discussing the book *Reading Wellness: Lessons in Independence and Proficiency* (Burkins & Yaris, 2014). Her principal agreed to provide funds to purchase the books. Once a week, their lunchtime together focused on their reflections of the week's reading. However, conversations about the book popped up during their daily lunches. Instead of complaining, the teachers were using the reflection questions from the book to try out individual lessons, discuss their experiences with one another, and bring in student work to share.

Book clubs provide a social and intellectual forum for teachers to share ideas, thoughts, feelings, and reactions to professional literature in relation to their own experiences (Burbank, Kauchak, & Bates, 2010; Flood & Lapp, 1994). Through reading about alternate perspectives, teachers are able to examine their own knowledge, beliefs, and practices (Burbank, Kauchak, & Bates, 2010; George, 2002). Book clubs accomplish two goals: (1) They allow for the introduction of new ideas into classrooms and schools, and (2) they foster teacher leadership as teachers develop ownership of ideas by talking with colleagues and comparing perspectives and practices.

Classroom Visits

Teaching is often described as an isolating profession (Flinders, 1988; Lortie, 1975; Schlichte, Yssel, & Merbler, 2005). U.S. teachers spend an average of 93% of their official workday in isolation (MetLife, 2009). Compared with teachers from other nations where students outperform the United States on international assessments, American teachers spend more time teaching students and have considerably less time to plan and learn together. The amount of high-intensity, job-embedded collaborative learning provided to teachers is significantly lower in the United States than in many European nations (Darling-Hammond et al., 2009; National Council of Teachers of English, 2011). In addition to the other professional development options described in this chapter to foster collaboration, classroom visitations empower teachers to open up their classrooms to their colleagues inside (intra-visitations) and outside (inter-visitations) their school.

Lab/model classrooms. With lab or model classrooms, a literacy leader and teacher work together over time to build an ideal teaching and learning space within the school and invite small groups of teachers to explore instruction during a series of classroom visits. The lab class is a "regular" classroom within the school, taught by an exemplary teacher interested in sharing his or her practice with others. The lab/model classroom teacher works closely with the literacy leader to build literacy content knowledge and refine the ways in which he or she communicates instructional decisions to others. Some questions to consider when choosing the lab class teacher include the following:

- Does the teacher view himself or herself as a learner?
- Is the teacher thoughtful in planning and teaching, and capable of discussing the purposes behind what he or she does with students?
- Does the teacher have the confidence to host visitors in his or her classroom?
- Is the teacher capable of discussing the purposes behind what he or she does with students? (Sweeney, 2003)

Because this is a classroom within the school, the teacher follows his or her normal routine with students. The difference is that the literacy leader and the teacher spend a great deal of time together organizing the learning environment, refining instructional routines and practices, discussing connections to published research, and planning how to use the lab/model classroom as a learning opportunity for other educators inside and outside the school and district.

Visiting teachers meet together before the visit to discuss their observational goals, what they are going to see, and where they want to focus their attention. The lab/model classroom teacher may lead this discussion, but more often, it is the literacy leader who provides an overview for the visit and guides visitors to specific points of interest, such as classroom arrangement, materials, transitions, and teacher–student interactions.

While visiting, teachers usually float around the classroom, listening to conversations and asking students questions about their work. Teachers also take notes during their visit, noting questions they may have and identifying structures, materials, and instructional practices that they found interesting and want to know more about. The lab/model teacher often vocalizes for visitors about the teaching practices that he or she is using.

After the visit, the teachers come together to debrief about their observations and wonderings. The lab/model teacher joins the group to answer questions and discuss what they learned about the students and their instructional needs. The teachers then draft next steps, because they are expected to implement the observed instructional practices in their own classrooms. See **Online Figure C** for suggestions for planning visitations to a lab/model classroom.

Intraschool visitations. Schools that value professional learning, and are built on collaboration and trust, encourage teachers to visit one another's classrooms. Intraschool visitations empower teachers to highlight the strengths of their practices. In order to be successful, literacy leaders need to support teachers as they refine their teaching strengths and develop ways to talk about their practices that support the learning of others (Wepner et al., 2012).

Interschool or district visitations. Sometimes teachers wish to learn about practices that are not happening at their own school. In this case, literacy leaders can empower teachers by planning classroom visitations in other schools and districts that are successfully implementing strategies teachers wish to learn more about or adopt. Schools with similar communities and classroom populations help teachers realize the potential or unsuitability of particular teaching methods and materials. The steps to planning a successful interschool visitation are similar to intraschool visitations (See **Online Figure C**). The Changing Suburbs Institute® (CSI) network at Manhattanville College has been a valuable source for teachers and leaders to collaborate and learn from one another about new teaching initiatives. As school leaders and teachers meet together at meetings and professional development events at Manhattanville, they learn about initiatives at each school and plan visits to one another's schools. This has been particularly useful for existing Professional Development Schools (PDSs) within the CSI network. Additionally, school leaders interested in making their school a PDS have brought groups of teachers to visit existing PDSs to learn about expectations. An example of a visit of a new PDS to an established PDS includes the following steps:

- Meeting with the administration to discuss the role of the principal in the PDS, and learn about the evolution of the PDS from the leader's perspective
- Meeting with the PDS leadership team to learn about the structure of the team and the role it plays in leading and supporting PDS initiatives
- Classroom visitations with various teachers who are working directly with PDS projects—for example, a field-based class and a student teacher–led parent workshop

Classroom visitations are powerful learning experiences for everyone involved. With careful planning and preparation, support for release time, and follow-up for implementation of new ideas, classroom visitations can lead to exciting and substantial changes in the classroom.

Mini-Practice Highlights/Demos

Caroline's school has infused short bursts of teacher-led professional learning through the use of mini-practice highlights or demonstrations during their monthly faculty meetings. All of the mini-practice highlights have been connected to the school's overarching goal to incorporate reading and writing workshop in all classrooms. Caroline and the principal have asked the teachers to highlight a practice they have been using in their classrooms. The mini-practice highlight topics of the past few months have included:

- taking conferring notes using Evernote (Apple, 2015);
- helping students engage in conversations in their partnerships and clubs;
- using think-alouds to model what students do as readers or writers; and
- trying interactive read-alouds to help students think about the strategies they use as readers.

During the mini-practice highlight on taking conference notes using Evernote, kindergarten teacher Maia walked teachers through her transition to using a digital platform to take conferring notes. Maia started by stating that her reasons for using the application included organization and space saving. Next, Maia demonstrated how she uses Evernote on the interactive whiteboard. This 15-minute mini-practice highlight piqued her colleagues' interest. Some teachers tried it out by themselves, and asked Maia questions along the way. Others sat down with Maia so she could walk them through the process of creating an account.

Caroline arranged for some of the teachers to visit Maia's classroom during writing workshop to see Evernote (Apple, 2015) in action. Mini-practice highlights build leadership capacity by emphasizing the strengths of individuals or groups and positioning them as a leading voice in the building on a particular topic.

Demonstration Lessons

Demonstration lessons are an important part of literacy leadership, especially when gradually releasing responsibility. A demonstration lesson is an authentic lesson taught by a literacy leader to students, while the teacher observes and takes notes. Demonstration lessons allow literacy leaders to provide clear and specific information while interacting with students and the teacher in a classroom setting. Many teachers appreciate observing new teaching techniques and strategies with "their own" students.

The literacy leader and the teacher meet for a "preconference" to discuss and plan the proposed lesson. The literacy leader then writes the lesson plan and provides the teacher with a copy before the actual lesson takes place. It is important to note that the demonstration lesson models lesson planning as well as teaching. The lesson is written in a way that allows any teacher to pick up the lesson and replicate it in his or her classroom, which often means that it is scripted. The demonstration lesson plan includes state standards (completely written out), goals or objectives for the lesson, a detailed plan of how the lesson will unfold, all necessary materials, and references and resources that apply to the content and/or structure so that the teachers can access them for more information or additional lesson ideas.

It is crucial to have pre- and post-conferences with the teacher so there is a commitment on the part of the teacher to learn about and try out the practices modeled in the demonstration. Otherwise, the literacy leader may find that while he or she is teaching the students, the teacher is using the bathroom, making phone calls, or working on the computer—doing everything but learning from the leader.

To help teachers focus their attention on the agreed-upon purpose, a demonstration lesson response sheet can be utilized (see Figure 5.3). This tool helps the teacher who is observing the lesson focus and record his/her observations, questions, and notes while watching the demonstration lesson. The response sheet also provides a written record of the teacher's thoughts and ideas and a guide for discussion during the post-conference future planning.

Janice, a literacy coach in New Jersey, reflects on her use of the demonstration lesson response sheet:

> When I first started conducting demonstration lessons, I found a few different things happened with my teachers. Oftentimes, they were into the lesson, but focused on something that I knew was their strength. I also found that they focused on something we had not discussed during the preconference or that did not match the purpose of the visit. Or, I observed teachers moving behind their desks and beginning to grade papers or work on their lesson plans. When I was introduced to this form, it made such a difference in my literacy coaching! Demonstration lesson

Figure 5.3. Demonstration Lesson Response Form

Classroom Teacher: _____   Literacy Coach: _____

Grade: _____   Lesson Date: _____   Post-Conference Date:

Demonstration Lesson Notes

Coach:	**Students:**	**Notes/Questions:**
List three things you saw the coach do that you would try with your students	Note student response and engagement	I was wondering about . . .

Post-Conference Notes

Next Steps: I'd Like More Information On:

Coaching Notes:

---

response sheets helped both the teachers and me focus on particular aspects of the demonstration that were central to our work together. I was more aware of particular aspects teachers were interested in and the teachers knew what to look for while they were observing. Using this form has helped tremendously!

Collaborative Lessons

Collaborative lessons are lessons that are co-planned and co-taught by the literacy leader and teacher, who teach side by side, and take responsibility for different aspects of the lesson. Collaborative lessons usually follow demonstration lessons as the teacher is learning to use a new practice. During teaching, responsibility may shift between the literacy leader and teacher, with the literacy leader modeling certain aspects of the lesson for the teacher, or the teacher taking the lead as the literacy leader gradually releases leadership by offering encouragement, giving reminders, and making suggestions.

Collaborative lessons are followed with debriefings about both teaching and student learning. In this discussion, the literacy leader and the teacher discuss the successful and unsuccessful aspects of the lesson evidence of student learning, and next steps for teaching. The teacher and literacy leader might plan additional collaborative lessons, or determine that the teacher can practice independently with the literacy leader observing and providing support.

Teacher Action Research

Teacher action research is a form of professional learning that supports teachers as they examine their own practice. It is primarily concerned with improving a particular context for learning and "balances a classroom culture that is personal, contextual, open-ended, and ever-changing with a research culture that is rigorous, structured, and systematic" (Caro-Bruce, 2004, p. 54). Action research helps teachers connect theory with practice, systematically collect and analyze data about the learning process, reflect about the outcomes, and become decisionmakers and knowledge-producers, (Baumann & Duffy, 2001; Cochran-Smith & Lytle, 1993, 1998; Mertler, 2006). Action research is a recursive cycle of collecting research, reflecting on the research, implementing change through action, and then reflecting on the action taken. The cycle repeats itself, as teachers' reflections about actions taken compel further research and, therefore, the start of a new cycle.

A literacy leader can facilitate a teacher action research group. Teacher-researchers begin their work by identifying and discussing pedagogical questions that arise from their teaching. The teachers then create action research questions. A literacy leader models how to locate relevant literature that grounds questions at the center of the teacher's inquiry. The literacy leader and teachers determine the data that should be collected and how the data can be analyzed to understand the phenomenon under investigation. As the group meets, teachers present their work and receive feedback from their colleagues. Teachers are encouraged to share their research within the school community at faculty assemblies as well as at local, state, and national conferences.

Teacher action research empowers teachers to examine their own practice in relation to data that have been collected and analyzed. Through action research, teachers are engaged in inquiry and theory building, and are a part of a professional learning community.

KNOW PROFESSIONAL DEVELOPMENT METHODS TO MEET TEACHER NEEDS

The professional development methods discussed in this chapter have the potential to build capacity and sustain real change in school. Literacy leaders must work with teachers to evolve into a school culture that values professional learning. In order to achieve this goal, it is essential to build in time for job-embedded professional development as a part of each teacher's workday. The professional development must connect to school and district initiatives and, more important, to teacher and student goals and needs.

LITERACY LEADERSHIP TOOLKIT

The two exercises in this toolkit help articulate teacher needs and identify professional learning experiences that subscribe to the school's and district's mission and goals for literacy.

Exercise 5.1:
Prompts for Creating a Professional Development Action Plan

This first exercise includes questions for creating a professional development action plan that relates to the district's and school's mission for literacy. Have your school's leadership team respond to these sample questions to help develop a plan that addresses teachers' needs.

Districtwide Literacy Mission:

- What is the mission for literacy teaching and learning at the district level?

Districtwide Literacy Goals:

- Which district-level initiatives must we follow?
- How do they connect to or impede our schoolwide mission?

Schoolwide Literacy Mission:

- What are our shared beliefs about families and students?
- What effective practices are currently being implemented?
- What do we mean by effective teaching and learning?
- What assessments are in place, how are they utilized, and by whom?

Schoolwide Literacy Goals:

- What is our school's goal this year for literacy?
- What is the school's long-term goal for literacy?

Schoolwide Professional Development Plan:

- How can we challenge our personal and shared assumptions about students and families in relation to our goals?
- What steps can we take to learn about the realities of our families' lives?
- What effective practices can we implement?
- How will these practices support our goal?
- What assessments can we use as benchmark indicators?
- Who will be responsible for each step?
- How can we assess our progress?
- How can the literacy leader and principal support the implementation of the steps?
- How can schoolwide professional development be structured to support our goal?
- How can grade-level professional development be structured to support our goal?
- How can individual teacher professional development be structured to support our goal?
- What is our target date for the completion of each step?
- Which teachers will be invited to participate?

Exercise 5.2:
Chart for Creating a Professional Development Action Plan

This exercise offers a template for a professional development action plan that your leadership team should complete to establish what can and should be done with and for your teachers. The chart specifies how your team's professional development goals will be met. Use responses to the questions from Exercise 5.1 to complete the first part of the chart. A sample professional development plan is included to demonstrate how the chart can be completed.

Professional Development Plan

Districtwide Literacy Mission:

Districtwide Literacy Goals:

Schoolwide Literacy Mission:

Schoolwide Literacy Goals:

Schoolwide Professional Development Plan:

Professional Development Goal	Action Steps	Person(s) Responsible	Resources Needed	Timeline	Evidence for Success
Strengthen conferring in writing workshop	Offer introductory workshops focused on conferring with writers Create teacher inquiry group to investigate conferring with writers Provide individual coaching in classrooms connected to workshop and inquiry groups	Literacy coach and teachers on literacy leadership team	Articles and books on conferring with writers Videos highlighting writing conferences Space and time for workshop and inquiry group	**Start date:** October 1 **End date:** June 20 The literacy leadership team will meet as a group every month to discuss progress, including successes and challenges	Observation of conferring in every classroom during writing workshop Conference notes from teachers as evidence of understanding students' strengths and needs Teacher reflections during and after professional learning experiences

CHAPTER 6

Know the Link Between Curriculum and Standards

- Literacy leaders consider the purpose of curriculum and what it means to be truly literate in the 21st century.
- Literacy leaders support teachers to create and revise curriculum that is *both* culturally responsive and standards-aligned.
- Literacy leaders guide teachers in how to navigate standards to support students as learners across the curriculum.

It is springtime, and eight reading specialists have just learned that they are such strong literacy leaders in the district that they are being asked to shift their roles from reading specialists to literacy coaches. District leaders have given considerable thought to the existing literacy programs and methods used in classrooms across the elementary schools in relation to the changing population of their district's classrooms. They have begun to ask questions about whether their program is best supporting students to be "core-ready" and whether the teachers have the curriculum and instructional methods needed to support all their students as literacy learners today and for the future. District leaders know that there have been limited authentic reading experiences, that their increasingly diverse student population is not represented in the texts featured in the curriculum, that teachers are either over-teaching or under-teaching books, and that they have had an unproductive focus on developing test-takers rather than readers. As a result of this critical reflection, district leaders have identified a group of reading specialists who have exhibited strong interpersonal relationships with teachers to support them in their classrooms with a new reading and writing curriculum for the K–5 schools.

What the district leaders propose is radical. They want to move the district away from basal readers and prepackaged curriculum and want the newly defined literacy coaches to write a reading and writing workshop curriculum that is Common Core–aligned, book-centered, and built upon research about what readers and writers really do. The specialists—now coaches—have the spring and following year to learn about coaching, write the curriculum, roll it out across the district, and provide teachers with job-embedded support.

EVALUATING EXISTING CURRICULUM

Some educators think of curriculum as a static entity, something that can arrive in a box or that lives in a binder. Other educators, including some curriculum theorists, turn to the Latin word *currere*, which means "to run the course," and define curriculum as the lived experiences we have with students as they learn new content, acquire new skills, and become citizens within their classroom and community (Connelly & Clandinin, 1988; Tyler, 1975). However, neither a static orientation nor a process-focused conceptualization of curriculum is sufficient. Curriculum is *both* the precise consideration of *what* is being taught as well as the *process* of experiencing and learning what is taught. Additionally, curriculum can also be defined as a set of beliefs "about how people learn, and the classroom contexts that best support learning" (Short & Burke, 1991, p. 6). Curriculum development is the process of teachers putting these beliefs into action through curriculum frameworks of teachers and students working together through negotiation (Bintz & Dillard, 2007). This relationship is dynamic and ongoing.

Curriculum theorist Pinar (2012) posed the question: "What knowledge is of most worth?" (p. 210). Although standards can give us some direction for defining what knowledge is expected and what teachers and students are accountable for demonstrating, standards do not tell us how to get there. Additionally, when considering what knowledge is of most worth, literacy leaders must also consider what is *not* in the standards but is essential knowledge, such as finding pleasure in reading and writing, knowing how to self-select books for various purposes, noticing connections and disconnections with a range of texts, and critiquing texts for sociocultural misrepresentation. Children's book author Katherine Paterson (2003) offers another question central to curriculum evaluation: "What does it mean to be truly literate?" (p. 8). Does it mean mastery of foundational skills or use of those skills across genres? Does it mean proficiency as a reader, writer, speaker, or listener? Or does it mean something much bigger—that we use literacy skills to improve our lives and the lives of others? As a literacy leader, how does one define "truly literate"? The eight literacy coaches described in the vignette are ready to consider what knowledge they believe is of most worth and how they define what it means to be truly literate in relation to current standards, and these leaders are taking steps to build on the best practices in their buildings.

What Knowledge Is of Most Worth?

How you answer this question depends on the values and beliefs of your local school community. This question is likely to be answered differently by principals, teachers, students, and families. There are also literacy-specific guiding questions that you can reflect upon to tailor literacy curriculum to meet the needs of 21st-century learners. Specifically, literacy leaders can consider: (1) Whose knowledge is valued in the school community? How do you know? (2) What kinds of reading and writing knowledge are valued? What forms of speaking and listening are valued? (3) In what ways do teachers and students share their love and knowledge of stories and other types of texts? Is there balance in the types of texts (picture books, traditional children's literature, contemporary and multicultural literature, poetry, nonfiction) being read aloud? (4) Is there a balance of text types (narrative, informational texts, argumentative, poetry) students write? (5) Are students supported to independently read to grow knowledge from interest? Are there culturally responsive resources to support independent reading? (6) Are students guided in small groups with culturally responsive texts at their instructional levels? How so? (7) How do students share their knowledge with authentic audiences? (8) Are there resources that reflect who students are, where they are from, and what they want to be? (9) In what ways is knowledge from students' lived experiences a part of their in-school literacy lives?

And, of course, many more questions could be asked when considering what knowledge is of most worth and to whom. As a literacy leader, consider your responses to these questions, and generate more questions with your teachers. Consider differing responses to them as you consider what curriculum exists, how it unfolds in classrooms, and what short-term and long-term goals you want to work toward with your teachers, students, and community to support different forms of knowledge.

What Does It Mean to Be Truly Literate?

Paterson (2003) connects being truly literate with the power of the humanities as a means of leading students into the "great adventure of the human mind and spirit" (p. 9). Paterson urges teachers and literacy leaders to emphasize critical thinking and foster inquiry through engagement with the humanities. Building on Paterson's framework, it is our belief that to be truly literate means not only having the essential foundational skills of reading and writing, but also using those skills to participate in the broader world to reflect, critique, challenge the status quo, and consider issues of power and privilege inherent in any text. An evaluation of curriculum must consider whether students are being supported in their literacy experiences not only to comprehend but also to critique. This chapter is based on the set of beliefs that literacy is not a discrete set of skills but a social practice that fosters communication and participation through reading, writing, speaking, listening, and viewing (Heath, 1983; Lewis, 2001; Luke, 1997; Street, 1999). Further, this chapter aligns with sociocultural perspectives that conceive of literacy as participation in a range of valued meaning-making practices influenced by our purposes, roles, and identities (Gee, 1996; Holland, Lachicotte, Skinner, & Cain, 1998; Moje & Luke, 2009). In short, the ways we participate as literate beings are shaped by who we are in a given context.

Drawing from research from after-school/out-of-school time settings, Hull and Moje (2012) identify the purposes, participant structures, and conceptions of literacy that provide a bridge between sociocultural perspectives and the goals of the Common Core. They advocate for thinking about the development of literacy in support of practices that "connect to learners' backgrounds, cultures, and communities; that capitalize on the social nature of learning; and that position young people to experience literacy as purposeful and themselves as skillful and confident makers of meaning" (p. 6). To be "truly literate" would start with literacy instruction and experiences that are personalized, culturally situated, and supportive of social and collaborative practices.

The eight literacy leaders described in the vignette and their teachers have begun to consider questions rooted in expanding what counts as knowledge and how they can make their literacy curriculum and instruction more participatory and culturally embedded while meeting the standards' requirements. They have begun to take action to support their students in making choices about what they are reading and for what purposes. They have begun to uncover and value students' multiple identities and interests as they support the students as literacy learners. They now make space for students' opinions on topics, issues, and texts. And they have begun to engage students as citizens of their classrooms and the community. They are redefining what it means to evaluate curriculum with their students in mind.

These eight literacy leaders are using examples from other schools with culturally and linguistically diverse students. They are following bloggers at sites such as Rethinking Schools (http://rethinking-schoolsblog.wordpress.com/) and Lee & Low Books' blog the Open Book (http://blog.leeandlow.com/) to learn from and reflect upon voices in the field grappling with issues of representation, equity, social justice, and literacy teaching and learning. They are figuring out ways to gather and share posts with their teachers to further consider the ways literacy can be more student-centered and culturally responsive in their buildings.

Teachers as Co-Evaluators

Literacy leaders are not the only evaluators of curriculum. Teachers must be a part of the curriculum evaluation process because they are the ones who create the curricular experiences that will impact student learning. To begin this process, ask teachers to reflect on an aspect of their teaching (a lesson sequence, a unit plan, a project) that positively impacted student learning and why it worked so well. Then, support teachers in reflecting on an aspect of their teaching (a lesson sequence, a unit plan, a project) that was less successful, and what you could do together to improve it. These reflections help build a foundation for more in-depth curriculum analysis, and open up conversations about what is being taught, why, and where teachers want to improve their practices for greater gains in student learning.

An important next step is to help teachers analyze specifically what is being taught across the curriculum to see where gaps and overlaps exist and where changes may need to occur. Following analysis of the existing curriculum, decide what to do about the gaps and overlaps that exist, and where curricular adjustments need to be made to support students as literacy learners.

THE COMMON CORE IS ABOUT BIG IDEAS

We are living in an era of big ideas. In education, the Common Core State Standards (CCSS) (National Governors Association Center for Best Practices & Council of Chief State School Officers, 2010) represent one such big idea. The standards are also a big experiment. Never before has this country overwhelmingly adopted a single set of standards. Debate remains about both the process of construction of the standards and their implementation across states, as well as their ties to state testing, federal funding, and the corporatization of education. As a literacy leader in a changing school, you must be well versed in both the particulars of the standards in your state and the big ideas behind them, with your students in mind. Although you may not be working in a state that has adopted the CCSS, knowing the guiding principles and shifts demanded by the standards are worth critically considering. In addition, the following sections have applications for knowing and working within a set of standards more broadly.

Many educators are asking what brought about the CCSS. The short answer is that today's jobs require different skills, and the country must consider the technological changes that have contributed to global competition for goods and services. But there also remains a critical social justice issue that the standards are attempting to address—that the gap between the wealthy and the poor continues to grow, limiting the social mobility students have access to when they are born into conditions of poverty. The literacies outlined in the CCSS are worthy of great consideration and are designed with these goals in mind. Yet, it is important to note that some critics have described the CCSS as a monarch—a centralized system counter to self-governance, choice, or alternative forms of education. The literacies the standards outline represent a particular view of literacy. This view is very important to consider, but may not represent all the literacies in which your students engage. This chapter describes the literacies advocated by the standards as well as ways to consider alternative views of literacy to support cultural, linguistic, and social diversity in your school.

The eight literacy leaders described in the vignette have a voice in deciding how the standards are framed in their schools. They certainly have reservations about whether their students are ready for more rigorous standards, how the standards impact assessment of student learning, and what the standards require of teachers. However, they believe they have an opportunity to support teachers through the standards to center students as learners so that they read widely and closely, engage with complex texts that are culturally and socially relevant, write across genres for authentic audiences, and use digital technologies to produce rather than simply consume media. They are considering how teaching to the standards can be about centering meaning; supporting ideas with evidence; providing arguments about issues that matter; mastering language critical to science, math, and social studies; and debating the messages within stories in ways that sustain student interest and motivation for learning.

As literacy leaders, we know that the task of determining what to teach can be overwhelming. The next sections provide information about college and career readiness, the key tenets of the standards, and how the standards are organized both vertically and horizontally, and also present a step-by-step approach for working with teachers to create units of study to support all levels of learners.

COLLEGE READINESS

The CCSS begin with the end in mind—college and career readiness defined as the acquisition of the knowledge and skills a student needs to enroll and succeed in credit-bearing first-year college courses without the need for remediation. The intention is that teachers and literacy leaders work backwards from that end goal to consider the skills and strengths needed at every grade level to get all our students to reach that goal. The CCSS are designed to give us a roadmap to support students from different geographic and social locations to be college and career ready. This has, perhaps, long been one of the goals of education in a democratic society, but our roadmaps thus far have varied from state to state.

Research continues to show that many students enter college without the reading, writing, speaking, and listening skills required to succeed in and complete college. The Condition of College and Career Readiness report by ACT (2012) states, "In 2012, 67% of all ACT-tested high school graduates met the English College Readiness Benchmark, while 25% met the College Readiness Benchmarks in all four subjects. Fifty-two percent of graduates met the Reading Benchmark and 46% met the Mathematics Benchmark. Just under 1 in 3 (31%) met the College Readiness Benchmark in Science" (p. 1). However, ACT data have found that there have been marked improvements in achievement in states that have created an educational culture focused on college readiness. Between 2010 and 2014, there was an 18% increase in the number of ACT-tested graduates. In addition, diversity has increased with more Hispanic ACT-tested graduates in 2014 than in 2010, and in 2014 18% were potential first-generation college students (ACT, 2014). Likewise, the College Board of the SAT reports that in 2014, there was an increase in overall participation and that nearly half of all students who took the exam, 47.5%, identified as minority students (College Board, 2015). However, data show that only 42.6% of test-takers achieved the SAT College and Career Readiness benchmark. This issue is especially acute among underrepresented minority students: 15.8% African Americans, 23.4% Hispanics, and 33.5% Native Americans met the benchmark.

The CCSS are pushing teachers of all levels and all subject areas to rethink which of their practices have been working and what needs to change to best support all learners from all backgrounds not only to enter college but also to thrive there. Debate remains around whether college readiness is a purposeful goal for all students and how the backwards mapping of standards negatively affects early childhood classrooms. As a literacy leader, consider your own beliefs about the educational experiences that can contribute to student growth at every grade level.

We also know that college readiness is about more than skills. It is also about believing you belong there—that college is an option for you. Roderick, Nagaoka, and Coca (2009) found in their study of college readiness and urban high schools that four essential indicators shape college access and performance: (1) content knowledge and basic skills, (2) core academic skills, (3) behavioral skills, and (4) "college knowledge." Our Changing Suburbs Institute® network includes 13 professional development schools with culturally and linguistically diverse students, many from low-income homes. Every year, one grade level at each school comes to our college campus to visit as part of a larger initiative to support students with the identity construction of "college bound." As a literacy leader, consider ways to support your students to see themselves as college ready in terms of their knowledge and skills and their belief in themselves. Some of our partnership schools have teachers hang their college pennants in the hallways. Others host local college students for special events to speak about the college experience. Still others host parent workshops in multiple languages in elementary schools to orient families to the college process.

CAREER READINESS

A career ready individual needs to be equipped to purposefully engage with the work before them, their colleagues, and the world. Speaking and listening are now playing equal parts with reading and writing as essential skills for career readiness. Educators are expected to give students more practice to voice their opinions, build arguments with evidence, and listen to the ideas of others in large- and small-group settings. As students move up through the grade levels, they are expected to demonstrate the ability to speak and listen with increasing independence as they develop knowledgeable discourse on a variety of topics.

Developing opportunities to practice speaking and listening will support students' career readiness and life readiness because whatever path they choose will likely involve social interactions in various contexts that ask them to communicate effectively and build on the ideas of others. As with college readiness, career readiness is about identity construction. What do your students want to pursue? What are the models within and beyond the community to support students to envision a world of opportunity beyond school? Consider hosting guest visitors who offer various perspectives on their career pathways and the choices they made that supported their success.

GUIDING PRINCIPLES FOR COLLEGE AND CAREER READINESS

The CCSS organize grade-level expectations for reading, writing, speaking and listening, and language, and provide guiding principles behind the standards. Allyn (2012) refers to these principles as *core capacities* that support *core learners* in our classrooms. Students who master core capacities outlined by the CCSS will be able to (1) demonstrate independence; (2) build strong content knowledge; (3) respond to the varying demands of audience, task, purpose, and discipline; (4) comprehend as well as critique; (5) value evidence; (6) use technology and digital media strategically and capably; and (7) come to understand other perspectives and cultures (National Governors Association for Best Practices & Council of Chief State School Officers, 2010). Consider how these tenets have value in your community. Although they are not all-encompassing, they do provide a framework worth considering. Share these tenets with teachers, and consider with them other capacities your school community strives to teach toward.

The literacy coaches described in the vignette are carefully considering and discussing these tenets with grade-level teams and at
full faculty meetings. Are their students mastering these capacities?
Are they supporting their students and one another to value these
capacities? And, what are the values within their own school community that might be missing from this list, such as literacy engagement
through the arts, literacy as purposeful play, and literacy as a path toward building empathy? As a literacy leader, consider how your program and school literacy vision support students in each of these core
capacities. Does the structure of how lessons are delivered support the
development of these capacities? What needs to change systematically
and culturally within your building to reposition these core principles
as essential tenets of your program across the grade levels? Consider
which of these capacities are already strong within your building.
Think of specific examples of how students exhibit these strengths.
Then, take on the more difficult challenge and consider the areas that
need to be re-evaluated within your program. This chapter and the
subsequent chapters on techniques and literacy programs will help
guide your thinking about action steps to turn the necessary changes
into reality.

KNOWING THE ENGLISH LANGUAGE ARTS STANDARDS HORIZONTALLY AND VERTICALLY

In addition to the guiding principles, it is important to gain familiar-
ity with the way your state's standards are organized and what they
call for across all grade levels. As a literacy leader, you want to speak
about standards from an informed position and confidently discuss
the changes your teachers and students are experiencing with the
shifts demanded by any set of standards.

Reading the Standards Horizontally: Themes Across the Standards

Reading standards horizontally means noting how each standard
adjusts from one grade level to the next. When we read standards
horizontally, themes begin to emerge that guide how literacy is positioned. The Common Core Anchor Standards provide us with an important tool for understanding areas of emphasis in literacy teaching
and learning, including reading complex texts closely, reading widely,

reading and writing in community, engaging purposefully with technology, writing, rewriting, revising, taking suggestions, and sharing.

Reading complex texts closely. Reading closely is something young children do naturally. They closely read adults' facial expressions, their best friend's tone, and leaves falling from trees. The CCSS call for students to read closely for a variety of purposes and articulate their understandings in writing and in speaking. Though close reading has been a practice at the secondary level, it is now a central component in how reading is defined at the elementary level as well. The first Anchor Standard for reading from kindergarten through 12th grade states, "Read closely to determine what the text says explicitly and to make logical inferences from it; cite specific textual evidence when writing or speaking to support conclusions drawn from the text" (National Governors Association for Best Practices & Council of Chief State School Officers, 2010, p. 10). This standard has caused debate around what close reading looks like, what texts are worthy of close reading, and the principles and practices teachers can use to implement close reading in their classrooms (Boyles, 2012; Cunningham, 2013; Gewertz, 2012). Fisher and Frey (2012) define close reading as "an instructional routine in which students critically examine a text, especially through repeated readings" (p. 179). In this way, close reading is about persistence, slowing down, and rereading with purpose. It is of increasing importance when readers are confronted by complex and unfamiliar texts. The Partnership for Assessment of Readiness for College and Careers (2011) states:

> A significant body of research links the close reading of complex text—whether the student is a struggling reader or advanced—to significant gains in reading proficiency and finds close reading to be a key component of college and career readiness. (p. 7)

Literacy leaders may find that close reading looks different across classrooms and that one of their increasingly important roles is to offer a framework for close reading that can work across the grade levels in their buildings. To set students up for success as close readers, teachers may find that they need support in what close reading looks like and which texts are worth reading closely. Fisher and Frey (2012) found that close readings of complex texts consist of short passages, limited frontloading, repeated readings, and text-dependent questions.

Cunningham (2013) advocates for supporting students to closely read print, visual, and multimedia texts to broaden the ways we define close reading. As a literacy leader, work with your teachers to develop your own set of suggestions for the kinds of texts and purposes that students can be supported to read closely.

The kinds of complex texts implied by the CCSS may have teachers of English learners concerned about how best to support them to make meaning if they have been challenged by below-grade-level and less linguistically complex texts. Fillmore and Fillmore (2012) advocate that teachers working with linguistically diverse students consider the differences in the structures between oral and written English, but not shy away from providing and supporting students with complex texts with embedded academic language. They advocate for teachers to use a single-sentence approach to help students see how language works in complex texts that are related to topics in science and social studies. By examining one content-rich sentence at a time, students learn how to make sense of texts that are linguistically and contextually complex with teacher support while working toward independence. Single sentences can be selected, analyzed, and interpreted in many different ways, including the parts of speech represented, sentence structure, word choice, and implied meanings.

As a literacy leader, consider engaging teachers in close reading clubs and supporting them to develop text-dependent and open-ended questions for a variety of print, visual, and multimedia texts, particularly multicultural text selections (see Chapter 9 for resource suggestions) and texts that are connected to science and social studies. Engage teachers in closely reading single sentences to notice structure, word choice, multiple meanings, and connections they draw.

Reading widely. To be a literacy leader is to have a wide reading life. Supporting children in reading widely and finding interest in a range of genres, authors, and series can transform their reading lives. While the first Anchor Standard calls for close reading, Standard 10 is about reading widely across the grade levels for both literature and informational texts. For example, the 3rd-grade Standard 10 for reading literature reads, "By the end of the year, read and comprehend literature, including stories, dramas, and poetry, at the high end of the grades 2–3 text complexity band independently and proficiently" (National Governors Association for Best Practices & Council of Chief State School Officers, 2010, p. 12). This standard is about reading across genres through a range of reading experiences. What does this mean for literacy leaders and teachers? They need to become readers across genres. They need to immerse themselves not only in picture books and novels for the age group they teach, but also come to know and value traditional texts such as fables, folktales, myths, legends, poetry, works of drama, and nonfiction. Our own reading lives are important models for what reading widely looks like. As a literacy leader, start with your own reading life. In what ways do you read widely? Is your nightstand or digital reader a collection of different types of readings? What books and other types of readings do you connect to and why? Consider creating a book club for teachers that is all about reading across genres over the school year. You could start the year with a favorite children's literature selection, and during the year read traditional tales, poetry collections, favorite blogs, news articles and editorials, and also discuss films. Consider opportunities for reading widely in texts written in languages other than English. Does the library have resources in languages represented in the school at various levels in various genres? Do families have access to a range of texts in different languages? Consider ways of extending wide reading between school and home, and celebrating the many ways people read in your community.

Reading and writing in community. We read and write to communicate and participate in the world. We read and write to learn about ourselves and others, form or further our interests, debate ideas, and engage with the world. When we read and write in community, we have the opportunity to voice our ideas and hear the ideas of others. To support students in doing this well, teachers need to give them models of how to agree and disagree with one another using academic language. Speaking and listening standards highlight the need for students to engage in a range of conversations and collaborations with diverse partners to build on others' ideas and express their own clearly and persuasively. Have teachers reflect upon how they purposefully and routinely have students discuss reading in partnerships, small groups, and as a whole class. What guiding questions do they design to support their students to read in community? What are the classroom spaces where they engage with one another around reading as a community? On the rug? At tables? In special book nooks? Online? Figure 6.1 is a helpful checklist for teachers to consider the ways they are establishing and growing a community of readers.

Figure 6.1. In What Ways Do Your Students Read in Community?

Configuration	Daily	Weekly	Monthly
Partnerships			
Small Groups			
Whole-Class Discussions			
Classroom–Classroom Partners			
Grade–Grade Partners			
Community Visitors			

Support teachers in establishing reading and writing partnerships in their classrooms, if they don't already have them. Help them organize partnerships into small groups for specific purposes, have more fruitful and engaging whole-class discussions, and partner with other classrooms, grade levels, or even the community to celebrate their reading lives. Encourage teachers to consider pairing children who share a native language and those who are emerging English learners (ELs) with native English speakers.

Engaging purposefully with technology. There is no doubt that the ways in which we read and write are changing with the increasingly digital lives we lead. Across the grade levels, there is an expectation that students engage purposefully with technology—that is, that they not only consume media but that they *critically* consume media as well as *produce* media for different purposes. There is no way to know what new technologies will emerge in years to come, but what we do know is that right now the digital landscape plays a crucial role in the ways we communicate and participate with the world. Teachers have different comfort levels when it comes to technology. To better understand your teachers' needs, consider developing a technology survey that asks about the types of social media they use and what they would be willing to try in their own classrooms. Figure 6.2 illustrates ways in which classrooms across the country are engaging students in technology. In addition, Chapter 9 includes several suggested resources for engaging students with blogging, digital storytelling, and social media.

Literacy leaders need to collaboratively direct the digital landscape of their school. The best way to learn how to teach with technology is to first engage with it yourself. Play around. Learn the language.

Figure 6.2. Communicating and Participating with the World Through Technology

Technology	Purpose	Curricular Connections
Blogs	Document learning; share writing; respond to texts and one another	Reading, writing, collaboration
Wikis	Collect research around topics; respond to one another's posts	Reading, writing, research, collaboration
Facebook	Communicate with families; share links	Reading, writing, collaboration
Twitter	Communicate with families; share links; reflect on learning; learn from those you follow	Reading, writing, collaboration
Tumblr	Document learning; great for book reviews	Reading, writing, collaboration
Pinterest	Gather ideas; create class pinboards	Reading, writing, research, curation
YouTube/ Vimeo	Share videos, watch videos	Reading, scripting, moviemaking, speaking, listening, collaboration
Digital Storytelling	Construct videos	Reading, writing, speaking, listening, collaboration
Podcasts	Construct audio files; reflect on reading; share in different voices; learn from others	Speaking, listening, collaboration
Doodlecast/ Screencast	Document learning; review lessons	Writing, storytelling

Have fun. And bring teachers along on the journey with you. There may already be teachers in your building who are leaders in technology. As one of us (Diane) did in one of our professional development schools, recruit these teachers to host a series of professional development sessions such as Lunch and Learns where teachers bring bagged lunches and learn about how to purposefully engage students with technology. Empower your teachers to be tech leaders, sharing their knowledge formally and informally with one another.

Writing, rewriting, revising, taking suggestions, and sharing. Writing is a social process. Starting in kindergarten, students can be supported to revise their work and take suggestions from their peers.

To do this successfully, teachers need to provide modeling, guided practice, and considerable support when students move to do this independently. Work with your teams of teachers to consider how to effectively and purposefully have students write, rewrite, revise, and take suggestions from peers. Then, work with your teams to consider the possibilities for sharing and celebrating writing at the end of each unit and throughout the curriculum.

Reading the Standards Vertically: The Staircase Approach to Skill Development

The CCSS have been designed with a staircase approach to the teaching of content, skills, and concepts. Yet, we know that not all students will be on the same step at the same time when we consider the stages of physical, social, emotional, cognitive, and linguistic development. Literacy leaders and teachers must advocate for best practices for their learners, and recognize that students need to be supported with texts that are appropriate for what they can read independently, instructionally, and during whole-class readings.

When supporting diverse students in classrooms, it is important to understand the staircase approach and consider the starting step for students as literacy learners. For some students, it will be critical that teachers know the standards below and above their grade level to adapt teaching points for one-on-one and small-group instruction to best support students from wherever their starting step happens to be.

SHIFTS DEMANDED BY THE CORE

When carefully analyzing the standards to design effective and purposeful curriculum for the range of students in our classrooms, it is important to be aware of the shifts that are demanded by the CCSS. The six major shifts that most schools are experiencing include directives to (1) read as much nonfiction as fiction, (2) learn about the world by reading, (3) read more challenging material closely, (4) discuss reading using evidence, (5) write nonfiction using evidence, and (6) increase academic vocabulary.

Literacy leaders can support teachers in meeting all these shifts through purposeful coaching. For example, to support students to read as much nonfiction as fiction requires making a wealth of informational texts available to teachers. Knowing what is available is an important place to start to best support teachers in scaffolding the reading of informational texts. You can, for example, register for newsela.com, an online news source for students in grade three and above, to find leveled articles based on current events or preview the *National Geographic* ladder series that allows students to engage with nonfiction topics at a few different Lexile levels, which measure the semantic and syntactic complexity of a text.

The publishing world is quickly realizing that students need content knowledge rooted in science and social studies, as well as content at varied reading levels. Consider which shift is a priority for your school right now and begin your own professional development around the topic through professional reading, conversation, and outreach.

CREATING UNITS OF STUDY THAT ARE STANDARDS-DRIVEN AND CULTURALLY RESPONSIVE

Curriculum comes to life through the decisions literacy leaders and teachers make that motivate students and personalize learning. Unit plans provide the roadmaps to make teaching decisions more purposeful. As classrooms continue to change technologically and demographically, curriculum documents can be seen as living, changing plans that require ongoing reflection and revision. Although there are many versions of curriculum mapping out there, a strong curriculum mapping process shares four essential elements: (1) providing essential questions and enduring understandings, (2) creating performance-based assessments, (3) sequencing teaching points, and (4) embedding academic vocabulary.

Developing Enduring Understandings and Essential Questions

McTighe and Wiggins (2005) developed the Understanding by Design (UbD) framework, which has shaped curriculum design both nationally and internationally. The UbD framework is based upon the concept of *backward design* as both a planning process and a structure to guide the development of curriculum, assessment, and instruction by beginning with the end in mind. That is, curriculum mapping begins by thinking about the desired outcomes you want students to achieve at the end of the unit and then considering enduring understandings and essential questions that guide instruction while supporting students toward those desired outcomes.

When you plan with the end in mind, the guiding question is: What should students know, understand, and be able to do? To answer this, there must be goals set for students, the established standards that apply, and a timeline for the unit. Assessments, particularly performance-based assessments, described in Chapter 7, are an integral part of the curriculum mapping process to determine students' success with your learning goals and areas in which reteaching and further support is needed. When establishing enduring understandings, you are thinking both within and beyond the unit. In this way, literacy leaders can support teachers to identify the knowledge and skills that will endure beyond the life of the unit and remain with students as big ideas. When educators develop essential questions, they are constructing questions that will guide the development of individual teaching points that are sequenced through the unit. Each teaching point should connect back to enduring understandings and essential questions. It is important as a literacy leader to engage teachers in the curriculum writing or revising process, and consider whether or not teaching is organized into units of study that are grounded by what you want students to know, understand, and be able to do. Figure 6.3 provides some examples of enduring understandings and essential questions written after the onset of the CCSS with schools that have culturally and linguistically diverse students.

Notice that these examples would be appropriate for a range of units, including print strategies for grades 1 or 2, characters in fiction for middle elementary grades, nonfiction texts, and research.

Sequencing Teaching Points

Strong units of study have clearly defined teaching points that are more than activities and emphasize what readers and writers *really* do when they apply strategies to ground their thinking. Consider the following three teaching points from a 4th-grade unit based on growing ideas about characters: (1) Readers determine who is telling the story; (2) readers get to know main characters and determine character traits by focusing on inner thoughts; and (3) readers make predictions about the main characters' future actions.

These are teaching points that can apply to almost any fictional text. They can be modeled with a sample text. They can be discussed,

Figure 6.3. Common Core–Aligned Culturally Responsive Enduring
Understandings and Essential Questions

Enduring Understandings	Essential Questions
Readers and listeners are active problem-solvers who use a variety of strategies to read and understand new and unfamiliar words. Readers and listeners use a variety of strategies to help them make meaning.	How do we use a variety of strategies in flexible ways to understand new and unfamiliar words when reading or listening? How do strategies help us read and listen for meaning?
Like real people, characters are complex and often change based on their life experiences, where they are from, and their need to overcome obstacles and challenges. Our understanding of characters in stories influences our interactions with others.	How can we analyze the characters in our reading and how does that thinking affect our understanding of the story? What do we understand about characters when we study their thoughts, feelings, and actions (hopes, fears, struggles, motivations)? How can we use our understanding of ourselves to help us better understand characters?
Different people have different interests and funds of knowledge. We can learn about the world from reading, viewing, and listening to diverse voices and perspectives. Readers, viewers, and listeners explore different kinds of informational texts to learn about the world. Readers, viewers, and listeners share their knowledge with others through speaking, drawing, and writing.	What kinds of information are different people interested in learning? What can we learn from reading informational texts or learning from experts in a range of fields? How do we share information we have learned?
Different sources hold different beliefs and values. We can learn to value different forms of information and critique them for accuracy and relevance. We can draw from different sources when sharing our research to synthesize information to communicate to our audience.	How do we value, critique, and synthesize information from multiple sources? How do we determine which information is important to share with different audiences?

debated, reconsidered, and determined. They can be written about or spoken about with text evidence. They are essential ways readers develop ideas about characters. Each teaching point can be tied back to an essential question and enduring understanding mapped out prior to the start of the unit. Each can be assessed through formative and/or summative performance-based assessments.

Embedding Academic Language

Academic language refers to the language used in school to help students acquire and use knowledge (Bailey & Heritage, 2008; Schleppegrell, 2004; Zwiers, O'Hara, & Pritchard, 2014). Academic language includes vocabulary, but it also encompasses particular sentence types, conventions, and discourses (Schleppegrell, 2004). Help teachers identify academic language as they craft or revise units of study. This includes the words and sentence structures related to the content area that teachers will highlight through instruction, either explicitly or in an embedded way. However, just identifying or highlighting these words and structures is not enough. Literacy leaders need to continuously model the use of academic discourse in a multitude of contexts and work alongside teachers to support students to use academic language independently in speaking and in writing in a variety of contexts. For example, a nonfiction unit on text features might use the following words as the academic vocabulary central to the unit: *article, caption, conventions, evidence, fact, features, glossary, index, informational text, main idea, opinion, sidebar, supporting ideas, table of contents*, and *visual features* (photograph, diagram, tables, and maps). These words can appear on a nonfiction word wall. They can be included in a nonfiction folder for each student. They can be highlighted with accompanying images. Yet, teachers need to create opportunities for students to use academic language in academic contexts.

Consider working with teams of teachers to build sentence frames to support students' use of academic language. Work with teams of teachers to find photographs and other images on Google Images to hang in the classroom on anchor charts or supply to some students who need additional reference. Develop lists of questions that teachers can incorporate into their instruction that support students in sharing their understandings of the words and ways to convey their understanding in speaking and writing. Consider focusing some of your coaching observations on academic language, and record the ways teachers model, provide guided practice, and support students to independently use academic language. When you do not see this process in place, consider volunteering to lead a demonstration lesson that includes a strong academic vocabulary component.

As a literacy leader in a changing school, you need to be aware of the academic language practices in your school, but you also want to ensure that teachers honor the natural process of language acquisition. All students, but especially ELs, need to explore the richness of language across genres and through different methods, including read-alouds, shared readings, guided reading, and independent reading.

REVISITING CURRICULUM THROUGH ONGOING REFLECTION

Curriculum development and curriculum revision require a reflective stance. Thinking, particularly reflective thinking, is essential for literacy leaders, teachers, and for students. However, it is often difficult to get a clear picture of what reflection looks like. How do we know when we are being reflective and why is it important? Over 100 years ago, Dewey helped give us a framework for thinking in *How We Think* (1910/1933). Rogers (2002) analyzed Dewey's work, and found four criteria that are aligned with critical reflection: (1) Reflection is a meaning-making process; (2) reflection is systematic, rigorous, and disciplined; (3) reflection happens in community; and (4) reflection requires attitudes that value the personal and intellectual growth of oneself and others.

So what does that mean for literacy leaders in changing schools? It means that reflection is part of the curriculum process. Devise for yourself a reflection schedule so that you set aside time to systematically and rigorously analyze what is going well within the curriculum, and what needs to change. Consider setting up a daily or weekly journal to routinize reflection with prompting questions such as: What am I grateful for in our school community? How will I support teachers today/this week to engage joyfully and purposefully? What are two amazing things that happened today/this week? How can I make my work with teachers better? Set aside time to work with teams of teachers so that your reflection is not based solely on your own thinking but on what your colleagues have to say. Finally, believe that your reflection matters and that you, your teachers, and their students will grow from the process. Being systematic and disciplined with your approach is an important part of the process. Consider where within your daily, weekly, and monthly calendar reflection plays a role. Set up your coaching calendar with a code for reflection, and take both the individual and collaborative time needed.

KNOW THAT YOUR CURRICULUM AND STANDARDS ARE ALIGNED

When you walk into a classroom that is full of learning and joy, you see hands in the air, questions asked and answered, books and devices in hand, evidence of thinking, and purposeful, clear teaching. Although curriculum development and oversight can be daunting, use this chapter to support yourself and your teachers to consider what is working within the curriculum, and what needs to change to be standards-aligned, technologically forward, and supportive of the learners and their sociocultural backgrounds in your school. Start with the big ideas, the gaps, and the overlaps, and then begin to develop or revise units that start with culturally responsive essential questions and enduring understandings. Curriculum development can easily lose the forest for the trees. So keep coming back to the big picture. When literacy leaders know the curriculum and support teachers to be curriculum-creators, students know that teaching has been planned and that their learning and their identities matter.

LITERACY LEADERSHIP TOOLKIT

The exercises below can help you assess the existing curriculum, consider action steps you can take with teachers, and reflect in systematic, rigorous, and disciplined ways. The toolkit is designed in two parts with one building upon the other. Like a photographer with an adjustable camera lens, begin by positioning yourself to think widely. Start with a panoramic view of your school's curriculum. Exercise 6.1 is designed to help you start big to consider what knowledge is of most value in your school, how you and your school community define what it means to be truly literate, what you see working, and where the gaps may lie. With this panoramic view in mind, you can begin to zoom in on specific standards to build a culturally responsive yet standards-aligned curricular framework. Exercise 6.2 is designed to support you in better understanding the key tenets of the CCSS and posing questions that will help you guide your teachers to support students with core capacities.

Exercise 6.1: A Panoramic View: Starting Big to Consider a Culturally Responsive Curriculum

---

As a first step in reviewing your school or district curriculum, reflect on the following questions. This exercise is designed to support you with big-picture thinking about knowledge, literacy, and best practices in your building as you support teachers to create culturally responsive yet standards-aligned teaching practices.

Step 1: What knowledge do you think is of most worth to your teachers? Your students? Your school community?

Step 2: How do you and your teachers define what it means to be truly literate?

Step 3: What within the curriculum that exists demonstrates culturally responsive curriculum and pedagogy? How can you leverage that building- or districtwide?

Step 4: What are the gaps and overlaps within the curriculum?

Step 5: What are the short-term and long-term goals needed to make the curriculum standards-aligned, student-centered, and culturally contextualized?

Exercise 6.2: Zooming In: Closely Reading the Standards to Analyze, Notice, and Reflect from a Culturally Responsive Perspective

---

Building on the panoramic view of your school's curriculum in Exercise 6.1, reflect on the performance indicators of the Common Core State Standards shown below, and consider the strengths and challenges they present to your school population. Use what you know from Exercise 6.1 to write reflections on the standards to further your thinking about what your school's literacy teaching and learning needs are within a culturally responsive framework. Turn your reflections into action statements to meet the standards through culturally responsive curriculum and pedagogy.

Performance Indicators	What to Notice	Your Reflections
CCSS for Reading		
Reading Literature • Key Ideas and Details • Craft and Structure • Integration of Knowledge and Ideas • Range of Reading and Level of Text Complexity	• The return to traditional literature • An emphasis on asking and answering questions • An emphasis on theme and central message • An emphasis on point of view • An emphasis on close reading	
Reading Informational Text • Key Ideas and Details • Craft and Structure • Integration of Knowledge and Ideas • Range of Reading and Level of Text Complexity	• An emphasis on main topic and supporting details • Connections across readings about people, places, and events • Importance of text features to locate information • Need for students to identify the reasons an author gives ideas • An emphasis on primary sources	Ex.: Do we prominently feature multicultural children's literature through ongoing study?
Reading Informational Text • Key Ideas and Details • Craft and Structure • Integration of Knowledge and Ideas • Range of Reading and Level of Text Complexity		
Foundational Skills • Print Concepts • Phonological Awareness • Phonics and Word Recognition • Fluency	• How print concepts are defined • The importance of hearing sounds in addition to reading/writing sounds • The need for a clear, systematic phonics program to achieve the standards	

Performance Indicators	What to Notice	Your Reflections
CCSS for Writing		
• Text Types and Purposes • Production and Distribution of Writing • Research to Build and Present • Range of Writing	• The importance of balance across text types: argument and opinion, informational and explanatory, narrative • The need for students to strengthen writing through revision and editing • The incorporation of digital tools as part of production and distribution of writing • How research moves from shared to independent	Ex.: Do students have opportunities to write family narratives or to research where they are from?
CCSS for Speaking and Listening		
• Comprehension and Collaboration • Presentation of Knowledge	• The need for partnerships, small groups, and whole-class discussion • The support students will need to negotiate when to speak and when to listen • The importance of clarifying for understanding • The importance of asking and answering questions based on what a speaker says • The need for students to express themselves clearly	Ex.: In what ways can we emphasize speaking and listening in multiple languages?
CCSS for Language		
• Conventions of Standard English • Knowledge of Language • Vocabulary Acquisition and Use	• A return to conventions including capitalization, punctuation, and spelling • The need for students to see themselves as wordsmiths • The need to choose words and phrases for effect • An emphasis on having tools for determining the meanings of unknown words, nuances, and multiple meanings of words	Ex.: What tools including visuals do we provide for vocabulary acquisition for emerging ELs?

Based on your observations and questions develop three to five action statements as short-term goals for supporting your teachers to use culturally responsive yet standards-aligned practices:

1._____
   _____

2._____
   _____

3._____
   _____

CHAPTER 7

Know Instructional Techniques

- Literacy leaders must have deep knowledge of literacy instructional techniques and practices.
- Literacy leaders support teachers as they make instructional decisions that best meet the needs of the diverse learners in their classroom.
- A balanced literacy framework offers practices and techniques that literacy leaders should model for teachers to help them with developing readers and writers.

Chrissy is a new kindergarten teacher at Park School, which has seen a growing population of English learners (ELs). She has taken a lot of time since the start of the school year to learn about the neighborhood, her students, and their families by walking around the surrounding community, talking with family members about their hopes and dreams for their children, and watching her students carefully as they negotiate their way through the school day. She has copious notes on each child that she has brought to her meeting with her literacy coach, Vanessa, who is helping her implement writing workshop. Each child has a folder with his or her name on it. Each folder has picture labels on the inside pockets to denote writing work in progress and work that is completed. Baskets are filled with writing utensils color-coded for each table. Paper choices (blank pages, pages with one line, and pages with two lines) are ready and in a place where students can replenish their supplies. She has her teacher notebook set up, and it even has a few lesson plans written out. Although Chrissy has all her materials ready, she is still apprehensive. She has not yet taught a single mini-lesson. She asked to meet with Vanessa to help address her fears about getting started. Chrissy starts by asking, "How are kindergartners supposed to write on their own, especially when some of them don't even know any letters? I just don't see how this can work with them all working on their own. I feel like I need to tell each of them exactly what to do and how to do it!"

> *Vanessa listens carefully to Chrissy and then replies, "I understand your concerns. Right now, let's talk about a few of your students. Tell me about Paola. What do you see as her strengths and needs?" Chrissy begins to describe Paola as a student who speaks Spanish at home and speaks English as her second language. She attended preschool, and adjusted well to the rituals of the classroom. Paola can identify the entire alphabet in both Spanish and English (in uppercase letters), and can write all of the uppercase letters. She knows about half of the sounds, and is starting to decode sight words such as* mom, dad, *and* dog. *As Chrissy takes a breath, Vanessa jumps in: "Great, Chrissy, you've learned a lot about Paola. Now let's move to Cole. Tell me about him." Chrissy shares what she has learned about each of her students over the past few weeks.*

The apprehension, fear, and questions that Chrissy expresses to Vanessa are not unusual for a new teacher or even an experienced teacher who is about to use writing workshop for the first time. In this particular situation, Vanessa has guided the conversation away from Chrissy's fears to focus on her students. She is helping Chrissy see that because her students have very different literacy strengths and needs, the writing workshop structure of mini-lessons, independent writing, guided writing, strategy groups, conferences, and share/debriefs will enable her to address students' needs.

INSTRUCTIONAL STRATEGIES AND TECHNIQUES

Literacy instruction is complex, multifaceted, and challenging; it requires that teachers know content, effective teaching practices, and assessment strategies. As the literacy leader in your school or district, one of your many roles will be to serve as a resource for all matters related to literacy to teachers and administrators, families, district leaders, and community members. Although no one expects you to know everything there is to know about literacy teaching and learning, it is imperative that you know how to guide others with instructional strategies and techniques, and where to find and access resources to support and extend others' learning. Some literacy leaders have set up a three-ring resource binder, while others have compiled a variety of literacy resources on a website. Your ability to access information quickly about various instructional practices helps you readily provide information, ideas, and materials that your teachers can use in their classrooms.

Chapter 6 posed two important questions: What knowledge is of most worth? and What does it mean to be truly literate? These two questions help a school or district's literacy team reflect on its beliefs and knowledge about literacy, and serve as a guide for its curriculum choices. Once you and your teachers have verbalized and agreed on beliefs about literacy instruction, you can help your teachers explore instructional techniques that support such beliefs. This chapter is an overview of literacy strategies and techniques that you can use to support your teachers' literacy instruction when working with culturally and linguistically diverse students.

Scaffolded Instruction

The literacy instructional framework that teachers use relates to their theoretical beliefs about teaching and learning. A balanced instructional literacy framework develops reading and writing skills simultaneously, meets the needs of students through scaffolded instruction, and provides gradual release for students' independence when reading and writing.

In Chapters 2 and 4, we discussed how successful teachers get to know their students and families well in order to provide literacy instruction that is culturally and linguistically responsive. They carefully observe their students and use the information gathered from their observations to make informed instructional decisions. They then use many of the strategies and techniques discussed in this chapter to meet their students' specific needs.

Many techniques, some of which are outlined below, are based on the belief that scaffolded instruction is at the core of literacy instruction. Wood, Bruner, and Ross (1976) explain that scaffolding "enables a child or novice to solve a task or achieve a goal that would be beyond his unassisted efforts" (p. 90). Just as a building under construction requires scaffolding to support the workers as they build upon and add new elements to the foundation, students need scaffolding to build upon what they already know to guide them to new levels of understanding. It is important to keep in mind that, as with the scaffolding on a building, instructional scaffolding is not permanent. When the construction work is completed, the scaffolding is removed. Likewise, scaffolded instruction must lead to the release of instruction so that students use their new knowledge and strategies independently.

"I do, we do, you do." This three-step, scaffolded literacy instruction technique can benefit students (Duke & Pearson, 2002; Fisher & Frey, 2008; Pearson & Gallagher, 1983). The *I do* step begins with the teacher modeling a literacy task proficiently. For example, Kristin's eldest son recently wanted to learn how to play tennis. First, he watched someone who excelled at playing tennis and discussed what he noticed about his playing. Kristin and her son studied how the player stood, held the racquet, and handled the ball. Next, Kristin picked up her racquet, and showed her son how she held the racquet and ball and stood to get ready to play. The *we do* step is a collaborative and supportive next step in the process. It was then Kristin's son's turn to pick up his racquet, hold it, and set his stance, using Kristin as a model. Together, Kristin and her son stood face-to-face, mirroring each other, talking, and working on their swings. Occasionally, Kristin's son's eyes peeked up from his stance to watch her closely before he returned to practicing. Kristin showed him how she could bounce the ball from the ground to her racquet, and then stood close to him as they bounced his ball slowly to the ground and tried to hit the ball to the ground again. The *you do* step is independent practice with support. As Kristin stood near her son, she talked him through what to do, and allowed him the space to try it on his own to begin to get comfortable with the feeling of the racquet, adjusting his grip and stance as needed.

Just as Kristin scaffolded tennis instruction for her son, teachers need to understand how to scaffold instruction so their students can learn how to be members of the classroom as readers, writers, speakers, and listeners. Scaffolded literacy instruction usually begins with a teacher demonstration (*I do*). Students watch as the teacher models how to use a literacy strategy proficiently, often verbalizing the strategy process by thinking aloud during the process and sometimes discussing the process after the demonstration. Modeling should be carefully planned and explicit, especially for striving readers, diverse students, and English learners. When working with a diverse population, teachers cannot leave student learning to chance. Teachers must be deliberate with their instructional planning, explicit with language, and must build on what *they actually know* about their students, not on what they might assume about them.

After the teacher has modeled the strategy, the next step is to have students experiment using the strategy. The responsibility of implementing the strategy is gradually released to the students as they try it out with teacher support. The teacher listens and watches closely, coaching students as they stumble and giving them positive feedback for their successes (*we do*).

Next, the students move to their ongoing independent work, adding the modeled strategy to their growing repertoire of strategies to be used in the appropriate situation (*you do*). As with many of the strategies within a balanced literacy instructional framework, this gradual release of responsibility is the cornerstone of teaching (Duke & Pearson, 2002; Fisher & Frey, 2008; Pearson & Gallagher, 1983).

BALANCED LITERACY INSTRUCTIONAL FRAMEWORK

Balanced literacy is an instructional framework that allows teachers to meet the needs of individual students through the use of a robust set of instructional practices and structures. Balanced literacy instruction consists of three instructional blocks: (1) language and word study, (2) reading workshop, and (3) writing workshop. This three-block framework helps literacy leaders guide their teachers to conceptualize and organize their time for literacy instruction. Figure 7.1 lists the components of each of these three instructional blocks.

This framework is interconnected and flexible; in fact, there are many instances when the skills and strategies are threaded throughout the blocks. For example, read-alouds appear in the language and word study block, but read-alouds can also be used as an instructional technique multiple times during the day and across the content areas.

Language and Word Study

Language and word study is the shortest of the three literacy blocks, usually running about 30 minutes in most classrooms, although it can run as long as 60 minutes. During this time, teachers choose an instructional technique based on the goals of the literacy unit and the needs of their students. The three Anchor Standards of the Common Core State Standards (CCSS) connected to language and word study are: (1) conventions of Standard English, (2) knowledge of language, and (3) vocabulary acquisition and use (National Governors Association Center for Best Practices & Council of Chief State School Officers, 2010). During the language and word study literacy block, literacy leaders should help teachers select the most appropriate of several techniques for a particular lesson.

Figure 7.1. Balanced Literacy Instructional Blocks

Language and Word Study	Reading Workshop	Writing Workshop

• Read-Alouds
• Interactive Read-Alouds
• Shared Reading
• Interactive Writing
• Word Study (Phonics, Vocabulary, Spelling)
• Storytelling
	• Mini-lesson
	• Independent Reading
	• Small Group Instruction
	  • Strategy Groups
	  • Guided Reading
	  • Book Clubs/Literature Circles
	• Conferring
	• Share/Debrief
		• Mini-lesson
		• Independent Writing
		• Small Group Instruction
		  • Strategy Groups
		  • Guided Writing
		• Conferring
		• Share/Debrief

Read-alouds. Read-alouds should be a foundational part of every literacy classroom. Fluent readers read aloud smoothly, with expression, and as if they are speaking (Partnership for Reading, 2001). The teacher models how a fluent reader reads so that students hear smooth and expressive reading of written language. In classrooms, read-alouds should include many different genres across different levels of texts (Cunningham & Allington, 2010). Read-alouds provide several benefits because they:

- help develop enjoyment for reading;
- provide an adult demonstration of phrased, fluent reading;
- develop a student's knowledge of text structure, increase vocabulary, and expand linguistic repertoire;
- build background knowledge; and
- establish known text to use as a basis for instruction through rereading (Fountas & Pinnell, 1996).

The American Academy of Pediatrics (2014) endorses read-alouds for children from birth to promote early literacy.

There are several ways in which literacy leaders can support teachers with read-alouds. First, read-alouds are a way for literacy leaders to introduce themselves into classrooms. Through modeling read-alouds, literacy leaders can demonstrate what a strong read-aloud looks like and can help teachers feel more comfortable with the literacy leader's presence in the classroom. Second, teachers often need support in choosing books for read-alouds. Read-alouds should connect to the teaching that is occurring throughout the day. Literacy leaders can introduce new books that are strong choices for read-alouds on a regular basis. By joining mailing lists of children's book publishing companies (e.g., Lee & Low Books, https://www.leeandlow.com/) or signing up for blogs (e.g., http://classroombookshelf.blogspot.com/), literacy leaders can stay abreast of newly released books. Finally, it is imperative that classroom libraries contain books for read-alouds that represent the cultural and linguistic backgrounds and experiences of students who are in the classroom. Literacy leaders can support teachers as they build their libraries with children and families in mind.

Interactive read-alouds with accountable talk. Many literacy experts support a more specific kind of read-aloud—the interactive read-aloud—because it scaffolds a specific strategy that good readers use automatically (Collins, 2004; Fountas & Pinnell, 2000; Hoyt, 1999). Interactive read-alouds are extremely important for diverse classrooms because they make explicit what is happening metacognitively, or inside a reader's head (Rea & Mercuri, 2006). Accountable talk occurs after the interactive read-aloud, and teaches students how to discuss texts and use language in academic settings. Resnick (1995) describes accountable talk as classroom conversation that raises the level of academic discourse by teaching students to ask for and provide evidence to support their claims.

During an interactive read-aloud, the teacher scaffolds student learning by stopping at predetermined sections of text to model the thinking process when reading (*I do*). After the thinking process has been modeled, the teacher stops at new predetermined sections of text, and prompts the students to think aloud while guiding and supporting them (*we do*). With the next set of predetermined sections in the text, students think aloud independently, without prompting (*you do*).

When incorporating accountable talk with an interactive read-aloud, teachers scaffold students' conversations by referring to specific parts of the text. Usually, the talk starts in partnerships, moves to small groups (combining partnerships), and gradually evolves into a whole-class conversation. During the talk, the teacher models and explicitly teaches conversational prompts to help students deepen their conversations. Figure 7.2 is an example of accountable talk prompts that hangs on the wall as a poster and is included in students' notebooks in

Figure 7.2. Accountable Talk Poster

Cory's 4th-grade classroom. Cory, who is a teacher in the same school as Chrissy from the opening vignette, has explicitly taught and modeled these conversational prompts to his students.

Providing time for talk is imperative for all students, but it is especially important for ELs to develop their academic language and vocabulary. Classroom talk allows students to explore ideas and negotiate meanings to deepen understandings and connections (Zwiers & Crawford, 2011). It also allows students to rehearse their ideas before they put pen to paper. As with strategies for reading and writing, strategies for classroom conversation need to be explicitly taught and modeled; we cannot assume that all students know how to engage in academic discussions.

Literacy leaders can help teachers plan for using interactive read-alouds with accountable talk. It is important that as you gradually release teachers to use this strategy, you actually model how think-aloud strategies are chosen, stopping points are planned, language is chosen, and students are scaffolded to independence. See **Online Figure D** for a guide to planning an interactive read-aloud with accountable talk.

Shared reading. Shared reading is an interactive process where students and teachers read together. The shared text can be big books, songs or poems printed on charts, text displayed on interactive whiteboards, or handouts of texts that each person holds (Cunningham & Allington, 2010; Robb, 2003). Shared reading introduces students to various authors and illustrators and the way they craft meaning. This entices students to become readers and writers (Parkes, 2000). During shared reading, students learn about print conventions, punctuation, phonemes, letter–sound relationships, words, syntax, and grammar. In diverse classrooms, teachers can use what they know about students and their families to help choose shared reading texts that connect to the students' lives and experiences. For example, Mike, a 1st-grade teacher at Park School, asked parents to share stories, songs, and poems that represented their families' traditions and culture. He worked with families to record the text. He then used these audio texts for shared reading. Mike reflected during a coaching debrief that his students sat up straighter and showed such pride at the realization that their families' stories and songs mattered in their classroom. Figure 7.3 lists some tools that teachers can use to help their students read the text during shared reading.

Figure 7.3. Tools for Shared Reading

- Highlighter tape
- Wikki Stix
- Post-it notes
- Correction tape
- Sentence strips
- Pocket charts
- Whiteboards
- Chart paper
- Sliding masks (Holdaway, 1979)
- Pointers (wooden finger pointers)
- Flyswatters (cut out at center to isolate letters, chunks, or words)

As a literacy leader, you can support teachers by creating a list of shared reading texts for teachers to borrow. Demonstrate ways in which shared reading can be used to teach specific skills. Support teachers who are new to shared reading by helping them focus their teaching on ways to prompt students during the reading process. For example, instead of saying, "Find a word that rhymes with *pop*," teachers can say, "Let's think about rhyming words. Whenever you hear or see words that rhyme, I want you to put a thumb up."

Interactive writing. Interactive writing is a teacher-guided activity designed to teach students how language works through the coauthoring of a meaningful text (Button, Johnson, & Furgeson, 1996; McCarrier, Pinnell, & Fountas, 2000). Interactive writing allows students to have an active role in the creation of text while giving teachers the opportunity to demonstrate concepts of print, processes for writing, and strategies that writers use while composing a message. It also provides opportunities for teachers to give immediate instruction at the point of student need (Button, Johnson, & Furgeson, 1996).

After Vanessa modeled an interactive read-aloud in Chrissy's classroom, Chrissy engaged her students in an interactive writing lesson by writing a thank-you note to Vanessa. Chrissy had the class sit on the carpet in front of the easel with chart paper and together they discussed the idea of writing a thank-you note. Chrissy used many techniques to help her students figure out how to construct a thank-you note, think about the message, and actually write the text. She had students work in pairs to exchange ideas on what to write, chose students to write specific words and phrases as other students wrote in the air, and had students read together what was written. This activity, which Vanessa had suggested, helped Chrissy observe ways in which her students were ready for writing workshop.

Lyons and Pinnell (2001) developed a scale for analyzing interactive writing. This tool helps literacy leaders analyze the planning and teaching of an interactive writing lesson in order to help teachers increase their effectiveness. The scale includes directions and focuses on different aspects of the lesson as well as functions of writing: composition (planning and deciding the precise text), construction (how print works and word solving), and reading connections (rereading). The scale can guide your observations of teachers' interactive writing lessons, and help you analyze your own planning and teaching.

Word study. There are several different approaches to word study, all of which are designed to teach and support students in phonics, vocabulary, and spelling. A list of strategies can be found in Figure 7.4.

Word study is typically conducted in small, flexible groups, depending on the skills students have mastered. Instruction can follow the *I do, we do, you do* pattern of scaffolding. For example, a word study lesson that uses picture or word sorts as literacy activities begins with a teacher demonstration (*I do*) of how to sort pictures or word cards by sound or pattern. The teacher supports students through the pronunciation of each of the words and their meaning. The teacher establishes the key words (e.g., *trapped*, *waited*, and *played*) to guide the sorts, and prompts students to think of categories (e.g., sounds that the ending *-ed* makes: *t* sound in *trapped*, *-ed* sound in *waited*, and *d* sound in *played*) that match the key word and speculate why the category and the word match. While the teacher models such an activity, he or she shares his thinking in the form of a think-aloud with the students. Next, the *we do* portion of the lesson has students sort a few more of the cards with guidance

Figure 7.4. Word Study Strategies to Teach Phonics and Vocabulary

Phonics	Ear to Eye Phonics (Johns & Lenski, 2001)
	Making Words (Cunningham & Hall, 1994; Fountas & Pinnell, 1998)
	Word Wall (Brabham & Villaume, 2001; Cunningham, 2000; Fountas & Pinnell, 1998)
	Word Sorts (Bear et al., 2011; Fountas & Pinnell, 1998; Ganske, 2013)
	Word Hunts (Barger, 2006)
	Nursery Rhymes
	Songs
	Chants
	Riddles
	Morning Message
Vocabulary	Word-a-Day
	Semantic Mapping
	Alphaboxes (Hoyt, 1999)
	Frayer Model (Blachowitz & Fisher, 2002)
	Semantic Feature Analysis (Johns & Lenski, 2001)
	Cloze Procedure (Blachowitz & Fisher, 2002)
	Word Play (Beck, McKeown, & Kucan, 2014)
	List, Group, Label (Blachowitz & Fisher, 2002)

from the teacher. For the last step, *you do*, students sort their own word cards or picture cards independently at their own pace. The teacher uses the *you do* phase to guide students to make discoveries and generalizations about the conventions of English orthography, and compare and contrast word features within categories. See **Online Figure E** for a list of different types of word sorting activities that you can help teachers to use with the *I do, we do, you do* technique (Bear, Invernizzi, Templeton, & Johnston, 2011; Ganske, 2013).

Moats (2010) developed a brief teacher's survey on language that can be used to gather information on a teacher's knowledge of language and word study to inform professional development needs. This tool can also help literacy leaders reflect upon their own knowledge about this important strand of literacy teaching and learning. As a literacy leader, you can support teachers as they learn about language, word study, and the developmental stages of spelling. Organizing students and materials for word study can sometimes be overwhelming for teachers. Guidance from the literacy leader on how best to manage the materials and facilitate student learning in a short block of time is essential in helping teachers be successful. Further, teachers often need support as they scaffold student learning in small groups.

Storytelling. Storytelling is a powerful component of language and word study that is often underutilized. "Storytelling is relating a tale to one or more listeners through voice and gesture" (National Council of Teachers of English, 1992, para. 2). Storytelling can be a window into students' lives outside of school, and allows teachers to learn about ways in which communication may be valued in their community (Gee, 2011; Heath, 1983). It promotes community within the classroom, and allows teachers to see the differences in students' linguistic and cultural backgrounds. Storytelling is found in every culture as a means to preserve cultural traditions, entertain a variety of age groups, and educate other members of the cultural group (Gee, 2011; Heath, 1983). Because storytelling reveals the language students use to tell stories, it can be used as the impetus for teaching about classroom and academic discourse. Further, storytelling helps students learn complex aspects of literacy such as motive for action, author and audience relationships, and nonverbal language skills (Berkowitz, 2011).

Teachers can use storytelling as a regular part of their classroom routine, and connect it to reading and writing workshop. As a literacy leader, encourage teachers to provide opportunities for students to tell their stories. Guide them to create a space and time to teach and investigate storytelling together. Encourage your teachers to develop a storytelling unit that is part of reading and writing workshop, and actually includes digital stories (see Chapter 9).

READING AND WRITING WORKSHOP

The reading and writing workshop approach to teaching literacy allows for teacher modeling, student independent work, small-group instruction, and individual conferencing. Students work at their independent reading and writing levels and at their own pace, as they learn new skills or strategies and apply them to their own reading and writing. Workshop teaching, which is part of a balanced literacy instructional framework, is not limited to reading and writing, and is often extended to language and word study.

Teachers who are accustomed to whole-class instruction or who have never taught before are often intimidated by a workshop approach, as Chrissy expressed to Vanessa in the opening vignette. Vanessa helped Chrissy realize that directed whole-class teaching would not allow each student to meet his or her potential. As described in the next section, Vanessa supported Chrissy in launching writing workshop.

Mini-Lessons

Mini-lessons, which last 5 to 15 minutes, focus on a procedure, skill or strategy, or craft from a unit or area of study that students need, based on information gathered from observations and assessments. There are three main categories of mini-lessons in reading and writing workshop teaching: procedural, strategy or skill, and craft (Dorn & Soffos, 2001).

- Procedural mini-lessons teach students about classroom expectations and routines as well as individual and collective responsibilities during the workshop. These mini-lessons are essential for a smooth-running workshop.
- Strategy or skill mini-lessons teach students how to use specific strategies and skills. Teachers demonstrate how skillful readers and writers use a specific strategy and coach

students as they try to implement the strategy themselves. Vanessa's mini-lesson focused on this category.

- Craft mini-lessons teach students about tools and techniques authors use. Craft mini-lessons help readers to navigate and understand texts, writers to compose texts, speakers to construct an argument, and listeners to deconstruct and comprehend a speaker's message. See **Online Figure F** for examples of mini-lesson topics for each of the three categories.

Mini-lessons scaffold instruction so that there is a gradual release for students' independence. The following mini-lesson framework supports this gradual release:

- *Connection*: Teachers activate students' prior knowledge by connecting today's teaching point to students' ongoing work.
- *Teach*: Teachers model the teaching point, showing students how and when to use the strategy or skill.
- *Active Engagement*: This is the guided practice part of the lesson. Students try the teaching point out, either with their own work or with the teacher's example. Teachers guide students by listening in and watching, carefully taking note of students who may be confused or need additional support.
- *Link*: The final part connects the mini-lesson to students' ongoing work (Calkins, 2010).

Teaching points in mini-lessons are narrow and specific. For example, a teacher might have taught the skill of adding details to one's writing as a whole-class lesson. In a mini-lesson, the teaching point is very specific. When Vanessa modeled the skill of adding details during a mini-lesson in Chrissy's writing workshop, she explained to the students how to add details. Her teaching point was very specific: "good writers add details to their stories by adding to their illustrations." See **Online Figure G** for the script of Vanessa's mini-lesson on adding details. This mini-lesson gave the kindergarten writers one specific strategy for adding details to their writing. That specific strategy then was added to their list of strategies that can be accessed when needed. As a literacy leader, guide your teachers in making decisions about choosing mini-lesson teaching points that are responsive to students' needs. Co-planning with teachers provides opportunities to discuss how to narrow a teaching point, choose language that is specific and clear for students, and balance the amount of teacher talk versus student talk. Literacy leaders can help teachers strengthen their mini-lessons by watching them teach such lessons and then following up with focused coaching on areas in need of improvement.

Independent Work

As with athletes, musicians, or dancers, readers and writers need time and space to practice and hone their craft. In workshop, practicing is done during independent work (which can range from 5 to 10 minutes at the beginning of kindergarten to as long as 45 to 60 minutes in the upper grades). As a literacy leader, guide your teachers to organize their schedules so there is ample time for students to think, talk, read, and write *every day*. Help them understand that independent work time is not time to check email, gather materials, and let students work on their own; it is a crucial time to *teach and guide* students. Independent work gives students the opportunity to apply strategies that have been introduced and taught. Help teachers so that they know how to teach small groups during this time and confer with students as they practice using newly acquired skills and strategies.

Independent reading. Independent reading is a time when students self-select books that are at their independent reading level, which means that students can read the text fluently, on their own, and with few errors (95% or above accuracy rate). Teaching students how to choose their own reading materials and giving them the space and opportunity to practice and apply strategies helps them become confident, motivated, and enthusiastic readers (Zemelman, Daniels, & Hyde, 2012). Research shows that the amount of time spent reading (reading volume) contributes significantly to increased vocabulary as well as overall reading achievement (Allington, 2009; Cunningham & Stanovich, 2003; Reutzel, Jones, Fawson, & Smith, 2008).

Literacy leaders can support teachers with strategies to learn about their students as growing readers. Careful observations of students, quick running records, and one-on-one conferences help teachers learn about the processes and behaviors that students are using and the areas in need of support. In the upper grades, many teachers have their students use reading logs to keep track of their reading. Literacy leaders can help teachers work with students to use these logs to create goals for themselves as readers (e.g., increasing volume, expanding to different genres, and reading more challenging texts).

Independent writing. During independent writing, writers work through the writing process at their individual pace, applying strategies learned as they compose, revise, edit, or publish their pieces. Topics are self-selected, motivating students to want to write and share their stories with others. During this time, writers may be reading, talking, or writing, all of which are important parts of the writing process. Having opportunities to talk while writing is essential for all students, but especially for ELs, because it is often through talk that learning is mediated (Ammon, 1985; Urzúa, 1986, 1987). Literacy leaders can support teachers in developing ways to learn about their students as writers through careful observations both in and out of the classroom, analysis of student writing, and conversations with writers.

Small-Group Instruction

Given that many classrooms are becoming increasingly more diverse, a wide range of flexible grouping strategies should be used to meet students' individual and collective needs. Although research suggests that groups should be flexible, fluid, and dynamic to reflect the learning goals (Caldwell & Ford, 2002), often children are grouped based on their reading level at the beginning of the school year and they remain in that same group for much of the year. We know that students develop as readers at different paces and perform at different rates. Therefore, it is vital to use a variety of grouping strategies, in addition to grouping by students' instructional reading level, that are determined both by the students' needs and the learning goals. Literacy leaders can help teachers use several types of small groups during independent worktime to focus reading and writing instruction: strategy groups, guided reading, guided writing, and book clubs/ literature circles.

Strategy groups. One way to flexibly group students for small-group instruction is to bring together students who need support in the same reading or writing strategy. These readers (or writers) may be on different reading (or writing) levels, but have difficulty using a specific reading (or writing) strategy. The strategy may have already been introduced to students in a mini-lesson, or it could be a new strategy that a small group of readers (or writers) is ready to attempt. The same structure described to teach a mini-lesson can be used in a strategy group.

Literacy leaders can show teachers ways to quickly assess the strategies that students can use independently and the strategies that students need to be retaught. Further, literacy leaders can help teachers set up a system for collecting and keeping track of information for forming small groups. They can also help them gather material and develop a library of leveled short texts, including texts that may be in students' first language or even bilingual texts that can be used for strategy work. In addition, literacy leaders can model how to follow up with students to ensure that the small-group learning transfers to independent work.

Guided reading. Flexible grouping for guided reading allows a teacher to support readers as they develop effective strategies for processing texts at their instructional level with 90–95% accuracy (Fountas & Pinnell, 1996). The main difference between strategy groups and guided reading groups is when a lesson is taught. With strategy groups, the mini-lesson is usually taught first, whereas with guided reading groups, students' reading occurs first. Guided reading focuses on the reading that was observed by the teacher, including the challenges posed in the text. There is more emphasis on text introduction, which not only engages the readers, but also provides information that will help students decode and comprehend the text (Fountas & Pinnell, 1996).

Selected texts are based upon the level of support and challenge they offer students. After the teacher introduces the text or book, students make predictions about the text. They then read their own copy of the text softly to themselves *at their own pace* as the teacher listens and provides support as needed. The teacher uses such strategies as discussion, retelling, and rereading to help students with comprehension and higher-order thinking skills (Opitz & Ford, 2001).

Lyons and Pinnell (2001) developed a scale for analysis of guided reading. As with their tool for interactive writing, this scale helps literacy leaders analyze teachers' planning and teaching of a guided reading lesson in order to help them improve their effectiveness. For example, literacy leaders can determine whether teachers are giving too much support to students as they read the text.

Guided writing. As with guided reading groups, guided writing groups allow teachers to pull together small groups of writers with similar needs to provide direct support. Guided writing often starts out with a brief, shared experience or a reflection of a shared experience (Gibson, 2008). For example, 4th-grade teacher Cory, mentioned above, wanted to support a small group of ELs in using transitional words. He had his small group of students tie their shoes and note the steps that they took. Together, they discussed the steps, highlighting the transitional words (e.g., *first, next, then, after, finally*). Cory and his students worked together to construct a short, shared text on how to tie a shoe, using transition words and phrases. Cory then asked the students to choose a piece to revise from their writer's notebooks. Cory "leaned in" to guide his students about their decisions and strategy use. Cory ended his guided writing lesson by asking his students to share one place where they added a transition word or phrase to their writing. Cory's ability to engage students in guided writing developed after many one-on-one sessions with Vanessa.

Book clubs/literature circles. Book clubs and literature circles are student-centered, collaborative groups in which members read the same text within an agreed-upon time frame (Calkins, 2000; Daniels, 2002). Members make decisions together, such as how much to read by a given point in time and how to manage and keep track of the conversations. The success of these groups depends on the degree to which students know and apply the procedures for working in a book club or literature circle, have the reading strategies and skills needed to lead and manage their work, and demonstrate the willingness to participate in conversations about texts.

Teachers monitor book clubs and literature circles, and coach students in the clubs as needed. Teachers should refrain from being a member of the group. Literacy leaders can support teachers by observing with them book clubs/literature circles in action and debriefing on points where students could use some additional teaching or support. For example, when Cory's 4th-grade students were meeting to discuss their books, Vanessa and Cory visited each group, watching students' interactions and taking notes on their discussions. They noted that, in at least three of the groups, students were talking about the large ideas in the chapter, but they were not returning to the text to provide evidence for their thinking. In one group, students were jumping from individual idea to individual idea, instead of developing the conversation. During lunch that afternoon, Cory and Vanessa came up with specific teaching strategies for developing a conversation and providing evidence from the text to deepen the conversation. The next day,

Cory started with a mini-lesson on providing evidence. He then sat for a few minutes with the book club that had struggled with this concept the day before to coach the students whenever there was an opportunity to provide evidence from the text.

Conferring

Conferring is often referred to as the heart of a workshop (Allen, 2009; Berne & Degener, 2015; Calkins, 1994). It also is one of the most difficult workshop components for teachers to use. Meeting with children individually offers teachers the opportunity to (1) learn how students are applying what they have learned to their independent work, (2) offer students concrete instruction that is directly tied to what they are working on right then and there, and (3) build students' confidence by providing positive feedback about a specific skill or strategy they are using well. As with all aspects of workshop teaching, conferences usually follow a common structure. At the beginning of a conference, the conversation between student and teacher allows the teacher to research what the student is attempting to do and how he or she is progressing. During this conversation, the teacher usually uncovers multiple teaching possibilities, but must decide the most important teaching point for this particular student at this particular point in time. Once the decision has been made as to what the teaching point will be, the conference moves to the teaching part. The teaching part of the conference is a conversation between the teacher and student rather than a series of teacher-directed questions.

As literacy leaders, you need to help teachers communicate their expectations for their students during a conference. You also need to support teachers in deciding what to teach and how to teach it. Bringing groups of teachers together to analyze student work can be helpful in deciding what students need and the best structures for teaching to those needs (see Chapter 5 for an example of examining student work). Audio or video recording of conferences and peer observations can help strengthen teachers' conferring practices.

Share

The end of a reading or writing workshop is usually called the "share" because it is a way to close the workshop while offering an opportunity to slip in additional teaching. It is a powerful time for reteaching or reviewing a strategy that was taught that day or a previous day by highlighting the work of a student who used the strategy successfully. To make sure that this is done efficiently, teachers usually prepare students ahead of time on what and how they should share or present their work to their classmates. Teachers can also close the workshop by revisiting the teaching point and reminding students of additional strategies they have discussed or have been taught. For example, when Vanessa modeled a strategy lesson for Chrissy, she could have closed the writing workshop in three different ways: She could have reinforced the mini-lesson teaching point by saying, "Writers add details to their stories by adding to their illustrations. First, they close their eyes and picture exactly what happened and ask themselves what do I see? They then check their illustration to make sure it matches the picture in their head. Remember, we also have learned that we can add details to our writing by___." A second way she could have ended the workshop is by asking the students to find a place where they added details to their story by adding to their illustrations and then having each student share that particular section with a partner or small group. Finally, Vanessa could have chosen one or two students who successfully used this strategy and had them share the way they used the strategy.

SELECTING APPROPRIATE ASSESSMENT TOOLS TO GUIDE INSTRUCTION

Assessment and instruction are inextricably linked. Chapter 4 discussed the concept of assessment in general terms in relation to getting to know your students. As a literacy leader, you should know and understand the different types of assessments and how to collaboratively choose the most appropriate assessment to meet the desired instructional goals. Figure 7.5 lists various types of assessments, the general purpose(s) of each type of assessment, and examples of each type of assessment.

Assessment can be daunting because literacy processes are so complex, assessment measures are so plentiful, and individual students are so diverse. A good place to start is to review the assessments that already are in place and the ways in which they are used. Before purchasing published assessments, think about ways teachers can work together to develop formative and summative assessments. For example, Vanessa worked with teachers of each grade in her school

Figure 7.5. Types of Assessment

Type of Assessment	General Purpose	Example(s)
Criterion-Referenced	Measures student performance against predetermined criteria or standards Usually reported as mastery (proficient) versus nonmastery	*Basic Reading Inventory* (10th ed.) (Johns, 2008) *Developmental Reading Assessment* (2nd ed.) (Beaver & Carter, 2006) *Observation Survey of Early Literacy Achievement, Revised* (2nd ed.) (Clay, 2006)
Norm-Referenced	Compares student performance with other students' performance on the same test Teachers use these measurements to determine whether a student's test performance is above average, average, or below average compared to classmates (local norms) or a broader group of like students (national norms) Teachers can also determine if a student's performance on the test is consistent with past performances	*Brigance Diagnostic Comprehensive Inventory of Basic Skills—Revised* (CIBS-R) (Brigance, 1999) *Gates MacGinitie Reading Tests* (4th ed.) (GMRT-4) (MacGinitie, MacGinitie, Maria, Dreyer, & Hughes, 2000) *Gray Oral Reading Test* (4th ed.) (GORT-4) (Bryant & Wiederholt, 2001) *Qualitative Reading Inventory* (5th ed.) (QRI-4) (Leslie & Caldwell, 2010)
Screening	Routinely given to students at the beginning of the year or when placed in a new environment Used to determine which students may need additional instructional support Results are typically not specific	*Phonological Awareness Literacy Screening 1-3* (PALS) (Invernizzi, Meier, & Juel, 2005)
Diagnostic	Given to students who were identified through the screening process Provides a more detailed view of students' strengths and needs	Informal Reading Inventories

Figure 7.5. Types of Assessment (continued)

Type of Assessment	General Purpose	Example(s)
Formative	Takes place during instruction Provides assessment-based feedback to teachers and students Helps both teachers and students make adjustments in teaching and learning	Observations Anecdotal Records Student Writing Running Records Student Work Exit Slips
Progress Monitoring	Students' current levels of performance are determined Goals are identified for learning that will take place over time Students' academic performance is measured on a regular basis Progress toward meeting the students' goals is measured Teaching is adjusted as needed	*Curriculum-Based Measurement* (CBM) (Deno, 1985) *AIMSweb* (n.d.) (http://www.aimsweb.com/) *Dynamic Indicators of Basic Early Literacy Skills* (6th ed.) (DIBELS) (University of Oregon, n.d.)
Benchmark	Measures students' progress against a specific benchmark (e.g., grade-level criterion, reading level, continuum of characteristics) Occurs at predetermined time of the year (beginning, middle, end)	*Fountas and Pinnell Benchmark Literacy Assessment System* (2nd ed.) (Fountas & Pinnell, 2010) Writing Continuums (e.g., Teachers College Reading and Writing Project)
Performance Based	Requires students to demonstrate and apply their knowledge or skills by creating a response or product	Creating a digital story as a personal narrative Writing a series of blog posts as a reader response
Summative	Takes place at the conclusion of a specific unit, semester, academic year Measures students' understanding	End-of-Unit Tests End-of-Term/-Semester Tests Standardized Tests

to craft a writing rubric, based on the adopted state writing rubric. First, teachers analyzed the state rubric and discussed the expectations at every level. The teachers then collected writing pieces from students and analyzed them in relation to the state rubric. Teachers also reviewed other rubrics they had designed or modified for each unit of study, and compared these rubrics to the state rubric. The teachers used this information to create a continuum of writing and benchmarks for writing at each grade level. This year-long inquiry into writing assessment helped clarify teachers' understanding of students as writers, create a shared understanding of expectations for student writing, and prompt conversations into many other aspects of the teaching of writing across the school.

THE IMPORTANCE OF KNOWING INSTRUCTIONAL TECHNIQUES

Balanced literacy provides teachers with an instructional framework that allows them to differentiate instruction to meet individual student needs by offering several different instructional techniques that combine interactive and direct approaches, flexible grouping, and modeling. Balanced literacy is particularly useful for ELs because it provides opportunities to develop academic oral language (O'Day, 2009). An essential component of literacy leadership is to support and guide teachers as they implement new or strengthen existing instructional techniques.

In addition, one of the most exciting aspects of being a literacy leader is the opportunity to keep learning about ways that instructional techniques and practices can be adapted to support all types of learners, especially those coming from culturally and linguistically diverse backgrounds. You are continually growing as professionals, constantly adding to your own knowledge base and to your practices, and deepening your understandings. No one should be positioned as knowing it all; you have expertise in literacy teaching and learning, and part of that expertise is knowing when and how to coach teachers to use different instructional techniques and practices in their classrooms.

LITERACY LEADERSHIP TOOLKIT

The Literacy Leadership Toolkit contains two exercises: a reflection tool to help guide you in evaluating your knowledge about literacy instructional practices and techniques, and a tool for selecting and evaluating assessments.

Exercise 7.1:
Literacy Practices and Teaching Techniques Self-Assessment

This tool will help you understand your areas of strengths and areas that need further development. As a literacy leader, it is important to have knowledge of various instructional techniques and practices. Take the time to look at this list, and mark each practice with the following codes:

✓ I feel confident in leading teachers in understanding and incorporating this practice.

+ I have some knowledge of this practice, but must do more to expand my knowledge and acquire resources before I can help teachers with this practice.

- I have to visit classrooms and schools that use this practice, attend conferences to learn more about this practice, and do as much reading as possible before I am ready to help teachers with this practice.

Use this self-assessment to create your own professional development plan for learning more about balanced literacy.

Literacy Practices and Teaching Techniques Self-Assessment

Language and Word Study	
	Read-Alouds
	Interactive Read-Alouds with Accountable Talk
	Shared Reading
	Interactive Writing
	Word Study (Phonics, Vocabulary, Spelling)
	Storytelling
Reading Workshop	
	Mini-lesson
	Independent Reading
	Strategy Groups
	Guided Reading
	Book Clubs/Literature Circles
	Conferring

Literacy Practices and Teaching Techniques Self-Assessment (continued)

	Reading Workshop	
	Share/Debrief	
	Writing Workshop	
	Mini-lesson	
	Independent Writing	
	Strategy Groups	
	Guided Writing	
	Conferring	
	Share/Debrief	

Exercise 7.2: Assessment Considerations

Before adopting published assessments or assessment systems, it is imperative that literacy leaders lead a small group of teachers and administrators in a review of the assessments. The following questions can guide you and your team to make informed decisions about current or proposed assessments. It is a good idea to create a spreadsheet to collate the answers to these questions, and compare the assessments to one another.

What is our goal or specific purpose for the assessment?	
Does the goal we have defined match the author or authors' stated goals about the assessment?	
How are the results reported?	
How will the results be used?	
What decisions are made based on the data?	
Who will receive the results?	
How can results be used for instruction?	
Which students will be assessed?	
How are assessments administered?	
Who will administer the assessment?	
Where will the assessment take place?	

When will the assessment take place?	
Who owns the data? Is the ownership external or with the district, school, grade level, content area, or classroom teacher?	
What professional development is needed? • How will the assessor be trained to administer the assessment? • How will the assessor and teachers be taught how to interpret results? • How will teachers be taught and supported in using the results to inform instruction?	
Where and how will the information be collected and stored?	

CHAPTER 8

Know Approaches and Programs to Language and Literacy Instruction

- Literacy leaders help teachers and building leaders evaluate which language and literacy programs will best meet the needs and build on the strengths of the students they serve.
- The evaluation of literacy programs should be systematic and comprehensive, and new programs should be adopted and adapted only after careful consideration of school and district goals and student and teacher strengths and needs.
- Districts can supplement their literacy program with additional support for students who would benefit from language development or intervention approaches.

Evie, a literacy coach in an all-girls school in the Northeast, has been working with her early grade teachers (kindergarten through grade 2) to assess the girls' strengths and needs in reading. Many of the teachers at Scholars' Prep have noticed that students are having difficulty decoding new texts, and with the push for students to be reading increasingly complex texts, the teachers are wondering how their students are going to be successful. Evie is sitting with the 1st-grade team today. Each teacher has a stack of his or her students' benchmark assessments (they use Fountas & Pinnell, 2010) and a chart of their overall analysis of the class assessments, showing each student's reading levels, specific strengths, and next steps for targeted teaching. Evie starts the meeting by moving right into the goal for their time together. "Thank you all for coming so well prepared today. We decided to have this meeting because, despite having developed and taught a series of mini-lessons focused on decoding texts, we are still noticing that many of our girls are struggling to decode unfamiliar words."

The four teachers around the table are nodding in agreement. Julie, the team leader for the grade level, speaks up: "I think our girls need something more focused than what we are doing in our mini-lessons and conferences. We designated time this year to focus on language and word work, but we all seem to be doing it differently. I know I have really spent that time on shared reading and interactive writing."

Jasmine chimes in: "And I have been spending the time teaching phonics more directly, but I really have no specific structure or way to know if what I am doing is right."

The conversation continues with each teacher describing what he or she is doing during language and word work as well as during individual conferences. The four teachers seem to agree that they need additional support and direction in providing students with more explicit instruction. Teachers share specific examples of students who are having difficulty to emphasize that the students have many needs. They think direct instruction in phonics will help their students reach their appropriate independent reading level.

Glancing at the clock, Evie concludes, "I am noticing the time, and I realize that this may be a bigger issue than just 1st grade. I am hearing similar comments in the kindergarten and 2nd-grade-level discussions. I think we need to investigate some of the published materials and different approaches to teaching phonics and word study. I am going to spend some time doing a bit of research this week. When we meet next week, I will have some information for us to review."

The teachers agree that this is a good next step, and they thank Evie as they hurry to pick up their students.

Evie's work with teachers is reflective of the experiences of many literacy leaders; when looking carefully at student assessment data, teachers notice a gap in their instruction and look to the literacy leader in the building for direction and resources to help them meet the identified student needs. This chapter discusses ways Evie and other literacy leaders can make informed decisions about different programs and approaches that best meet the needs of the students they teach.

WORKING WITH LITERACY APPROACHES AND TECHNIQUES

Although they use a culturally responsive literacy framework to teach literacy, the teachers at Evie's school realized from their analysis of the student assessments that they need to focus a chunk of their literacy teaching on phonics and word study. There are several different approaches to the teaching of phonics and word study. Most programs offer structure and resources for teaching. As a team, teachers and literacy leaders must work to analyze these different approaches and programs before making a decision about which approach they believe will both work best with their students and will complement the current ways in which literacy is taught in the school.

Quite often, a specific method or program is growing in popularity in the surrounding districts or within a literacy leader's network of schools. Although paying attention to these trends is instructive, it is imperative that, as a literacy leader, you research what is available that best meets the needs of the school and the students. A method's popularity is not a measure of its appropriateness for a given school and its students.

Reviewing Programs

The first step Evie took after her discussion with the early-grade teachers was to research the instructional resources that would meet the needs of both the students and the teachers. Evie knew from the assessment data and teachers' observations that many students were struggling with decoding unfamiliar words. Evie also noticed (and had not yet shared in larger groups) that students were struggling with spelling. This struggle was also appearing in students' writing. She was aware that there was no formal spelling instruction taking place in the school. Thus, Evie looked for an approach to teaching phonics, spelling, and vocabulary that would enhance (not replace) her school's current curriculum, while also meeting the needs of a culturally and linguistically rich and diverse student body.

Purpose. Choosing materials to use in a classroom or school is not an easy task. This complex work must take many factors into account. At the most basic level, the decisionmaking process should include the needs and wants of students, teachers, administrators, and community members. The process for material selection might require approval from school boards, boards of trustees, parents, or community members. As the literacy leader, it is likely your responsibility to research what the district's policy and process is, and design procedures that align with these guidelines. In Evie's case, there are no formalized protocols, and it is up to her as the literacy leader to research the programs, present them, and review them with the teachers. At the same time, she needs to keep the instructional leadership team (which includes other specialists and the principal) informed. At the end of the process, Evie and the teachers will recommend a first and second choice to the instructional leadership team, with the principal having the final decisionmaking power.

   Questions to ask. A logical starting point for the process of selecting one or more programs to support language and literacy learning is to consider the questions that should guide the inquiry. The Literacy Leadership Toolkit at the end of the chapter contains a chart with a list of questions to use in both formal and informal vetting processes. These questions allow Evie and her committee of teachers to take notes, and track the similarities and differences across the different programs they review during the selection process. Evie also can share these questions with the administrators, teachers, and community members who are involved in the selection process.

   The questions vary from inquiries that address concrete questions about lesson structure and delivery to more abstract queries about goals. They provide a first step toward helping Evie and her colleagues organize what might otherwise be an overwhelming amount of information. Further, if nearby schools are using a program under review, it is beneficial for a group of teachers and administrators to visit the school, see different aspects of the program in practice in several classrooms and grade levels (if applicable), and debrief with teachers and administrators about their experiences with the program and materials.

FOUNDATIONAL LITERACY PROGRAMS

Over the past decade, several significant studies of reading have supported the importance of the effective teaching of what the Common Core State Standards (CCSS) is now calling foundational skills (National Governors Association Center for Best Practices & Council of Chief State School Officers, 2010). In the CCSS, foundational skills are identified as print concepts, phonological awareness, phonics and word recognition, and fluency. Research has shown that teaching foundational skills is *one aspect* of a comprehensive literacy framework (see Chapter 7). There are several approaches to teaching foundational skills, specifically focusing on phonological awareness, phonics, and word recognition. Figure 8.1 describes the six different approaches.

These approaches, which vary in their focus on letters, phonemes, and other sound–symbol relationships, are not absolute and are sometimes combined for instructional purposes. When evaluating the options for teaching foundational skills, Evie and her colleagues consider which program(s) will best complement their school and district's existing structure of teaching and assessment, and help teachers close gaps in student learning. Two of the most popular approaches to teaching phonics are multisensory approaches and word study approaches.

Multisensory Approaches

Multisensory approaches encourage and teach students to use more than one of their senses to learn: visual (sight), auditory (hearing), tactile (touch), kinesthetic (movement), usually referred to as VAKT. Although many teachers employ multisensory *activities* in their teaching,

Figure 8.1. Approaches to Phonics Instruction

Synthetic Phonics	Children learn how to transfer letters or letter combinations into sounds, and then how to blend the sounds together to form identifiable words.
Analytic Phonics	Children learn to analyze letter–sound relationships in previously learned words. They are not taught to pronounce individual sounds in isolation.
Analogy-based Phonics	Children learn to use parts of word families they know to recognize words they don't know that have similar parts.
Phonics Through Spelling	Children learn to segment words into phonemes and to make words by writing letters for phonemes.
Embedded Phonics	Children are taught letter–sound relationships during the reading of texts.
Onset Rime Phonics	Children learn to identify the sounds in the onset and the rime. The onset is the part of the word before the vowel; not all words have onsets. The rime is the part of the word including the vowel and what follows it.

Adapted from Eunice Kennedy Shriver National Institute of Child Health and Human Development, 2001.

there are specific programs that incorporate systematic multisensory approaches to teach foundational skills. Figure 8.2 provides a visual for the principles of instruction found in many of the multisensory structured language programs. Many were originally designed for students who were experiencing severe difficulties with reading and who had been identified as having a learning disability, such as dyslexia, dysgraphia, and/or dyscalculia. These approaches are based on the work of Orton, a child neurologist, and his curriculum collaborators Gillingham and Stillman. They developed an instructional approach for students with dyslexia (Ritchey & Goeke, 2006). Their work provides a foundation for many, if not all, of the multisensory approaches to teaching reading. See **Online Figure H** for detailed descriptions of different multisensory approaches and **Online Figure I** for ways that a specific multisensory approach, the Spalding Method, has been developed into a graduate program for practicing teachers.

Orton-Gillingham-based approaches have become increasingly popular in schools and classrooms. Although the International Dyslexia Association (2014) acknowledges the importance of multisensory approaches for students diagnosed with dyslexia, it also affirms that multisensory approaches have "not yet been isolated in controlled comparison studies of reading" (p. 2). Evie knows that, before she invests in such a program, she needs to work with her colleagues to

Figure 8.2. Principles of Instruction in Multisensory Language Programs

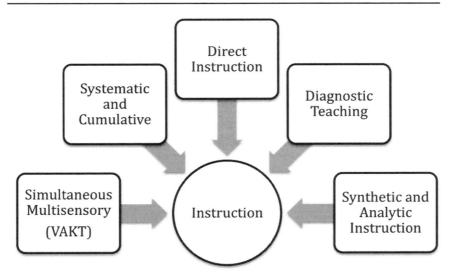

determine whether their students would benefit from a multisensory approach. They need to investigate the programs that other schools with similar demographics are using, the types of students who are benefitting, the instructional time that is devoted to these programs, and specific outcome measures. Evie understands that she needs to determine for whom and in what settings Orton-Gillingham–based methods are most effective. Figure 8.3 lists multisensory program approaches based on Orton-Gillingham.

DEVELOPMENTAL WORD STUDY APPROACHES

While the multisensory phonics programs focus on helping students memorize rules about how sound–symbol relationships work within the English language, another option Evie and her team are exploring involves developmental word study approaches that guide students through active inquiry of word families in context. A word study approach focuses on the three layers of English orthography, with each level building upon the other. The three layers include alphabet/sound, pattern, and meaning. The alphabet/sound layer is based on the relationship between letters and sounds. It shows how to build words by joining letters together, either singly or in pairs, in order to

Figure 8.3. Additional Multisensory Approaches

- Alphabetic Phonics (Cox, 1992)
- The DuBard Association Method (DuBard & Martin, 1994)
- Fundations® (Wilson, 2005)
- The Herman Method (Herman, 1993)
- Lindamood-Bell (Lindamood & Lindamood, 1975)*
- Preventing Academic Failure (Bertin & Perlman, 1998)
- Project Read (Enfield & Greene, 1997)
- The Slingerland Multisensory Approach (Slingerland & Aho, 1994-1996)
- The Spalding Method (Spalding & North, 2012)
- Starting Over Multisensory Reading Program (Knight, 1995)
- The Wilson Reading System® (WRS) (Wilson, 1988)

*Lindamood-Bell is a multisensory approach that purports not to be Orton-Gillingham–based.

form sounds from left to right. For example, in the word *pit*, a single letter represents each sound. Students blend the sounds for /p/, /i/, /t/, to read the word *pit*. The pattern layer overlays the alphabetic layers because, in the English language, there is not a single sound for each letter, unlike Spanish, which does have a one-to-one correspondence between letters and sounds. Therefore, students must begin to look for patterns in the words they analyze—for instance, the consonant–vowel–consonant–silent e pattern, which usually creates the long vowel sound (e.g., *kite*).

The meaning layer concentrates on groups of letters that represent meaning directly, such as prefixes and suffixes. When students learn that groups of letters can represent meaning directly, it helps them when they encounter unusual spellings. Prefixes, suffixes, and Greek and Latin stems are examples of groups of letters that help us understand meaning. For example, students may wonder why the word *composition* is not spelled *compusition*, but by studying the roots of words, they recognize its relationship to the word *compose* (Bear, Invernizzi, Templeton, & Johnston, 2011).

In word study, students are taught to explore the sound, pattern, and meaning relationships among words using compare-and-contrast strategies known as word sorts. They discover consistencies that enable them to generalize their understandings to other words and thereby learn to read, spell, and write more efficiently (Ganske, 2013). Because this approach builds upon what students already know, it works from a strength perspective, using students' funds of knowledge (Moll, Amanti, Neff, & Gonzalez, 1992) as a place to start and develop learning. This is especially important for ELs, who have often been framed as having language and literacy deficits.

In addition to reviewing multisensory approaches to teach foundational skills, Evie and her team have been investigating two popular developmental word study approaches to phonics, spelling, and vocabulary instruction: *Words Their Way* (Bear, Invernizzi, Templeton, & Johnston, 2011) and *Word Journeys* (Ganske, 2013). Both approaches are based on the idea that the brain is a pattern recognizer and classifier, and they use word sorts as a main activity. A spelling inventory and writing samples are used to place students along a developmental continuum (Bear et al., 2011; Ganske, 2013; Henderson, 1990). Instruction is scaffolded using small groups, and is planned to meet students' needs. The approaches are structured so that students have to pay close attention to the words and their sounds instead of relying on memorization, which is typical of many spelling programs. Because students are taught the words ahead of time in a teacher-directed sort, students can concentrate on analyzing the words, rather than decoding them. Further, students analyze the words using words they know to determine the patterns that can be transferred in the future when they encounter new or unknown words in context. See **Online Figure J** for a detailed description of *Words Their Way* (Bear, Invernizzi, Templeton, & Johnston, 2011) and *Word Journeys* (Ganske, 2013).

USE OF COMMERCIALLY PREPARED MATERIALS

Whether you are using a structured multisensory phonics program such as the Spalding Method or implementing a word study approach such as *Words Their Way*, these commercially prepared programs should not be allowed to supplant the teacher's insights and instructional expertise. McMasters et al. (2014) explored ways to balance teacher fidelity and teacher flexibility. They offer several questions to guide customization of a commercially prepared product:

- Why is it important to become proficient in implementing core components before making specific program changes?
- Which program components might require fidelity checks throughout implementation?
- Which components would you consider modifying in your classroom and why?
- How will you measure student progress to evaluate the benefits of your changes?
- How will you decide to make adjustments if students are not making progress in response to instruction? (p. 174)

LANGUAGE DEVELOPMENT PROGRAMS

In addition to multisensory and word study approaches to teaching foundational literacy skills, many districts opt to offer ELs specialized programs designed to promote language development. At a diverse school such as Evie's, many of the students speak languages other than English in their homes. As discussed in Chapter 4, diverse students have particular needs related to their cultural and linguistic backgrounds as well as their proficiency level in English. Language development programs can help meet those needs. Literacy leaders like Evie should be familiar with these programs not only to help classroom teachers better meet the needs of the students participating in them, but also to be able to make recommendations to building and district leaders about student placement and the selection and prioritization of the programs themselves. Exercise 8.2 in the Literacy Leadership Toolkit contains some key questions and considerations to guide this inquiry process. Decisionmakers will need to consider concrete factors such as the size and composition of the EL population, the availability of funding, and the potential for appropriate staffing as well as more intangible measures such as school and community buy-in (Honigsfeld, 2009).

Native Language Instruction

If her school wishes to consider programs that offer native language instruction, Evie may have to begin the selection process by addressing some common misconceptions about these programs. Perhaps because it contradicts "commonsense" notions of how to learn a second language, the role of native language instruction in the acquisition of English is often misunderstood. Conventional wisdom postulates that the fastest path to fluency in English is to be completely immersed, but research in the field of second-language acquisition affirms the affective as well as the cognitive benefits of native language instruction (Cummins, 1979, 1980; Krashen, 1981, 1999; Thomas & Collier, 2003). Although in the past 15 years states such as Arizona and Massachusetts have passed legislation limiting native language instruction in public schools, research continues to indicate that the structured English immersion programs promoted in these laws are among the least effective programs available for ELs (Center for Research on Education, Diversity & Excellence, 2003; Honigsfeld, 2009; Mahoney, MacSwan, & Thompson, 2005). The misunderstandings that plague bilingual education and its effectiveness may be the result of confusion over the distinct types of programs and their purpose.

Bilingual Programs

Bilingual education programs have been controversial in the United States, but leaders in the field of second-language acquisition such as Cummins and colleagues (1979, 1980, 2005) and Krashen (1981, 1999) affirm their value when they are properly implemented. Though the public rancor against bilingual education often treats these programs as a single entity, there are vast differences in goals and outcomes between transitional bilingual programs and maintenance bilingual programs. Transitional programs offer ELs instruction in their first language for the first year or so of schooling until they can be mainstreamed into traditional classes. Their goal is a rapid transition to monolingual instruction. Maintenance programs offer long-term instruction in both languages with the goal of developing academic English while maintaining or developing the primary language. The goal of these programs is to produce bilingual and biliterate students, leading to fluency in English as well as in another language such as Spanish or Mandarin.

Krashen (1999) offers three conditions that must be met in order for a program to be accurately labeled bilingual: (1) content-area teaching in the primary language without translation until such instruction is comprehensible in the second language, (2) literacy development in the primary language, and (3) comprehensible input in the second language. He asserts that in most of the research that questions the effectiveness of bilingual education, these conditions were not met, particularly in regard to the duration and depth of the native language instruction being offered in transitional programs. One type of program that does adhere to these more rigorous standards is dual-language immersion.

Dual-Language Programs

A proven method of bilingual instruction is dual-language instruction, or programs in which the school day is divided into segments according to the language of instruction. Students split their time between two teachers who use only one of the languages to teach content as well as the language itself through a language arts block. Often, these programs begin with up to 90% of the day being offered in the nondominant language (e.g., Spanish or Mandarin) before eventually moving to a more balanced 50-50 model after a few years. Although dual-language programs are popular in districts that serve large immigrant populations, they are also effective with monolingual speakers of English. These programs have been proven especially effective when they mix students with dominance in both of the targeted languages—for example, Spanish-speaking immigrants and U.S.-born speakers of English can both benefit from the same dual-language immersion program. Both groups of students are first- and second-language learners. Park Avenue School, described in Chapter 2, is an example of such a school.

Thomas and Collier (2003, 2012) advocate for balanced dual-language immersion programs, but they offer clear guidelines for the programs. Figure 8.4 lists the components of an effective dual-language program. The researchers have documented the effectiveness of this approach, when properly implemented, across different regions in the United States.

Dual-language programs are more common in districts with a substantial EL population, so it may be a viable option at Evie's school if she and her colleagues believe there will be sufficient community buy-in and support. Not all districts have the means or the inclination to offer dual-language programs, even if there is a large EL population, but many of their strengths, such as access to comprehensible content and linguistic scaffolding, can also emerge through effective sheltered instruction.

SHELTERED/CONTENT-AREA PROGRAMS

Students who do not have access to or who opt out of native language instruction can be placed in sheltered programs that offer content instruction in an environment that acknowledges the linguistic needs of ELs. More formally known as Specially Designed Academic Instruction in English (SDAIE), these programs make content comprehensible for ELs while actively promoting the acquisition of academic English.

Sheltered Instruction Observation Protocol (SIOP)

The Sheltered Instruction Observation Protocol (SIOP) is a well-known model of sheltered instruction. Originally designed by Echevarría, Vogt, and Short (2008) as an instrument for recording observations of teachers offering sheltered content-area instruction to ELs, the creators of the protocol expanded its scope as a result of feedback from teachers to include the planning and delivery of lessons. The SIOP model includes a lesson planning and delivery system and an instrument to observe, rate, and provide feedback on lessons.

Figure 8.4. Components of an Effective Bilingual Education Program

- At least 6 years of bilingual instruction
- A focus on core academic content
- High-quality language arts instruction in both languages presented thematically
- Separation of the languages with no translation of lessons
- Use of the non-English language at least 50% but as much as 90% of instructional time
- An additive bilingual environment
- Promotion of positive interdependence among students and between teachers and students
- High-quality personnel proficient in the language of instruction
- Active community–school partnerships.

SIOP consists of eight general components with 30 more specific features divided among them, which together help teachers address ELs' language and content needs. Many of the components, such as lesson preparation and building background, are familiar to all teachers, while others—such as comprehensible input—reflect SIOP's focus on language learners. Together, they offer a comprehensive scaffold on which to plan and/or evaluate language-based content instruction. If Evie and her team decide to adopt the SIOP model, they will be able to find considerable support from both the printed materials and professional development available commercially, including videos on each component available on YouTube.

Cognitive Academic Language Learning Approach (CALLA)

Chamot and O'Malley (1994) developed the Cognitive Academic Language Learning Approach (CALLA) to support ELs who have basic communication skills but need help acquiring academic language. The approach views learning as an active process and distinguishes among three types of knowledge: (1) declarative or knowledge of facts; (2) procedural or knowledge of process or how to do something; and (3) metacognitive or knowledge of how to relate current tasks and problems to past knowledge and procedures.

CALLA is grounded in the development and implementation of comprehensive, scaffolded lesson plans in which content is used to determine the academic language selections and learning strategies to be taught. For example, students might learn to use the language of comparison in the context of a science lesson on different types of plants. These lessons rely on instructional supports when concepts and skills are first introduced, but students work toward independence through the gradual removal of scaffolds as they develop greater proficiency, knowledge, and skills.

ACADEMIC LANGUAGE INSTRUCTION

Chapter 4 introduced the distinction between the language demands of basic conversations and academic discussions. The word study and language development programs described above were designed to help students bridge any potential gaps between these ways of using language. For culturally and linguistically diverse students to be successful in rigorous academic settings, they will need to be supported in their acquisition of academic language. Whichever literacy program Evie and her teachers choose, they will need to make sure they are also working to provide support as students acquire the language they need to succeed in school. As a literacy leader, you must help teachers understand the different dimensions of academic language.

For many educators, vocabulary is the most obvious component of academic language, and ELs typically need support to master both the structure and functions of language. Zacarian (2013) asserts that educators should reframe the "achievement gap" as an academic language gap, a shift in thinking that focuses not on deficit views of culturally and linguistically diverse students and their families, but instead on how teachers can help all students gain the linguistic tools they need to succeed in rigorous standards-based classrooms. Literacy leaders like Evie can help teachers close this language gap by helping them deepen their understanding of the different elements of academic language.

Vocabulary

Many studies have revealed that culturally and linguistically diverse students, particularly those from impoverished backgrounds, have smaller working vocabularies than their mainstream peers. At times, this research has been used to justify deficit views of these children and their families. Literacy leaders working in diverse schools need to help teachers ignore rhetoric that blames families and instead focus their energy on helping students acquire the two key components of academic vocabulary: (1) content-area terminology and (2) sophisticated words used to organize ideas and build arguments in complex texts. For example, to plan a unit on plant science for 3rd-graders, a teacher will not only need to teach the term *photosynthesis*, but he or she will also have to make sure that students understand general academic terms such as *observe* and *describe* as well as more science specific terms such as *hypothesize*. These words are best learned in context by planting and nurturing seeds as well as through comprehensive vocabulary exercises such as the Frayer Model (Frayer, Frederick & Klausmeier, 1969), List-Group-Label, Semantic Feature Analysis, and Semantic Mapping. These methods ask students to consider words holistically, asking not only for definitions but also examples, nonexamples, relationships to other words, and other dimensions of meaning that can help students gain deeper understanding.

Literacy leaders should help teachers remember that, although culturally and linguistically diverse students might lack the vocabulary to discuss plants academically, those from rural areas might actually have hands-on knowledge about the natural world. For example, a 2nd-grader who arrived from Mexico at the end of kindergarten whose father works as a landscaper will be able to talk and write about plants with more detail than many of his peers if he is given access to the official language with which to do so.

Syntax

Written and spoken academic language involves more than appropriate words; it also requires the construction of sentences that are often more complex than those used in everyday language. Syntax is the arrangement of words and phrases to create sentences, a task that can be challenging for culturally and linguistically diverse students who are used to different word orders from those typically found in English. The challenge is often exponentially greater when these young people must make meaning from the complex, multiclause sentences that characterize academic texts. In order to succeed in a U.S. school, language learners need the support of teachers to understand how English works in its simplest and most complex forms. As mentioned in Chapter 4, teachers who know that in Spanish the adjective comes after the noun are better equipped to help Spanish speakers master basic syntax. Similarly, educators who teach their students about how clauses are strung together to convey ideas and construct arguments within a complex sentence are providing their students with a powerful tool to both read and write academic texts. All too often, language learners are not exposed to complex texts, denying them the opportunity to acquire academic language through written input. Wong-Fillmore and Fillmore (2012) share their work on teaching academic language at the sentence level by asking ELs to make meaning from a single sentence from a complex text such as Dr. Martin Luther King's (1963) "Letter from Birmingham Jail." Students can thus be exposed to complex language in accessible chunks. As discussed in Chapter 4, reading is a powerful source of input for language learners, when it is made comprehensible. Teachers can also support students to produce output using academic language through scaffolds such as word walls and sentence frames.

Discourse

If syntax focuses on the sentence level, discourse involves more extended messages and texts. Every discipline has its own discourse patterns, although there is often overlap. For example, whereas many history texts are likely to be arranged chronologically, science texts often feature a cause-and-effect structure. Students need to be familiar with both general and content-specific discourse structures to be able to write an academic text or participate actively in an academic conversation. Culturally and linguistically diverse students often require extensive support to produce an extended written or oral text. Graphic organizers that highlight the different sections of an expository text are useful in this situation, particularly when they highlight key rhetorical features such as topic sentences and transitions, which can be included as sentence frames embedded in the tool.

RESPONSE TO INTERVENTION (RTI)

In addition to the literacy programs offered to all students and the more specialized language development programs designed to meet the needs of culturally and linguistically diverse students, literacy leaders like Evie may be called on to plan and provide programming for students who require additional interventions. The reauthorization of the Individuals with Disabilities Education Act (IDEA) in 2004, codified in Response to Intervention (RtI), recommends a tiered process of instruction and increasingly supportive intervention services with a deliberate progress monitoring component. RtI provides an alternative to using a discrepancy model for deciding special education eligibility, which has often been referred to as a "wait to fail" model (Donovan & Cross, 2002; Fuchs, Mock, Morgan, & Young, 2003). Instead, RtI focuses on intervening early through a multitiered approach where each tier provides interventions of increasing intensity.

Given the role of culture and language in both learning and teaching, the curriculum and instruction delivered in Tier 1 must be grounded in culturally and linguistically responsive practices (King-Thorius & Sullivan, 2013). Brown and Doolittle (2008) suggest a cultural, linguistic, and ecological framework for addressing the strengths and needs of ELs that incorporates the nuanced consideration and investigation of individual student factors (e.g., immigration patterns), the general education classroom context, and culturally responsive curriculum and instruction, along with assessment and interpretation of student progress (Brown & Doolitle, 2008; King-Thorius & Sullivan, 2013).

Tier 2 goes beyond instructional adjustments (which occur in Tier 1) to include additional instruction time with targeted interventions, usually provided by a specialist (literacy specialist, speech and language specialist, and so on). Instructional interventions for ELs should be both linguistically and culturally appropriate. A student who makes expected gains may cycle back to Tier 1 with close observations and, conversely, a student who makes slow or no progress would move into Tier 3.

If Tiers 1 and 2 have been effective, there should only be a small number of students moving to Tier 3, which provides (most often) different and more intensive instruction. In this tier, instruction is often small-group or one-on-one. In some cases, Tier 3 is considered special education, whereas in some models students would receive intensive individual interventions while being assessed for special education services, which would occur in a fourth tier.

Figure 8.5 includes guiding questions for each tier of instruction for ELs. These questions help educators gather information about the child and family as well as reflect on instructional decisions and the classroom context to help ensure that culturally, linguistically, and experientially responsive instructional decisions have been made.

If Evie and her colleagues opt to adapt RtI, they will have access to considerable resources through both research journals and commercial publishers as they learn the new system and determine how it should work within their building.

Figure 8.5. Guiding Questions for the Three Tiers of RtI and ELs

Tier 1 All students General education setting	Is consideration given to students' cultural, linguistic, socioeconomic, and experiential backgrounds? Is instruction targeted at students' level of English proficiency? Is the concern examined with the context (i.e., language of instruction, acculturation)? Have the parents been contacted and their input documented? Have accurate baseline data been collected on what the students' strengths are as well as the students' needs? Is language proficiency monitored regularly? Have the ecology of the classroom and school been assessed? What were the students' preschool literacy experiences? Have hearing and vision been screened? What tasks can the students perform, and in what settings? Have specific Tier 1 interventions that are culturally, linguistically and experientially appropriate been developed?
Tier 2 Students who need different and more intensive instruction than provided in Tier 1 Small-group setting	Will instruction in a small-group setting lead to success? Has the student's progress been compared to his or her previous performance using data collected over time and across settings? Does the student's learning rate appear to be lower than that of the average learning "true peer"? Is the student responding to intervention? Will alternate curriculum help the student succeed?
Tier 3 Students who need different and more intensive instruction Alternate setting	How many rounds of Tier 2 has the student had? Is there evidence of progress from previous interventions? Is the student successful with different curriculum, teaching approaches, and an individualized setting? Does the student differ from similar "true peers" in their level of performance? Learning slope? What are the student's functional, developmental, academic, linguistic, and cultural needs? If additional assessments are used, are the instruments technically sound, valid, and used appropriately for EL students? Are test results interpreted in a manner that considers students' language proficiency and their level of acculturation? Do assessments include information in the students' native language and English? Have the students received continuous instruction (e.g., the student is not continually absent)?

Adapted from Brown & Doolittle, 2008.

MAKE INFORMED DECISIONS

As the literacy leader at Scholars' Prep, Evie assumed a leadership role when teachers and administrators decided to evaluate their existing language and literacy programs. She understood that such an important change should not be made hastily, without considering how the shift would impact her colleague teachers and their students. As she makes recommendations, she is taking into account district goals, the school culture, and the cultural and linguistic backgrounds of the students. She also knows to use the program review chart and guiding questions from the Literacy Leadership Toolkit with her colleagues as an overview of key elements to consider. At the end of the process, Evie and her colleagues will be confident in their choice and ready to embrace the new program(s) to better meet the needs and build on the strengths of the students they serve.

Evaluating and choosing literacy programs may be one of the most crucial responsibilities of a literacy leader like Evie because the consequences are far-reaching for teachers, administrators, and students. The process will likely be challenging and should not be taken lightly. Though choosing the right program can help teachers better meet students' needs, literacy leaders must help administrators avoid the trap of buying into costly, trendy programs that promise results they cannot deliver. Once chosen, the programs themselves should be implemented with the proper degree of fidelity, but they should not supplant teacher knowledge. The right program can and should be customized to meet student needs once teachers can implement it with confidence. Programs are just one variable in the equation behind building and maintaining an effective literacy program that is responsive to student needs.

LITERACY LEADERSHIP TOOLKIT

When literacy leaders help make decisions about selecting and adapting literacy programs, they will want to collect focused and organized data to inform their choices. The charts below help committees record key information they will need to evaluate their different options.

Exercise 8.1: Literacy Program Review Chart

This chart assists the selection committee in keeping track of the key features of the different literacy programs under consideration.

	Program Name #1	Program Name #2	Program Name #3	Program Name #4	Program Name #5
1. Who is the intended audience?					
Primary K–2					
Intermediate 3–6					
Middle Grades 7–8					
High School					
English Learners					
Students in Tier 2					
Students in Tier 3					
2. What are the goals of the program?					
3. What type of program is it?					
Prevention					
Intervention					
General					
4. How is instruction delivered?					
Whole group					
Small group					
Individual (1:1)					
Mix of the above					
5. What assessments are included, and how are they used?					
6. How has the program been researched?					
Has a third party conducted studies of validity and reliability?					
Was the population of students included in the research similar to the population in your school or district?					

	Program Name #1	Program Name #2	Program Name #3	Program Name #4	Program Name #5
7. How does the program connect with the standards?					
8. How does the approach to teaching complement the school's current approach?					
9. What types of family components are included?					
10. What does the program propose to do to meet the needs of culturally and linguistically diverse students?					
11. How are lessons structured?					
12. How are lessons differentiated?					

Exercise 8.2: Guiding Questions for Selecting a Language Development Program

This chart assists the selection committee in collecting information to help make an informed choice about which language development program to implement at the school or district level.

Institutional Considerations	
How many ELs does the program/school/ district serve?	
What is the budget for the program?	
What facilities/space can the school/district provide for the program?	
What is the desired goal of the program? (i.e., for students to become bilingual or for students to exit the program rapidly?)	

Language Considerations	
Which languages are spoken in the school/district?	
What is/are the preferred language(s) of instruction?	
What attitude do teachers and administrators have about native language instruction?	
Can the school district provide qualified native language instruction?	
Instructional Considerations	
Who will provide instruction?	
Can the school district provide qualified English language teachers and aides?	
What is the school/district philosophy regarding collaboration between English language specialists and other teachers?	
What type of materials and methods of instruction will be used?	

CHAPTER 9

Know Materials and Resources to Support and Deepen Learning

- Literacy leaders must evaluate existing materials and how they are used, and consider the resources needed to more accurately reflect our nation's culturally and linguistically diverse student population.
- Literacy leaders can support teachers to build culturally relevant, multimodal, and multigenre text sets that fuel student interest and learning.
- Literacy leaders must consider our increasingly digital lives and classrooms, and embrace the ways in which new technologies can empower and transform students as literacy learners.

When Mrs. O'Neil entered her new 2nd-grade classroom, her eyes widened when she saw all the books on the shelves. A lover of children's literature, she greatly anticipated being able to put great stories and nonfiction texts into her students' hands to support them as they grew as readers and writers. She began to organize the books into baskets by topic, author, genre, and level. She knew her students would be excited to "shop" the shelves and find books that matched their interests and levels. Yet, as she surveyed each of the titles and book covers, she began to realize that she did not have books in her classroom library that reflected who her students were or that affirmed their cultural heritage. She partnered with her building's literacy leader to learn more about how to find and share books that represented where her students were from, their rich cultural heritages, their family dynamics, their communities, and their languages. As new titles came in that supported the identities of her culturally and linguistically diverse students, Mrs. O'Neil was invigorated by her students' enthusiasm for reading and their strengthened proficiency. With a growing core set of texts that represented the diversity of students in her classroom, Mrs. O'Neil gained the confidence and knowledge to build text sets that were multimodal and multigenre to support her students with thematic and issues-based studies. She found that bringing a culturally responsive approach to resources better supported her students to read with engagement, write with purpose, and speak and listen with interest.

TAKING STOCK OF LITERACY RESOURCES

When you look at the resources you use to support students as readers, writers, speakers, and listeners in your classroom or building, do the resources mirror where the students are from, what their strengths are, and what their needs may be? One of the first priorities for someone new to the role of literacy leader is to take an inventory of the resources in the building—to take stock. Taking stock of literacy resources, however, is about far more than knowing how many books are in each classroom and how they are being used. Taking stock is critically analyzing whether the collections and resources you have are student-centric. It starts by knowing who your students are (see Chapter 4) and what resources will support them to listen intently to stories, devour books, critically discuss complex ideas, engage meaningfully with new technologies, develop as writers, and increasingly participate and further develop oral and written language both in their native languages as well as in English.

Observing Material Use

As a literacy leader, a first step in taking stock is determining what resources exist and how teachers perceive they are using them to support the learners in their classrooms. In partnership with classroom teachers, build an inventory document or spreadsheet that catalogs what books, magazines, technologies, and other resources are used in the building. This should include books for read-alouds as well as books available for independent and instructional reading. This should include magazine and newsprint subscriptions, online subscriptions, family members who serve as guest speakers, community members and businesses who share their expertise with teachers and students, and partnerships that provide essential resources. Ask teachers to indicate how the resources are used and what level of impact (low, medium, high) they believe the resource has on student engagement and learning. See **Online Figure K** for an example of a sample inventory table. Consider creating a table, spreadsheet, or Google Form to gather and collate your findings. See **Online Figure L** for a sample inventory Google Form.

Once data are collected and shared with teachers, it is time to consider whether the data match your observations of how resources are used in the building. Think of your observations as an ethnographic study that requires an ongoing presence in classrooms rather than basing your ideas on "snapshot" observations. To build an ethnographic approach, adhere to the culture of peer observation that exists in your school or district and consider the suggestions given in Chapter 4. Once you have collected your own data regarding resource use, revisit teachers' inventory data and use this as an opportunity to revise their initial input.

As the year progresses, continue to come back to the document with their inventory data, revising what resources are being used and in what ways, with particular emphasis on resources that feature culturally and linguistically diverse characters, topics, and authors. Although there will never be a complete list of resources, it is essential to continue engaging with the teachers in your building(s) or district around the resources that are being used. Find out why the resources are being used, how they are being used, and what resources are needed to better support culturally and linguistically diverse students with rich and authentic texts, speakers, and opportunities to engage with technology.

CLASSROOM LIBRARIES

Think about libraries that you like to visit. What are some of the features they have? Likely, there will be well-organized sections of fiction and nonfiction collections, recommendations from librarians, new books, magazines and newspapers, and compelling displays that appeal to a wide variety of interests readers have when seeking new books. Great libraries invite readers in. They encourage us to pick up a stack of new titles, make decisions for ourselves, get into the reading zone, and perhaps, share our thinking with others. Our classroom libraries must do the same for children. They are a constant and compelling reminder that reading is valued. Our classroom libraries can help foster a love of books; here students learn how to care for books, how to select books independently, how to navigate across genres, and how to talk about and interact with books.

One of the most important roles a literacy leader serves is to ensure a large, varied, and updated collection of books for classroom libraries to support reading performance and a school culture that is enthusiastic about literacy learning. Research continues to show that the more contact children have with books and a literacy-rich environment, the better readers they become (Allington, 2012; Neuman, 1999). Research also suggests that the physical arrangement of the classroom can promote greater time spent with books (Morrow & Weinstein, 1986; Neuman & Roskos, 1997). This involves the selection of materials that will facilitate language and literacy opportunities, reflection around classroom design, and intentional instruction and support by teachers and staff (Burns, Griffin, & Snow, 1999). By providing access to a classroom library, teachers promote greater volume of reading, increased frequency, and more diverse reading experiences across genres, topics, authors, and series.

Neumann (1999) conducted a large-scale study of classroom libraries with high-quality books that were placed in more than 350 schools to enhance the language and literacy environment of 18,000 economically disadvantaged children. Her study found that

- time spent reading increased by 60% compared with the control group;
- literacy-related activities more than doubled, from an average of 4 interactions per hour to 8.5 interactions per hour; and
- letter knowledge, phonemic awareness, concepts of print and writing, and narrative competence rose 20% more than the control group after a year, followed by continued gains 6 months and 12 months later.

These are compelling data that emphasize the research-based need for greater access to books for children from socioeconomically disadvantaged positions. Yet, as a literacy leader, how will you know when the classroom libraries in your school are varied, being used effectively, and reflect our diverse society?

One place to begin is to look at the number of books available in each classroom library. Experts agree that volume matters, with most recommending at least 300 books in a classroom library (Fountas & Pinnell, 1996; Hack, Hepler, & Hickman, 1993; International Reading Association, 2000; Neuman, 1999).

Yet, volume alone does not mean that the selections included in classroom libraries represent our diverse society in ways that affirm cultural heritages and the everyday experiences of young people, their communities, and their families. According to the Center for Public

Education (2012), birth and immigration records indicate that soon there will be no majority ethnic group in America (www.centerfor-publiceducation.org). Census data show that 37% of the United States population consists of people of color (United States Census Bureau, 2012). Nevertheless, our classroom libraries do not reflect these demographic shifts. The children's book publisher Lee & Low Books (2012) found that over the past 20 years, despite demographic and classroom shifts, children's books plateaued, with approximately 10% containing multicultural content. What does this demographic and publishing data mean for you as a literacy leader? Given the publishing world's plateau with multicultural content in children's literature, it requires more investment and determination on the part of a literacy leader to support teachers and ultimately students with literature that is more representative of our increasingly culturally and linguistically diverse student population. It is imperative that children have access to high-quality literature that represents who they are and where they are from with compelling stories, authentic characters, and accurate historical information. Children also deserve writers and illustrators from their own cultural background. When teachers come from different sociocultural backgrounds than their students, it is essential that they have professional development opportunities to learn about books that feature diverse characters, settings, authors, and illustrators.

Use the inventory data you collected to determine what Neumann (1999) refers to as "core" collection needs. Establish a plan for a regularly replenished "revolving" collection that is updated at determined intervals. This collection should include a variety of genres, including greater balance between fiction and nonfiction, a range of reading levels, and new books with appealing covers with multicultural content and characters from various sociocultural backgrounds. Often, building and maintaining classroom libraries requires a multiyear, phase-in plan, reaching out to community partners, and generating community investment. Consider generating a multiyear plan that is specific to your building's needs.

Our communities vary greatly in terms of available resources and potential partnerships. Consider community resources when determining classroom library needs as they fit into your specific plan. Wholesale book distributors such as BookSource can help you match your budget with your specific needs. Individual publishing houses that specialize in books that feature social, cultural, and ecological diversity can do the same. Some examples are included in Figure 9.1.

Figure 9.1. Independent Publishing Houses Focused on Multicultural Children's Literature

Publishing Companies	Multicultural Focus
Lee & Low Books and their imprints: • BeBop Books • Tu Books • Children's Book Press	• Early readers with multicultural content • Fantasy and science-fiction books with multicultural content • Multicultural picture books
Cincos Puntos Press	Children's literature focused on Latino/a content
Just Us Books	Black interest books for children
The Roadrunner Press	Children's literature focused on the American West and Native American nations
Barefoot Books	Children's literature focused on art and storytelling

It is also helpful to consider the annual American Library Association awards and other children's and young adult literature awards that are chosen by librarians and educators to reflect high-quality literature, illustrations, and authentic content. Beyond the Caldecott and Newbery winners, look to the winners and notable honor winners of the following children's literature awards to build classroom libraries that more authentically represent our diverse society:

• Coretta Scott King Award for African American–centered books
• Pura Belpré Award for Latino/a-centered books
• Asian Pacific American Award for Literature
• Middle East Book Awards
• American Indian Youth Award
• Rainbow Project Reading List
• Notable Books for a Global Society

In addition to being selective about text choices, consider fundraising within your community for classroom libraries. Mrs. O'Neil, as described in the vignette, knew that her classroom library needed to better reflect the cultural and linguistic backgrounds of her students. She turned to her literacy leader for help, but they both knew that even with a multiyear, multiphase plan, financial resources were going to be a challenge. In partnership with her literacy leader, Mrs. O'Neil attended local library book sales and let the staff know her goals. Mrs.

O'Neil realized that library sales have a "bag day" toward the end of the event where you pay one price for everything you can fit into a bag. She reached out to local consignment and charity shops, and let them know of her needs. As a frequent visitor to local bookshops, she asked the managers and owners about discounts for her school. She also reached out to community businesses to see if they would sponsor a set of books for a particular grade level. She also did some comparison shopping and considered ebooks that are free as well as those that have minimum subscriptions such as free-ebooks.net (http://www.free-ebooks.net/) or Scholastic's Storia app (http://www.scholastic.com/storia-update/). Finally, Mrs. O'Neil and the literacy leader in her building developed a pamphlet on research that shows the importance of classroom libraries and literacy-rich environments with others. This helped build community awareness around the power of books and the urgency of providing access to award-winning and multicultural books for their students. As a literacy leader, consider ways you can support teachers to grow their classroom libraries, all the while ensuring that classroom libraries reflect an equitable distribution of district resources that are based on classroom needs.

Multicultural Children's Literature:
Moving from Cultural Awareness to Disruption

When selecting children's literature for the classroom, literacy leaders need to consider the cultural models that are upheld or resisted through their choices. Ching (2005) argues that multicultural children's literature offers an opportunity not just to focus on racial harmony but rather to look closely and critically at issues of power in children's literature: "Selection criteria for multicultural literature typically promote cultural awareness and sensitivity, and often overlook the control, deployment, and management of power" (p. 129). Fox and Short (2003) draw from multicultural theorists including Banks (2001) and Nieto (2002) to suggest that multicultural children's literature that portrays authenticity addresses the intersection of power, race, and culture. Sims (1982) has found that African American children's literature (and one could argue any children's literature that could be considered multicultural) falls into three distinct categories: "melting pot," "social conscience," and "culturally conscious." As a result, multicultural children's literature often focuses on traits such as historical accuracy, positive character portrayal, authentic portrayal of individuals and groups, and resistance to stereotypical representations of people of color and other minorities. As a result, deeper issues of power are often overlooked by teachers when selecting multicultural children's literature. A cultural awareness perspective is not enough.

Discuss with the teachers in your building the authenticity of the texts they are using and whether they are upholding cultural models or disrupting them. Start by sharing essays from Fox and Short's (2003) *Stories Matter: The Complexity of Cultural Authenticity in Children's Literature.* Select essays that model diverse perspectives on multicultural children's literature and begin a discussion about what children's literature is being used, and for what purposes. Analyze whether the selections provide connections for students, promote cultural awareness and sensitivity, and/or facilitate discussion of issues of power in society at large.

In addition to the texts themselves, literacy leaders need to think differently about the ways we teach with multicultural children's literature to include more interactive and culturally responsive methods (Gangi, 2008; Gangi & Ferguson, 2006; Heath, 2004; Ladson-Billings, 1994). Such methods are often arts-based, and include collaboration such as readers theater, choral reading, and collaborative meaning-making arts interpretations. Consider working with teachers to develop a signature experience that showcases students' response to literature or their own storytelling at each grade level that is culturally responsive, arts-based, and rooted in multicultural children's literature.

Balancing Leveled and Non-Leveled Books

Research shows that supporting students with books at their level is an essential component of building a classroom library that fosters greater automaticity, fluency, comprehension, and stamina (Allington, 2012). However, children routinely strive to read things beyond their level. We want all students to find books that grab their interest, spark their imaginations, and compel them to learn new kinds of information. Consider the students you know who may be below-grade-level readers but absorb information from a nonfiction illustrated encyclopedia or who carry a well-worn copy of a *Harry Potter* book under their arm to show others that they are part of the culture of reading that their peers value. Providing a balance of leveled and non-leveled books is an important characteristic of a classroom library. As a literacy leader, work with teachers to develop classroom routines that foster independent reading of books at students' independent reading levels while also establishing routines for choice reading from any text of interest.

Text Selection for Small-Group Instruction: Supporting Students to Lean in to Learn

The resources needed for effective small-group instruction in reading will depend on the reading levels of your students and the small-group instruction structure teachers use, including guided reading, strategy groups, partnerships, and book clubs. One of our Changing Suburbs Institute® partnership schools with a culturally and linguistically diverse student population recently engaged in a series of professional development sessions to determine the structures and resources they would need to rethink their use of a basal series to support small-group reading instruction. In 2010, the student population was composed of 55% students of color; 14% of the students had documented limited English proficiency and over 35% of the students were eligible for reduced-price or free lunch (www.city-data.com). At that time, the district administration turned away from a literature-based curriculum to a basal curriculum to meet the needs of their diverse student population. After 3 years of a basal program, they found that by 3rd grade the teachers were overly focused on skills and strategies during small-group instruction and were not building a love of reading in their students. There was also a disconnect between the reading students did in their basal readers and their independent reading. During professional development sessions with one of us (Katie), the teachers reflected on how they planned less with their basal program because the plans were already in place and, as a result, they knew less about their students as readers. They wanted to return to a more personalized approach to curriculum with resources to support students to not only read proficiently but also to want to read. They needed to rethink the structure and purposes of their small-group reading instruction and they needed new resources that would appeal to students' enthusiasm about a range of texts. As a literacy leader, you want to work with your teachers to determine what is working with their small-group structures and what their goals are for small-group instruction to support skills acquisition, strategy support, and engagement.

Small-group instruction is a time to support students with strategies to build reading skills, but it is also a time to come together to nurture a small reading community. Consider whether the texts being used for small-group instruction provide a balance between short and long texts. Some students will be more engaged by short, manageable texts from sources such as newspaper and magazine articles, short stories, comic strips, and essays from projects such as National Public Radio's "This I Believe" project (2005–2014). Though short texts provide opportunities for targeted strategy instruction, we also want students within a small group to read longer, extended texts where they can apply strategies across a whole book, and discuss the book with their peers. Such small groups can use a guided reading structure or take the form of partnerships or book clubs. Consider engaging a cohort of teachers in a professional book club focused on small-group instruction to facilitate goal setting for structuring their small groups to feel like reading communities. Have teachers share with one another the texts they are reading with their small groups. Are the texts supporting students to lean in to learning? Do the texts have characters that represent the lives their students lead? Are they building a love of reading alongside the acquisition of skills and strategies?

Read-Aloud Texts That Support Units of Study and Identity Connections

Trelease (2006) discusses the essential mechanics of reading, or phonics skills, as the "how-to" of reading. But he advocates for teachers and families to equally value the "want to" of reading. Read-alouds build "want to" motivation in our students. Trelease (2009) states:

> We read aloud to students for the same reasons we talk with them: to reassure; entertain; bond; inform; arouse curiosity; and inspire. But reading aloud goes further than conversation when it conditions the child to associate reading with pleasure; builds background knowledge; builds "book" vocabulary; and provides a reading role model. (p. 2)

To provide more context, the U.S. Department of Education Commission on Reading took into account more than 10,000 studies and issued a report, *Becoming a Nation of Readers* (Anderson, Hiebert, Scott, & Wilkinson, 1985). The report stated that the most important activity for building the skills and background for eventual success in reading is reading aloud to children. All children need to hear complex language to gain new types of content knowledge, understand syntax and structure, and gain new vocabulary before they will be able to access these words in print themselves. Supporting teachers with suggestions for read-alouds for the heart of their units of study is a key component of literacy leadership.

When supporting teachers to choose texts for reading aloud, consider the quality of the books as well as the ways in which read-alouds can support units of study and their corresponding essential questions and enduring understandings. Books that are well written, with engaging and authentic characters and compelling plots, offer many opportunities to model fluent and expressive reading and foster interest and enthusiasm. In addition, selecting books that foster connections for children from culturally and linguistically diverse backgrounds is essential. Proficient reader research (Anderson & Pearson, 1984; Duke & Pearson, 2002; Harvey & Goudvis, 2007; Keene & Zimmerman, 2007; Miller, 2012) has greatly influenced the way reading comprehension is taught in schools. Teachers now routinely model and explicitly teach ways to question, activate prior knowledge, determine importance, infer, synthesize, visualize, and make connections. However, research also continues to show that "since children must be able to make connections with what they read to become proficient readers, White children whose experiences are depicted in books can make many more text-to-self, text-to-text, and text-to-world connections than can children of color" (Gangi, 2008, p. 30). When we model think-alouds and support students to share their thinking during our read-alouds, we must consider whether the texts themselves help students make connections and gain proficiency as readers. The read-alouds we share with our students matter. Work with your teams of teachers to consider the use and effectiveness of read-alouds tied to units of study as well as the ways the texts are supporting positive constructions of identity in their students.

Building Culturally Relevant, Multimodal, Multigenre Text Sets

Individual stories can transform students' lives, but potentially even more powerful and transformative are text sets that explore issues, themes, and questions that connect to students' lived experiences. Since the 1990s, text sets have emerged with a variety of models and definitions. Yet, diversity in text types has been a key component of text set construction to support students to understand, think critically about concepts, and form connections across topics, issues, and ideas (Nichols, 2009). As a literacy leader, you may be wondering what kinds of texts to include and how to build a text set that is not only diverse in its text types but represents diverse voices, views, and sociocultural locations.

One model for text set construction is to pair nonfiction texts with fiction texts that share a common theme, issue, or question that is relevant to students' lives. Consider pairing an informational text with a fictionalized biography about someone culturally relevant to your students, or pairing a historical fiction text about a time period of interest to your students with a primary document from the time period.

To build text sets that are more complex in text type and purpose, consider bridging print texts with multimedia or visual texts to create multimodal and multigenre text sets. According to Cappiello and Dawes (2012), a multimodal and multigenre text set is

> a versatile tool constructed by a teacher or team of teachers and ideally, a school or public librarian that can be applied at any grade level, from pre-kindergarten through high school, and can be used as a means of achieving the goals of a unit of study. Text sets themselves are not the focal point of the curriculum or unit of study; whatever it is that holds the text set together—a topic, connect, theme, or question—is the focal point. (p. 21)

Reading aloud a novel, pairing it with a map of the region featured in the story, and viewing an online book talk by the author can serve as an example of what Cappiello and Dawes (2012) refer to as multimodal and multigenre. Supporting a core text with a variety of print, visual, and multimedia texts can build interest and engagement for students as they form connections, ask questions, and generate new ideas. In addition to multimodal and multigenre possibilities, another critical consideration in text set construction is the perspectives and positions represented within the texts themselves. McGee and Richgels (1996) found that students need to be exposed to a range of language, topics, genres, and perspectives that reflect our diverse and multicultural society, which text sets can naturally lend themselves toward supporting.

To build a multimodal, multigenre, *and* culturally relevant text set, consult resources such as children's literature blogs. Examples include the following:

- *The Classroom Bookshelf* (www.classroombookshelf.blogspot. com)

- *Interesting Nonfiction for Kids* (I.N.K.) (http://inkrethink. blogspot.com/)
- *School Library Journal* (http://www.slj.com/)
- *The Children's Book Cooperative* (http://ccbc.education.wisc. edu/)
- *Living Barefoot* (http://blog.barefootbooks.com/)

Consult blogs that specifically feature multicultural children's literature:

- *The Open Book* (http://blog.leeandlow.com/)
- *The Brown Bookshelf* (http://thebrownbookshelf.com/28-days-later/blog/)
- *Latinos in KidLit* (http://latinosinkidlit.com/)
- *Bookdragon* (http://smithsonianapa.org/bookdragon/)
- *Diversity in YA* (http://diversityinya.tumblr.com/)
- *Rich in Color* (http://richincolor.com/)
- *Colorín Colorado* (http://www.colorincolorado.org/)
- Any number of others from the now formalized Kidlitosphere

Speak with your school and local librarians about recently released texts as well as their favorites. Look for online periodicals, video clips, and podcasts. As a starting place with teachers, gather existing read-alouds and organize them according to theme or genre. Notice and note culturally relevant works, and spotlight them as core texts. Work with teachers to consider additional book and online resources that can support core texts that are already part of the existing curriculum, and consider themes central to your school's mission as a way of building text sets unique to your school setting.

TECHNOLOGY AND DIGITAL MEDIA

It is undeniable that our literacy lives have changed and continue to change through new technologies. This section provides context and suggestions for how to authentically incorporate and maximize the use of technologies and digital media to enhance student understanding about topics, issues, and ideas, and how to support students as critical consumers and producers of media.

How Technology Is Changing Our Lives

In our New Technologies and Critical Literacies course, we ask teacher candidates to track the literacy events they experience in a day. It is typical for our students to write about how they hear their alarm clocks; check their emails; scroll through their Instagram, Twitter, and Facebook accounts; and select music from Pandora all before leaving bed. The Internet and mobile technology have changed the nature of how people interact, how they work, and the ways we learn. In fact, technology allows nearly 24-hour media access as we go about our daily lives.

For young people, access to media is widespread. According to the Kaiser Family Foundation Survey (Rideout, Foeher, & Roberts, 2010), the amount of time young people spend with entertainment media has risen dramatically, especially among minority youth, since their 2005 survey. In 2005, 8- to 18-year-olds devoted an average of 5.5 hours a day to entertainment media. Four years later, the survey found that the same age group devoted an average of 7 hours, 38 minutes to using entertainment media across a typical day (more than 53 hours a week). This represents an increase of one-third of media time in just 4 years of survey data. In addition, Common Sense Media (Rideout, 2012) has found that almost a quarter of teenagers access social media sites at least 10 times a day, and more than 50% use social media once a day.

In addition, recent data from Pew Research Center (in Madden, Lechart, Duggan, Cortesi, & Gasser, 2013) found that one in four teens are "cell-mostly" Internet users and that 78% of teenagers, ages 12–17, have a cellphone, with almost half of those smartphones. Those who fall into lower socioeconomic groups are just as likely and in some cases more likely than those living in higher socioeconomic households to use their cellphone as a primary point of access.

In another survey from the Pew Research Center, Lenhart et al. (2008) found that 97% of teenagers, ages 12–17, play computer, web, portable, or console games. They also found that, for most teens, gaming is a major component of their overall social experience. Those teens who take part in the social interactions of games (e.g., comment sections) also frequently engage civically and politically, as evidenced by their tendency to persuade others to vote in an election, raise money for charities, and commit to other civic participation.

How Technology Is Changing Our Classrooms

As technology impacts our students' lives (and our own) outside of school, it continues to have the potential to impact our classrooms in important ways. Video, audio, images, and interactive features provide opportunities to learn about worlds and cultures that we were limited to learn about from books alone in the past. Perhaps most important, new technologies give teachers and families tremendous power to support students to tell their stories and learn from the stories of others. When students share their ideas and stories online, there is potential to connect in ways that mirror the world outside of school and support them to be more globally connected. Our students are already part of online social networks and use new technologies in a myriad of ways. Our classrooms can further support all learners through technology to read widely, write purposefully, and engage with others in the exploration of ideas.

As a literacy leader, consider hosting a series of events that offer opportunities for teachers to share their perspectives on technology. Teachers who engage with technology in their personal lives may be more comfortable making technology an integral part of their classroom, giving students opportunities to engage with technology as consumers and producers. Reach out to find out which teachers host their own classroom websites to update families and with what frequency, or which teachers support students in blogging. Consider offering differentiated or even teacher-led professional development sessions on technology in the classroom.

Many of the changing schools we work with now harness the possibilities of three technologies, in particular, on a regular basis to support all of their students: blogging, digital storytelling, and social media. Figure 9.2 provides information on how these digital tools are used.

As with all new technologies, check your district and school policies regarding blogging and social media use to make sure you are recommending digital engagements that adhere to these policies.

Blogging. Blogs give teachers and students the opportunity to write content that often blends information with opinion and the power of narrative. Blogs hook their readers to follow them over time because their voice connects you to their thinking. Blogs allow authors to post as little or as much information as they would like. Blogs also use a multimodal approach to convey their topic and opinion through photos, images, videos, and words. Ayres and Overman (2013) write that classroom blogs

Figure 9.2. Digital Resources and How They Are Used

Digital Resource	How They Are Used	Best Features
Blogging Tools • Google's Blogger • Wordpress • Tumblr	• To recount events • To share an opinion • To provide information to an audience • To comment on posts and build dialogue around a topic	Blogger: links with other Google tools Wordpress: easy to navigate features Tumblr: has an array of visual features and grid layouts
Digital Storytelling Tools • Windows Moviemaker • iMovie • Animoto	• In response to texts • As a form of interpretation • To share one's own story	Windows: best tool for PC iMovie: can be used on a phone, tablet, or computer as a filming and editing tool Animoto: free and online tool
Social Media Sites • Facebook • Twitter • Instagram • Pinterest • Snapchat	• To connect with others • To communicate an idea and solicit a response • To share ideas through minimal words, visuals, and short videos	Facebook: most widely used site Twitter: best supports students to say more with less; hashtags link topics in conversation threads. Instagram: supports students to tell visual stories with a range of filters for effect; hashtags link topics in conversation threads Pinterest: supports students to create digital interest boards; especially useful for gathering images, text, and hyperlinks for research Snapchat: allows for instant image sharing; images are not saved; emphasis on process rather than product

can be fancy or simple, but they all have a common purpose: to give students an audience for their writing and an outlet for their voices. Blogging empowers students to use their voices and share their stories, opinions, and interests. (p. 43)

Through blogging, students can share their thinking with one another, their families, other classes within the school, or with the global community.

As a literacy leader, consider gathering a group of teachers interested in starting up or fine-tuning the purposes and practices of blogging in their classrooms. Determine the purposes of the blogs for students, including to document learning; to share their writing independently, in partnership, or in small groups; to comment and respond to posts; to reflect on effective writing techniques; to celebrate their ideas and their writing; to serve as text critics in response to texts; or to evaluate what they read or view from a culturally responsive position. Consider a topic, issue, or text as the focus for new blogs, or support teachers to ask students what they think about what would make a compelling blog and co-construct a rubric with blog criteria. And, of course, as a literacy leader, consider hosting a literacy blog for your school community to follow that includes notes from the field of literacy, examples of student writing, and information about what people are reading around school and the community. Look to models in the field such as the *Nerdy Book Club* (http://nerdybookclub.wordpress.com/), Vicki Vinton's *To Make a Prairie* (http://tomakeaprairie. wordpress.com/), or any of the children's literature blogs described earlier in the chapter. Blogging can be a powerful vehicle for honoring the voices of students and teachers, and your own voice. It also gives the community an opportunity to comment and respond, furthering the diverse representation of ideas and perspectives.

Digital storytelling. Digital storytelling uses technology tools, including video, photographs, animation, audio, and illustrations, to tell a story, share a moment, report on a topic, or persuade an audience. The beauty of digital storytelling lies in its simplicity. The composer decides on the purpose of his or her story, such as a digital summary and review of a text read, an argument about an important topic, or a reflection on a life experience. Like all great stories, digital stories typically have a lead, which can be a question, phrase, or image that pulls viewers in and connects them to the message and purpose. Digital stories have a compelling message or idea. And they end powerfully to leave the viewer with something to remember, ponder, or debate.

As a literacy leader, consider ways to support teachers to use digital storytelling as a means of better understanding their students. What if students shared who they were or what they wanted to be through digital stories at the start of the school year? What images would students choose? Which soundtrack? Which words and for what reasons? What if each class chose a favorite multicultural read-aloud to interpret as a shared digital story? What if students composed their own digital stories that critiqued a text by describing how the text did or did not mirror their own life?

Consider using digital storytelling to strengthen student writing in the text types advocated for by the Common Core State Standards: narrative, argument, and informational texts. Work with teachers to consider which units and text types could be strengthened through an additional layer of digital storytelling so that students compose written and digital texts to demonstrate understanding. Like all forms of writing, digital storytelling benefits from structure and craft. Digital stories have hooks, a logical sequence of ideas, and powerful conclusions that leave viewers thinking about texts and issues in new ways. View student-created digital stories on sites such as YouTube and Vimeo, and support students to notice the craft techniques digital storytellers use to make their messages understood. Preview websites and apps for tablets and smartphones such as Popplet, Scholastic Story Starters, Shadow Puppet EDU, Book Creator, Toontastic, Voice Thread, and Adobe Voice. Follow ClassTechTips on Twitter for near-daily suggestions for digital storytelling tools as plug-ins to the writing process, as engaging and authentic tasks, and as ways to strengthen content knowledge.

Social media. There are several platforms for social networking, and more and more surface with each year. It can be overwhelming to know where to begin or which to utilize in the classroom. Yet, the power of social media is rooted in the idea that literacy itself is a social practice—that we read and write in community, that we want to share our ideas with our networks, and that we have different identities depending on the platform, audience, and purpose of our posts.

Increasingly, the schools we work with have noted how students are engaged in visually driven social media platforms such as Tumblr, Instagram, Snapchat, and Pinterest (see Figure 9.2). These platforms are particularly engaging for students whose native language is other than English because of the process used for the selection and interpretation of spaces that are provided. Even print-based spaces such as Twitter can support all learners to fine-tune their word choice and grammar. With no more than 140 characters, every word counts for saying something significant in a concise way. Harnessing the capabilities of visually driven and print-limited social media platforms frees students to engage creatively and critically with their ideas and the ideas of others.

As a literacy leader, guide teachers to consider the what, why, and how of selecting social media platforms that will support student learning and engagement. Tapping into every possibility will often leave students overwhelmed, but being selective and having a culturally responsive purpose can build a more inclusive literacy environment for all learners. What kinds of guided learning must take place to guide students to be responsible contributors on social media spaces? Can students be supported to take or find visuals that describe a feeling as a prompt for writing? Can students respond to a text that is read or viewed through a tweet? Can students research a topic through Pinterest as a valid and valued starting place? Can students design their own Tumblr pages as an ongoing reader response log?

To encourage students to engage in social media platforms as part of their academic lives requires that teachers and families feel comfortable with the process. Consider drafting a sample letter to families that indicates the online communities that will be used for academic purposes in the school for students to learn content as well as how to interact with others online. Invite families to follow the news feeds generated through classroom engagements and respond to the kinds of learning they see happening. Take an interest survey of your teachers. Discuss the goals teachers have for their students as digital producers and critical consumers and the pedagogies and platforms that can be used to reach their goals. Congratulate teachers and students as they share themselves, their ideas, their writing, their creativity, and their research. Let them know their voices are heard.

WHAT'S IMPORTANT TO REMEMBER?

This chapter is designed to guide you as a literacy leader to identify and use culturally responsive resources in books and beyond. Like any new initiative, the most important place to begin is with reflection on what resources your teachers already use and which are best for supporting students as readers, writers, speakers, listeners, and viewers. Too often, we find that expensive resources purchased by literacy leaders, administrators, or classroom teachers end up in closets and do not get into students' hands. It is our perspective that it is not important to have the latest and greatest resource at your disposal, but it is important to have resources that support students to make connections, engage with ideas and one another, and build community within and beyond the walls of the school. We believe that capitalizing on children's literature, harnessing the power of technologies that students already use in new ways, and supporting teachers to share and learn from one another are the most student-centered and culturally responsive places to start.

LITERACY LEADERSHIP TOOLKIT

Once you have taken stock of the literacy resources in your building, it is time to develop a multiyear, phase-in plan to prioritize your building's resource needs. The following exercises are designed to support you in this process.

Exercise 9.1: Multiyear Phase-In Resource Plan

Start with the suggested priorities on the left-hand side of this table, and consider our recommended phase-in approach using our sample as a guide. We recognize that not every building will be able to follow this plan exactly because of district needs. Circle the greatest priorities your building has for each of the 5 years included below. Use this as a working document to share with other building and district leaders, teachers, and families as you increase the volume of texts, variety of texts, genre balance, reference books, leveled texts, small-group resources, and storage needs for your building.

Priorities	Year 1	Year 2	Year 3	Year 4	Year 5
Volume					
Variety of Texts					
Fiction					
Nonfiction					
Reference Books					
Leveled Texts					
Multiple Copies for Small-Group Instruction					
Multigenre and Multimodal Text Sets					
Storage					

Sample Multiyear Phase-In Plan

Priorities	Year 1	Year 2	Year 3	Year 4	Year 5
Volume	+50–100 titles per classroom	+50–100 more titles per classroom	+50–75 titles per classroom	+25–50 titles per classroom	+15–25 titles per classroom
Variety of Texts	Greater balance between fiction and nonfiction Picture books, wordless books, and big books, K–2 Picture books and read-aloud novels, 3–6	Greater balance between fiction and nonfiction Traditional stories Poetry	Historical fiction Fantasy Biography	Incorporate magazine subscriptions to each class	Evaluate variety needs
Fiction	40–50% of collection Focus on diverse authors, illustrators, and themes Recent award winners	40–50% of collection Focus on diverse authors, illustrators, and themes Recent award winners	40–50% of collection Focus on diverse authors, illustrators, and themes Recent award winners	40–50% of collection Focus on diverse authors, illustrators, and themes Recent award winners	40–50% of collection Focus on diverse authors, illustrators, and themes Recent award winners
Nonfiction	40–50% of collection Variety of topics	40–50% of collection Variety of topics	40–50% of collection Variety of topics	40–50% of collection Variety of topics	40–50% of collection Variety of topics

Sample Multiyear Phase-In Plan (continued)

Priorities	Year 1	Year 2	Year 3	Year 4	Year 5
Reference Books	5% of the total collection dictionaries, thesauruses, almanacs, atlases, and encyclopedias	5% of the total collection atlases	5% of the total collection almanacs	Add reference texts as needed	Add reference texts as needed
Leveled Texts	5 titles at each independent reading level	5 titles at each independent reading level	5 titles at each independent reading level	5 titles at each independent reading level	Evaluate leveled text needs
Multiple Copies for Small-Group Instruction	2–3 sets for each level	2–3 sets for each level	1–2 sets for each level	1–2 sets for each level	Evaluate small-group instruction needs
Multigenre and multimodal Text Sets	Begin 1 text set per grade level.	Generate 1–2 text sets per grade	Generate 1–2 text sets per grade	Generate 1–2 text sets per grade	Evaluate text set needs based on evolving units of study
Storage	Bookshelves Leveled book bins Genre bins	Leveled book bins	Add storage as needed	Add storage as needed	Add storage as needed

Exercise 9.2: Culturally Responsive Lenses
for Evaluating Print and Multimedia Resources

This exercise, which is based on work of Cunningham and Enriquez (2013), helps you evaluate children's literature and other materials to ensure that they accurately represent our diverse society. When evaluating a book, digital or multimedia resource, consider the following questions as guides to help you think about the impact and purpose of the resources to support and deepen students' learning about themselves, the world, and topics and issues they care about.

Lenses	Questions to Ask Yourself	What to Do
Language Lens	Are there words that will expand your students' academic vocabulary? Y_____/ N_____ Is the language accessible for the age group? Y_____/ N_____ Does the author choose words that are culturally sensitive and accurate? Y_____/ N_____ If the language is problematic, whose perspective does these words represent? _____	Order classroom copies _____ Order classroom copies with recognition of problematic language to explore _____ Do not order _____
Thematic Lens	Is there an identifiable central message, lesson, or moral conveyed through key details? Y_____/ N_____ Does the text encourage a vision for a better, more just world? Y_____/ N_____ If not, how can issues of power and perspective be explored? _____ How does the story promote understandings of our diverse society? _____ Does the story promote reflection? Y_____/ N_____	Order classroom copies _____ Order classroom copies with recognition of issues of power and perspective to explore _____ Do not order _____
Plot Lens	Is the story engaging for children? Y_____/ N_____ How do events develop over the course of the text and in what ways can your students retell the story for deeper understanding? _____	

Lenses	Questions to Ask Yourself	What to Do
Plot Lens (continued)	Do the events in the story accurately reflect cultural customs? Y_____ / N_____ If not, whose representation of cultural customs is presented, why does it matter, and what power does this perspective hold? _____	Order classroom copies _____ Order classroom copies with recognition of misrepresentation of cultural customs to explore _____ Do not order _____
Character Lens	Are the characters relatable to students? Y_____ / N_____ How do the characters respond to major events and challenges throughout the story? _____ What identifiable character traits support your students' understanding of characters as unique individuals? _____ In what ways can students compare their point of view with that of the characters? _____ Does the author avoid attributing stereotypical cultural or racial characteristics to characters? Y_____ / N_____ If not, what purpose do those stereotypes serve? _____	Order classroom copies _____ Order classroom copies with recognition of stereotyping to explore _____ Do not order _____
Visual Lens	Do the illustrations enhance the characters, setting, plot, themes, and tone of the story? Y_____ / N_____ Are the illustrations visually appealing and interesting? Y_____ / N_____ Do the illustrations accurately depict unique cultural aspects? Y_____ / N_____ If not, could the illustrations be used to encourage discussion about cultural representation? _____	Order classroom copies _____ Order classroom copies with recognition of inaccurate cultural representations to explore _____ Do not order _____

CHAPTER 10

Putting It All Together

- Effective literacy leaders use their unique self-acknowledged strengths to learn as much as possible about their context in order to support teachers with their curriculum development, instruction, assessment, and parent outreach.
- Effective literacy leaders are skilled at working with principals, vice principals, teachers, and other administrative and instructional staff to tailor their own short-term and long-term goals to the school's literacy plan.
- Effective literacy leaders have the wherewithal and talent to sustain momentum with their constituencies to positively impact a school's literacy program.

Laurie Pastore is a literacy leader in one of the K–6 professional development schools in our Changing Suburbs Institute® network. She is responsible for supporting all classroom teachers in the development of literacy. She spends 80% of her time working with teachers and 20% of her time working in a remedial setting with culturally and linguistically diverse students. As a self-professed "geek" when it comes to standards, Laurie takes great pride in the standards-based curriculum plans that she has written for teachers. She came to this job after spending 11 years as a literacy consultant for other schools in the New York region to plan, design, and write curricula. Laurie meets weekly with her principal and vice principal to identify and address literacy objectives for the building. She might be asked to support one teacher, an entire grade level, or a particular topic such as writing about reading. Her work with teachers involves planning meetings, classroom demonstration lessons and observations, and follow-up meetings. During a testing window, Laurie works with teachers to help them know how to score tests and analyze test scores. She believes that her job is to help her colleague teachers—whether through one-on-one coaching, small-group meetings, or in-class sessions—to be as successful as possible in a school where three-fourths of the students do not speak English as a first language.

BRINGING PERSONAL STRENGTHS TO LEADERSHIP

This last chapter presents ideas for putting together the tenets from the previous nine chapters so that you can function effectively as a literacy leader in a K–6 school. Laurie Pastore (personal communication, July 2, 2014) is a seasoned literacy leader who enjoys the diversity of her school, appreciates the dedication and commitment of her principal, and thrives on working with her colleague teachers on literacy development. She knows that she has not yet been able to help every single teacher in her building, but she keeps trying to build bridges with teachers so they are amenable to developing professionally. Laurie came to her position as an outsider. However, because she is included on the principal's cabinet and communicates regularly with the principal and vice principal, she does not feel she is at a disadvantage in her ability to work strategically and effectively with teachers.

Mary Shannon (personal communication, June 27, 2014), on the other hand, had been in the same school as a 2nd-grade teacher nearly 20 years before she became a full-time literacy coach. Her principal, who was intrigued with the way she was using reading and writing workshop to develop students' literacy, gradually removed teaching periods from her schedule so she would be available to work with other teachers. Eventually, she made the transition to working full-time with teachers. Because her school has more than doubled in size since she began as a classroom teacher, there are many new teachers in her building who need help. She spends one period a week with each new teacher individually, and is in and out of classrooms to observe and help with lessons. Mary meets monthly with the principal and assistant principal to discuss the school's literacy goals, and has worked closely with the principal to develop standards-based unit plans that incorporate the arts into literacy. Mary is quite proud of her ability to help teachers succeed, especially those who had been struggling.

Similar to Mary, Karen Brenneke (personal communication, June 30, 2014) was an internal hire. She had been a 6th-grade teacher for 7 years before becoming a literacy coach who is primarily responsible for providing staff development to teachers in grades 4–6. The district administrators wanted someone who knew the school's culture to help the district as a whole transition from a cottage industry curriculum that was a "mile wide inch deep" to a balanced literacy approach with authentic reading and writing. Her suburban school, though not as diverse as Laurie's and Mary's schools, does have a growing English learner population and a large special education population. Karen finds that every day as a coach is different, from conducting multiple demonstration lessons to working with teachers individually on student achievement strategies. She discovered that book studies are an excellent means for building opportunities for learning. She usually runs two book studies during the year on topics such as close reading or the Common Core State Standards (U. S. Department of Education, Office of Elementary and Secondary Education, 2010). She meets with teachers after school every couple of weeks after they have read assigned portions of a book and engaged in a homework assignment in their classrooms related to that section of the book. The teachers share experiences about the assignment's relevance to their classrooms. Karen reports directly to her assistant superintendent about her progress in the position.

Laurie, Mary, and Karen have their own unique styles of serving as literacy leaders, based on their situations and themselves. They take pride in their inroads with teachers, even with the pockets of resistance they have encountered in different ways at different times. They focus on slightly different achievements, based on their own strengths. Laurie is proud of the curriculum units she has created that are being used by the teachers. Mary is proud of the change in the way reading and writing are taught, especially with a focus on the arts. Karen is proud that her students can articulate what they are doing with reading and writing. These three literacy leaders acknowledge that time constraints, varying teacher strengths, and unpredictable teacher responses to professional development affect their ability to accomplish their goals. However, they truly believe that their efforts to build rapport and engender trust with teachers help in appealing to teachers' professional development needs.

Laurie, Mary, and Karen illustrate ways they are incorporating the recommendations from the previous nine chapters into their roles and responsibilities as literacy leaders. They understand how to use their school district community as an asset for their students. They know their teachers well enough to engage them in useful professional development. They are so well versed in professional development options that they know how to use them differently for individual teacher needs. They know their students and the learning strengths and challenges that they bring to the classroom. They use their knowledge of the school's balanced literacy approach (e.g., guided reading, read-alouds, shared reading and writing, and independent reading and writing) to help their teachers use and adapt these components with the appropriate materials so their students can develop as readers and writers. They constantly assess teachers' development and students' achievements, informally and formally, to determine their next steps. They also continue to develop as leaders as a result of their experiences with the teachers in their building and their earnest and constant attempts to self-reflect about their impact on the teachers. Although not necessarily aware of their administrators' intentions, they have worked with their administrators to create and follow action checklists that subscribe to their school's literacy plans to build capacity in their schools. The next two sections describe components of a literacy plan and how it can serve as a springboard for a literacy leader's action checklist.

LITERACY PLANS AS FRAMEWORKS FOR BUILDING CAPACITY

A literacy plan provides a blueprint for students' learning. Some literacy plans are developed at the district level, some are developed at the school level, and some are developed at both levels. When developed at both levels, school-based literacy plans typically support district plans. Literacy plans usually include a mission, goals, a curriculum description, professional development plans, an assessment plan, and parent outreach initiatives to communicate ways the plan's mission is being accomplished.

Mission and Goals

Missions are statements that envision what all students in a school can accomplish and become, and what all teachers need to do to facilitate such accomplishments. For example, an elementary school with a diverse student population in Eagan, Minnesota, has as part of its mission to ensure that "every child is literate" (http://www.glacialhills.org/cms/lib6/MN01001111/Centricity/Domain/1/Glacial%20Hills%20Elementary%20School%20Literacy%20Plan%205-12.pdf). Another diverse elementary school in Umitalla, Oregon, has as its mission to build and sustain "a school culture in which high quality reading instruction for all students is our most important priority" (http://mhes.umatilla.k12.or.us/scott-smith/literacy-plan).

Missions are accompanied by reading goals that delineate how a mission will be accomplished. For example, the school in Eagan, Minnesota, includes goals about providing for the five essential components of reading (vocabulary, phonemic awareness, phonics, fluency, and comprehension), explicit and systematic instruction (direct instruction, modeling, guided practice, and application), reading support strategies (interactive read-alouds and literature discussions, shared reading, and guided reading), and independent reading expectations. The school in Umitalla, Oregon, includes goals about the implementation of a schoolwide beginning reading model to help every child read at grade level or above by 3rd grade and continue on through 5th grade, the need to support those who have difficulty meeting the schoolwide goal, and a commitment to teaching children in their native language, especially those students whose first and strongest language is Spanish.

Curriculum

Schools interpret variously the concept of curriculum development and implementation. Some schools develop their own curricula. Au, Strode, Vasquez, and Raphael (2014) discuss how elementary school teachers develop a "staircase" curriculum, aligned with standards, that reflects what their elementary students should be able to do as readers and writers when they graduate from their school. Some schools adopt statewide curriculum guides that have been developed to support standards, and some purchase ready-made, commercial curricula that have been developed in accordance with standards. The instructional techniques and materials that are used are part and parcel of the curriculum framework. Chapter 6 discusses critical elements of a curriculum in relation to standards. Chapter 8 describes different approaches and programs to teach foundational skills, an important element of the curriculum, and Chapter 9 presents ways to ensure that the materials and resources support the curriculum.

Professional Development Plans

Professional development plans range from brief overviews to comprehensive descriptions of what a school does and will do to provide teachers with the necessary knowledge and skills. The most effective professional development plans honor the principles of adult learning by understanding that teachers draw upon their experiences to aid their learning, by involving teachers in planning and evaluating their instruction, and by ensuring that teachers can apply what they learn to their teaching situations. The three literacy leaders—Laurie, Mary, and Karen—focus on providing relevant, ongoing, and consistent professional development that builds on their teachers' strengths and supports them as they work to improve their teaching practice (Bean, 2014; Mraz & Kissel, 2014). Chapters 3 and 5 describe the many different types of professional development opportunities that are available for your teachers.

Naturally, an important consideration for teachers' professional development is time. Teaching assistants, other support staff, administrators, community partners, volunteers, or members of teaching teams can serve as substitutes for teachers (Tallerico, 2014). Some principals and district administrators bank teachers' contact time with students so that teachers spend additional time some days to then have blocks of time for professional development on other days. One of our CSI districts, Bedford Central School District in Bedford, New York, has created an intern program where our teacher candidates serve as substitute teachers in the elementary schools so that the teachers can be released from teaching to have time to engage in professional development. These same paid student interns, when not assigned as substitute teachers, assist students with a partner teacher before, during, and after the school day.

Assessment

An assessment plan includes ongoing evaluation of reading programs and interventions, ongoing assessments of students' strengths and needs that are built around standards, frequent formative assessments to inform instruction and meet student needs, and multiple formative and summative assessments to assess abilities and developmental levels. Chapters 4 and 7 discuss how different types of assessments can be used in a literacy plan to ensure that students receive appropriate instruction and support services.

Parent Outreach

Parents' level of involvement with their children's education usually depends on their social, cultural, and linguistic capital (Bourdieu 1986; Edwards, Paratore, & Sweeney, 2014; Lareau, 1987). Differentiated parent outreach strategies need to be included in a literacy plan so that they take into account the needs of the entire school district parent population (Edwards, Paratore, & Sweeney, 2014). Many suburban school districts that are changing demographically have nondiverse, upwardly mobile elementary schools and diverse, socio-economically challenged schools. The former have active PTAs with significant fundraising abilities to provide extraordinary resources for the schools. The latter have minimal parent involvement and limited resources provided by the parent community. Literacy plans need to address each school's reality.

Challenges with parent outreach are accompanied by challenges with teachers who have difficulty adjusting to changing student populations. Chapter 2 offers ideas and exercises that help teachers examine their core beliefs and attitudes so they better understand the students they are teaching and can connect to students and parents from backgrounds that are different from their own (Delpit, 1995; Edwards, Paratore, & Sweeney, 2014).

USING LITERACY PLANS AS A SPRINGBOARD TO A LITERACY LEADER'S ACTION CHECKLIST

If a school-based literacy plan exists, it offers a school a basic template for *what* should be accomplished to promote students' literacy development. It does not necessarily provide specific information about *how* it will happen, *when* it will be accomplished, and *who* will help accomplish the plan. As a literacy leader, you have the ability, but not necessarily the authority, to implement a plan over time. You should collaborate with your principal, vice principal (as appropriate), and teachers to develop a loosely configured "scope and sequence" for the plan so that eventually many to most teachers are subscribing to what is desired for the school and the students. Your own action checklist can bring a school's plan to life. For example, if a literacy plan states that teachers will receive professional development on data-driven instruction, you can determine what each teacher actually needs, and then organize professional development opportunities for different teachers at different times based on individual needs. Even if your school does not have a plan, your action checklist can serve as the catalyst for moving forward in an organized, thoughtful, and realistic way.

Action Checklist

Figure 10.1 provides the basic topics that should be addressed in your action checklist. These topics encompass essential components of a successful literacy program. These topics are not weighted in any way

332

Figure 10.1. Action Checklist for Serving as a Literacy Leader

1. Know Yourself as a Literacy Leader

Current Status:

Long-Term Goal:

Goal for ___ (year):

2. Know the Community

Current Status:

Long-Term Goal:

Goal for ___ (year):

3. Know the Teachers

Current Status:

Long-Term Goal:

Goal for ___ (year):

4. Know the Students

Current Status:

Long-Term Goal:

Goal for ___ (year):

5. Know Your Professional Development Options

Current Status:

Long-Term Goal:

Goal for ___ (year):

6. Know the Link Between Curriculum and Standards

Current Status:

Long-Term Goal:

Goal for ___ (year):

7. Know Instructional Techniques

Current Status:

Long-Term Goal:

Goal for ___ (year):

8. Know Approaches and Programs to Literacy Instruction

Current Status:

Long-Term Goal:

Goal for ___ (year):

9. Know Materials

Current Status:

Long-Term Goal:

Goal for ___ (year):

for importance, nor do they need to be addressed in any specific order or timeline. They simply need to be considered when developing, implementing, or reconfiguring a literacy program.

Connection Between a Literacy Plan and an Action Checklist

A schoolwide literacy plan speaks broadly about goals, intentions, actions, and opportunities over multiple years. Your action checklist is tailored specifically to an existing literacy plan as well as the individual stakeholders affiliated with the plan. It includes both specific, annual activities and general, multiyear goals and intentions. Both documents offer guidance and direction for your immediate, ongoing, and eventual responsibilities. Figure 10.2 shows how the two documents interface with each other.

Any and all efforts to develop students' literacy should subscribe to a plan's mission and goals. Your ability to help accomplish the plan's mission and goals comes from your willingness to honestly assess and continuously develop the needed knowledge, skills, and dispositions

Figure 10.2. The Interface of a School's Literacy Plan and a Literacy Leader's Action Checklist

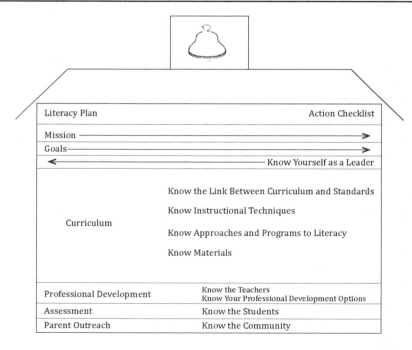

for the job. Such knowledge and skills are reflected in your facility with helping teachers link their grade-level curricula with standards and use appropriate instructional techniques, programs, materials, and assessments. Your capacity to provide differentiated professional development opportunities emanates from your knowledge of teachers' values and instructional patterns, combined with your knowledge of professional development options. Your participation in as many professional development opportunities as possible, such as conferences, workshops, symposia, book clubs, and coursework, contributes to your repertoire of strategies to use with teachers.

Knowledge of the students—from their achievement patterns to their family lives—helps teachers develop, use, and interpret assessment tools and techniques so that students continue to develop. An understanding of the strengths and needs of culturally and linguistically diverse students helps teachers select and use appropriate assessments prior to, during, and after instruction.

Sample Action Checklist

Figure 10.3 indicates how to complete an action checklist. This particular checklist has as its theme the need for the literacy leader to have an impact on additional teachers in the building, especially because of the increased diversity in the school and the growing achievement gap between the haves and have nots. Sam, the literacy leader who completed this checklist, wants to make inroads with the primary teachers who have been teaching in the school for at least 20 years. These teachers were eminently successful with their primarily White, middle-class student population. They now are frustrated by their students' lack of basic literacy skills. These teachers have been making comments in the teacher's lounge and elsewhere about these students' lack of preparation and inadequate family support. These same teachers have not been willing to try new programs, instructional techniques, or grouping patterns to help these students. As Sam's checklist indicates, he is going to start by working with the principal to identify three teachers who, because of some type of incentive (additional funds for teaching materials or travel funds for a conference), will be willing to work with him. Sam intends to work with his literacy colleagues in other schools to identify professional development strategies that could work with these teachers since they do not seem ready to have him conduct demonstration lessons in their classrooms or be coached on different

Figure 10.3. Ideas for Completing a Literacy Action Checklist

1. Know Yourself as a Literacy Leader

Current Status: Working with about 60% of the teachers.

Long-Term Goal: Work with over 90% of the teachers.

Goal for ___ (year): Work with the principal to identify three teachers in the primary grades (teachers X, Y, and Z) who have been resistant to any type of assistance with literacy. Figure out ways to communicate your accessibility and willingness to help so that they invite you into their classrooms to work with you on their instructional needs. Analyze their responsiveness to you and your ideas, discuss your findings with the principal and other colleagues, and identify additional ways to engage these teachers. Continue to use this cycle of self-reflection throughout the year.

2. Know the Community

Current Status: Using basic outreach strategies with parents of culturally and linguistically diverse students that are not really working.

Long-Term Goal: Involve this segment of the parent population in the life of the school.

Goal for ___ (year): Develop new approaches for reaching out to parents of culturally and linguistically diverse students. For example, offer a range of times for them to attend school events, develop written notices and offer programs in their home languages, and use their local organizations to make announcements of school events (Edwards, Paratore, & Sweeney, 2014). Make an effort to track any increased level of involvement of the parents of the children in the three teachers' (teachers X, Y, and Z) classrooms because of your efforts with these teachers (see #3 below).

3. Know the Teachers

Current Status: Know the teachers who have invited me into their classrooms, but only have superficial knowledge about the strengths, challenges, interests, concerns, and goals of those teachers who have not reached out. Have a hunch that those who have not reached out might have some biases toward those students who are culturally and linguistically diverse because of comments that I have heard from them and other teachers.

Long-Term Goal: Form a close working relationship with all those teachers who have not engaged me so that they are comfortable reaching out to me, especially when it comes to working with culturally and linguistically diverse students.

Goal for ___(year): Work with the principal to learn as much as possible about the three teachers in the primary grades (teachers X, Y, and Z) to find out what would motivate them to allow me to work with them. Use

Figure 10.3. Ideas for Completing a Literacy Action Checklist (continued)

the ideas to create opportunities to meet with them individually and in small groups, visit their classrooms, or possibly form a book club.

4. Know the Students

Current Status: Have a general sense of students' achievement patterns, and continue to be perplexed about the ever-widening achievement gap between the haves and have nots.

Long-Term Goal: Understand firsthand—through observations and conversations with students, discussions with the teachers and the principal, and parent interaction—reasons why the school's culturally and linguistically diverse students struggle to achieve. Develop and implement a plan with the teachers and principals to begin to narrow the achievement gap.

Goal for ___ (year): Observe students in the three primary classrooms (teachers X, Y, and Z) to understand their learning patterns and challenges. Work with the teachers, the principal, and learning specialists to modify instructional practices. Monitor student progress.

5. Know Your Professional Development Options

Current Status: Know how to engage teachers who are willing to work with me, but still struggling with identifying useful, job-embedded professional development opportunities for resistant teachers.

Long-Term Goal: Know how to use a more robust array of professional development options that can work with even the most resistant teachers.

Goal for ___(year): Work with colleagues in other schools and districts to identify at least two new professional development strategies that will work with the three primary teachers (teachers X, Y, Z) so that they begin to open up about what is happening in their classrooms that is causing them so much frustration. Try these strategies to see if they work.

6. Know the Link Between Curriculum and Standards

Current Status: Working with teachers by grade level to help them understand how to incorporate nonfiction books into their reading and writing curriculum.

Long-Term Goal: Ensure that the K–6 teachers are using nonfiction texts within and across grades for reading and writing workshop.

Goal for ___(year): Work with the principal to ensure that nonfiction texts are plentiful within and across grades, that teachers understand the importance of their use, and are readily using them for reading and writing instruction. Work with the three primary teachers (teachers X, Y, and Z) to ensure their use of nonfiction texts for all students in their classrooms. Help them adjust the way in which they use the texts for their ELs.

Figure 10.3. Ideas for Completing a Literacy Action Checklist (continued)

7. Know Instructional Techniques

Current Status: Working with teachers as a group on the concept of a balanced reading approach, K–5, but concerned that they still do not understand how to use small-group work for strategy work and guided reading.

Long-Term Goal: Help all teachers in the building to effectively use all components of a balanced reading approach.

Goal for ___ (year): Identify those teachers ("expert" teachers) who are working effectively with students on strategy work and guided reading during small-group instruction. Work with these teachers to develop a workshop for the other teachers in the building and then arrange to have the other teachers visit the "expert" teachers to observe what they do. After eventually getting to work directly with the three primary teachers (teachers X, Y, and Z), create opportunities for them to work with the "expert" teachers as well.

8. Know Approaches and Programs to Literacy Instruction

Current Status: Working with some of the primary teachers on implementing the school's multisensory, phonics-based reading program to help with foundational literacy skills, but am concerned that the resistant primary teachers are not using it the way it is intended to be used.

Long-Term Goal: Ensure that all primary teachers are using the school's multisensory, phonics-based reading program with all primary students.

Goal for ___ (year): Study primary students' achievement patterns for phonemic awareness, phonics, and fluency to underscore differences between the primary teachers who are using the school's phonics program and those who are not. Share the results with the principal and the teachers. Work with the principal to develop a plan to get the primary teachers (teachers X, Y, and Z) to use the program as expected.

9. Know Materials

Current Status: Do not feel comfortable advising teachers on different ways to use blogs, wikis, online search techniques, and social media for critical and joyful reading.

Long-Term Goal: Develop enough expertise in using current technology to be able to coach teachers at all grade levels.

Goal for ___ (year): Learn in-depth three new technology applications, and work with willing teachers to implement these applications. Have teachers then demonstrate to other teachers how they are using these applications to develop students' new literacies (Leu, Forzani, & Kennedy, 2014).

instructional techniques. He is thinking of bringing them together as a group to begin to address their biases. He wants to start by asking them to read "Unlocking the Research on English Learners" (Goldenberg, 2013). Perhaps a small-group discussion will prompt them to freely admit their concerns and brainstorm ideas for addressing some of the challenges that they are encountering.

Sam also wants to work with the principal and other teachers on the achievement gap between the haves and have nots. He wants to help teachers incorporate nonfiction texts, implement all elements of a balanced literacy program, and use a multisensory, phonics-based approach in the primary grades. He plans to help himself with new professional development ideas and current uses of technology. Sam's action checklist is ambitious, yet focused on what he believes will help.

FORM A LEADERSHIP TEAM

As a literacy leader, you cannot do it alone. You need to be involved with some type of leadership team that makes recommendations and decisions about the school's literacy program and the literacy leader's role in the program. The size of the leadership team does not matter. It could include as few as two people (the literacy leader and the principal) or as many representatives as possible—for example, the principal, vice principal, grade-level teachers, dual-language teachers, special education teachers, learning resource teachers, and media specialists. The members of the leadership team also can vary. Whereas some teams are school-based, others are districtwide. For example, Karen Brenneke's leadership team includes the assistant superintendent and other literacy coaches in the district. A leadership team should meet at least monthly to ensure that recommendations and decisions are implemented and assessed for their impact. As a literacy leader, you should work with your principal to guide the team to create a focus for each year, set the agenda for meetings, ensure that information from the meeting is shared with the school staff, and help implement the team's literacy goals (Literacy Leadership Team, 2011). A leadership team should serve as an important guide for the types of initiatives pursued with teachers in relation to student progress. A team provides the opportunity to connect to and collaborate with others about important decisions and priorities for the school's literacy program.

SUSTAIN MOMENTUM

As Laurie, Mary, and Karen have discovered, it often is difficult to sustain momentum with different projects and different teachers because of interferences from, for example, testing, unanticipated teacher absences, changes in administration, newly discovered principal concerns, and districtwide shifts in expectations. Frustration can set in because of the inability to make progress in any area. Laurie, Mary, and Karen keep in mind the expression that "when one door closes, another opens" every time they are disappointed with a failed attempt to work with a specific teacher or introduce a new strategy to a group. They know that they need to be patient and, at the same time, begin to work with other willing teachers and pursue different projects. They also know to remain hopeful that, at some point, they will figure out a way to accomplish what they originally set out to do, or develop an even better idea for their colleague teachers.

Hurdles, obstacles, resistance, and disappointments are part of the leadership landscape because leaders are trying to shepherd people to do what they may or may not want to do. Serving as a literacy leader can be particularly trying because the concept of developing students' literacy continues to elude many teachers as a result of the constant mix of programs, strategies, and materials that appear in their classrooms for different types of students.

The wherewithal to sustain momentum comes from a deep belief in the importance of the job and confidence in one's ability to do the job. As Chapter 1 highlights in its discussion of literacy leadership, it is about your disposition—that is, your attitudes, values, and beliefs demonstrated through your verbal and nonverbal behaviors toward others. Also important for sustaining momentum is your appreciation for the school and the teachers' desire to change, coupled with assurance of support from an administrator. Even if certain conditions are not obvious from the start, it is critical for you as a literacy leader to sustain momentum—no matter what—in order to positively impact a school's literacy program.

TAKING OWNERSHIP OF YOUR PLAN

As previously expressed, a patented formula for effective literacy leadership does not exist. As a literacy leader, you must blend a unique combination of your talents and skills with a distinctive set of school characteristics to strengthen teachers' pedagogy in order to improve students' achievement. To be effective, you must know how to create just the right mix of professional development opportunities for teachers that fulfill their needs in relation to a school's mission. This tall order can begin to be filled when you, in concert with your principal, have a holistic view of the school in relation to its component parts (e.g., community, teachers, students, and curriculum). This whole-to-part-to-whole view contributes to creating a realistic and doable plan that accounts for the school's profile. Your effectiveness as a literacy leader becomes obvious when you take ownership of such a plan through your own short-term and long-term goals (referred to in this chapter as an action checklist), and use your intellectual, social, and psychological capital to ensure that each initiative is attempted and eventually accomplished. In other words, you know how to capitalize on your own strengths within a specific context, and for a specific purpose, to elicit other people's strengths.

LITERACY LEADERSHIP TOOLKIT

The following ideas can be used with individual teachers or small groups of teachers, especially those who are having difficulty with culturally and linguistically diverse students. These exercises can be used during one-on-one coaching or during "Lunch and Learn" or "Eat and Explore" sessions to help teachers identify and address challenges.

Exercise 10.1: Then/Now Chart

Have teachers complete a Then/Now Chart to put into words differences from when they first began to teach to their current teaching situations. Include five to seven items in the chart.

	Then	Now
1. Student Population		
2. Community		
3. Curriculum		
4. Instructional Techniques		
5. Materials		
6. Expectations of Teachers		
7. Expectations of Students		

Exercise 10.2: Framed Paragraph for Three Goals and Three Wishes

Have teachers use their responses from the Then/Now Chart to complete the Framed Paragraph. Use their responses to the "goals" and "assistance" sections to develop a professional development plan for them. If working with a small group, look for overlaps to streamline your professional development plans for them. Explain what you have discovered and seek their permission to move forward accordingly.

Now that students are _____ and the community is _____, I need to _____. I know that I am expected to _____. I feel _____ about these expectations. In order to meet these expectations, I will have to _____. If I do what I think I need to do, I will _____. In the next _____ (month/year), I want to accomplish the following three professional goals for myself: (1) _____; (2) _____; (3) _____. To do this, I wish to have assistance in the following three ways: (1) _____; (2) _____; (3) _____.

Exercise 10.3: Framed Paragraph for Progress Monitoring

Have teachers complete this Framed Paragraph on a monthly or bimonthly basis so that you can monitor their progress. Review their responses and look for any patterns that emerge. Provide feedback on what you have learned about their discoveries.

Since _____ (put in date), I have learned that _____. I am quite _____ with what I have discovered because _____. To keep making progress with _____, I need to _____. I continue to need assistance with _____. I would like _____ so that I have the assistance I need.

Exercise 10.4: Framed Paragraph for End-of-Year Growth

Have teachers complete this framed paragraph at the end of the year so they can reflect about their accomplishments and future goals. Once you review their responses, provide them with feedback about their perceived growth and ways you will help them with future goals.

Now that it is the end of the year, I believe that I have learned to _____. I am particularly pleased with my progress with _____. In the future, I would like to _____. I plan _____ to accomplish this goal for myself.

References

ACT. (2012). *The condition of college and career readiness 2012.* Available at http://media.act.org/documents/CCCR12-NationalReadinessRpt.pdf?_ga=1.6848 1618.257848270.1421423129

ACT. (2014). *The condition of college and career readiness 2014.* Available at http://www.act.org/research/policymakers/cccr14/findings.html.

Aimsweb. (n.d.). Available at www.aimsweb.com

Allen, P. (2009). *Conferring: The keystone of reader's workshop.* Portland, ME: Stenhouse.

Allington, R. L. (2009). If they don't read much . . . 30 years later. In E. H. Hiebert (Ed.), *Reading more, reading better* (pp. 30–54). New York, NY: Guilford Publishers.

Allington, R. L. (2012). *What really matters for struggling readers: Designing research-based programs.* New York, NY: Pearson.

Allyn, P. (2012). *Be core ready: Powerful, effective steps to implementing and achieving the Common Core State Standards.* Upper Saddle River, NJ: Pearson.

The American Academy of Pediatrics. (2014). Policy statement: Literacy promotion: An essential component of primary care pediatric practice, *Pediatrics, 134*(2), 404–409. Available at http://pediatrics.aappublications.org/content/134/2/404.abstract?rss=

American Council on the Teaching of Foreign Languages. (2013). *NCSSFL-ACTFL can do statements.* Fairfax, VA: Author.

Ammon, P. (1985). Helping children learn to write in English as a second language: Some observations and some hypotheses. In S. W. Freedman (Ed.), *The acquisition of written language* (pp. 65–84). Norwood, NJ: Ablex.

Anderson, C. B. (2008, December). One conversation: Exploring the role of culture in coaching. *Literacy coaching clearinghouse.* Available at http://www.literacycoachingonline.org/briefs/One_conversation_brief_12.13.08.pdf

Anderson, R. C., Hiebert, E., Scott, J., & Wilkinson, I. (1985). *Becoming a nation of readers: The report on the commission of reading.* Washington, DC: National Academy of Education.

Anderson, R. C., & Pearson, P. D. (1984). A schema-theoretic view of basic processes in reading. In P. D. Pearson, R. Barr, M. L. Kamil, & P. Mosenthal (Eds.), *Handbook of reading research* (pp. 255–291). White Plains, NY: Longman.

Appalachia Regional Comprehensive Center. (2009). *Effective practices for teaching English language learners: A resource document for North Carolina's ELL work group.* Charleston, WV: Advantia. Available at http://sites.edvantia.org/publications /arcc/effectiveellpractices031109.pdf

Apple. (2015). *Evernote* Version 7.6.5. [Mobile application software]. Available at http://itunes.apple.com

Armand, G. (2011). *Love twelve miles long.* New York, NY: Lee & Low.

Asher, J. (1969) The total physical response approach to second language learning. *The Modern Language Journal, 53*(1), 3–17.

Atkins, J. (2008). *Get set! Swim!* New York, NY: Lee & Low.

Au, K. H., Raphael, T. E., & Mooney, K. C. (2008). Improving reading achievement in elementary schools: Guiding change in a time of standards. In S. B. Wepner & D. S. Strickland (Eds.), *The administration and supervision of reading programs* (4th ed., pp. 71–89). New York, NY: Teachers College Press.

Au, K. H., Strode, E. V., Vasquez, J. M., & Raphael, T. E. (2014). Improving literacy achievement in elementary schools: The standards-based change process and the Common Core. In S. B. Wepner, D. S. Strickland, & D. J. Quatroche (Eds.), *The administration and supervision of reading programs* (5th ed., pp. 74–84). New York, NY: Teachers College Press.

Ayres, R., & Overman, C. (2013). *Celebrating writers: From possibilities through publication.* Portland, ME: Stenhouse.

Bailey, A. L., & Heritage, M. (2008). *Formative assessment for literacy, grades K–6: Building reading and academic language skills across the curriculum.* Thousand Oaks, CA: Corwin/Sage Press.

Ball, D. L., & Cohen, D. K. (1999). Developing practices, developing practitioners: Toward a practice-based theory of professional development. In G. Sykes & L. Darling-Hammonds (Eds.), *Teaching as the learning profession: Handbook of policy and practice* (pp. 30–32). San Francisco, CA: Jossey-Bass.

Banks, J. (2001). *Cultural diversity and education: Foundations, curriculum, and teaching.* Boston, MA: Pearson, Allyn, & Bacon.

Barger, J. (2006). Building word consciousness. *The Reading Teacher, 60*(3), 279–281.

Baumann, J. F., & Duffy, A. M. (2001). Teacher-researcher methodology: Themes, variations, and possibilities. *The Reading Teacher, 54*(6), 608–615.

Bean, R. M. (2014). Developing a comprehensive reading plan (pre-K–Grade 12). In S. B. Wepner, D. S. Strickland, & D. J. Quatroche (Eds.), *The administration and supervision of reading programs* (5th ed., pp. 11–29). New York, NY: Teachers College Press.

Bear, D. R., Invernizzi, M., Templeton, S., & Johnston, F. (2011). *Words their way* (5th ed.). Upper Saddle River, NJ: Pearson.

Beaver, J. (2012). *Developmental reading assessment 2* (2nd ed.). Upper Saddle River, NJ: Pearson.

Beaver, J. M., & Carter, M. A. (2006). *The developmental reading assessment* (2nd ed.) (DRA2). Upper Saddle River, NJ: Pearson.

Beck, I. L., McKeown, M. G., & Kucan, L. (2014). *Bringing words to life: Robust vocabulary instruction* (2nd ed.). New York, NY: The Guilford Press.

Berkowitz, D. (2011). Oral storytelling: Building community through dialogue, engagement, and problem solving, *Young Children, 66*(2), 36–40.

Berne, J., & Degener, D. C. (2015). *The one-on-one reading and writing conference: Working with students on complex texts.* New York, NY: Teachers College Press.

Bertin, P., & Perlman, E. (1998). *Preventing academic failure: A multisensory curriculum for reading, spelling, and handwriting.* White Plains, NY: Monroe Associates.

Bialystok, E. (2011). Reshaping the mind: The benefits of bilingualism. *Canadian Journal of Experimental Psychology/Revue canadienne de psychologie expérimentale, 65*(4), 229–235.

Billings, J. (2014, February 11). Children are the priority. Change is the reality. Collaboration is the strategy. *School Improvement Network* [SI-NET]. #edchat [Tweet]. Available at https://twitter.com/sinetedivation /status/433372655807254528

Bintz, W., & Dillard, J. (2007). Teachers as reflective practitioners: Teacher stories of curricular change in a 4th grade classroom. *Reading Horizons Journal, 47*(3), 203–227.

Blachowicz, C.L., & Fisher, P.J. (2011). Best practices in vocabulary instruction revisited. In L. Morrow & L. Gambrell (Eds.), *Best practices in literacy instruction* (4th ed., pp. 224–249). New York, NY: Guilford Press.

Blank, M. J., Melaville, A., & Shah, B. P. (2003). *Making the difference: Research and practice in community schools.* Washington, DC: Coalition for Community Schools. Available at http://www.communityschools.org/assets/1/page /ccsfullreport.pdf

Bourdieu, P. (1986). The forms of capital. In J. G. Richardson (Ed.), *Handbook of theory and research for the sociology of education* (pp. 241–258). New York, NY: Greenwood Press.

Boyles, N. (2012). Closing in on close reading. *Educational Leadership, 70*(4), 36–41.

Brabham, E., & Villaume, S. (2001). Questions and answers—building walls of words. *The Reading Teacher, 54*(7), 700–703.

Bracco, C., & Rabinovitch, A. (2014, October 2). *Latino youth and their families.* Paper presented at the meeting of the Putnam/Northern Westchester BOCES Regional ELL Needs Assessment Forum, Yorktown, NY.

Bridges, L. (2013). Make every student count: How collaboration among families, schools, and communities ensures student success. *Family and community 2013 engagement research compendium.* New York, NY: Scholastic. Available at http:// teacher.scholastic.com/products/face-new/pdf/research-compendium/family -involvement.pdf

Brigance, A. H. (1999). *Brigance diagnostic comprehensive inventory of basic skills—Revised.* North Billerica, MA: Curriculum Associates.

Briggs, K. C., & Myers, I. B. (1998). *Myers-Briggs type indicator: Form M.* Edmonton, Canada: Psychometrics.

Brown, J. E., & Doolittle, J. (2008). A cultural, linguistic, and ecological framework for response to intervention with English language learners. *TEACHING Exceptional Children, 40,* 66–72. Available at http://www. nccrest.org/Briefs /Framework_for_RTI.pdf

Bryant, B. R., & Wiederholt, J. L. (2001). *Gray oral reading tests* (4th ed.). Upper Saddle River, NJ: Pearson.

Bunch, J. (1991). The storyboard strategy. *Training and Development, 45*(7), 69–71.

Burbank, M., Kauchak, D., & Bates, A. (2010). Book clubs as professional development opportunities for preservice teacher candidates and practicing teachers: An exploratory study. *The New Educator, 6*(1), 56–73.

Burgess, T. (2006). A frame work for examining teacher knowledge as used in action while teaching statistics. In A. Rossman & B. Chance (Eds.), *International Conference on Teaching Statistics 7 Proceedings* (ICOTS-7), 1–6. Available at https://www.stat.auckland.ac.nz/~iase/publications/17/6F4_BURG.pdf

Burkins, J. M., & Yaris, K. (2014). *Reading wellness: Lessons in independence and proficiency.* Portland, ME: Stenhouse.

Burns, M. S., Griffin, P., & Snow, C. E. (Eds.). (1999). *Starting out right: A guide to promoting children's reading success.* Washington, DC: National Academy Press.

Button, K., Johnson, M. J., & Furgeson, P. (1996). Interactive writing in a primary classroom. *The Reading Teacher, 49*(6), 446–454.

Calderon, M. E., & Minaya-Rowe, L. (2003). *Designing and implementing two-way bilingual programs: A step-by-step guide for administrators, teachers, and parents.* Thousand Oaks, CA: Corwin.

Caldwell, J., & Ford, M. (2002). *Where have all the bluebirds gone? How to soar with flexible grouping.* Portsmouth, NH: Heinemann.

Calkins, L. (1994). *The art of teaching writing* (2nd ed.). Portsmouth, NH: Heinemann.

Calkins, L. (2000). *The art of teaching reading.* Upper Saddle River, NJ: Pearson.

Calkins, L. (2010). *The nuts and bolts of teaching writing.* Portsmouth, NH: Heinemann.

Cappiello, M. A., & Dawes, E. T. (2012). *Teaching with text sets.* Huntington Beach, CA: Shell Education Publishing, Inc.

Caro-Bruce, C. (2004). Action research. In L. B. Easton (Ed.), *Powerful designs for professional learning* (pp. 53–60). Oxford, OH: National Staff Development Council.

Center for Comprehensive School Reform and Improvement. (2009). *Professional learning communities.* Washington, DC: Author. Available at http://www.centerforcsri.org/plc/elements.html

Center for Public Education. (2012). *Changing demographics at a glance.* Available at http://www.centerforpubliceducation.org/Main-Menu/Staffingstudents/Changing-Demographics-At-a-glance

Center for Research on Education, Diversity & Excellence. (2003). *A national study of school effectiveness for language minority students' long-term academic achievement.* Available at http://crede.berkeley.edu/research/crede/products/print/research_briefs/rb10.shtml

Chamot, A., & O'Malley, M. (1994). T*he CALLA handbook: Implementing the Cognitive Academic Language Learning Approach.* New York, NY: Addison-Wesley.

Ching, S. H. D. (2005). Multicultural children's literature as an instrument of power. *Language Arts, 83*(2), 128–136.

Clair, N. (1993). *Beliefs, self-reported practices and professional development needs of three classroom teachers with language-minority students.* Unpublished doctoral dissertation, Teachers College, Columbia University, New York.

Clay, M. M. (2006). *An observation survey of early literacy achievement* (2nd ed.). Portsmouth, NH: Heinemann.

Coady, M., & Escamilla, K. (2005). Audible voices, visible tongues: Exploring social realities in Spanish speaking students' writing. *Language Arts, 82*(6), 462–471.

Cochran-Smith, M., & Lytle, S. L. (1993). *Inside/outside: Teacher research and knowledge.* New York, NY: Teachers College Press.

Cochran-Smith, M., & Lytle, S. L. (1998). Teacher research: The question that persists. *International Journal of Leadership in Education, 1*(1), 19.

College Board. (2015). *2014 College Board program results: SAT.* New York, NY: The College Board. Available at https://www.collegeboard.org/program-results/2014/sat

Collier, V. P. (1995) Second-language acquisition for school: Academic, cognitive, sociocultural, and linguistic process. In J. E. Alatis, C. A. Straehle, B. Gallenberger, & M. Ronkin (Eds.), *Georgetown University round table on languages and linguistics 1995* (pp. 311–327). Washington, DC: Georgetown University Press.

Collier, V. P., & Thomas, W. P. (2009). *Educating English language learners for a transformed world.* Albuquerque, NM: Dual Language Education of New Mexico Fuente Press.

Collins, J. (2001). *Good to great: Why some companies make the leap . . . and others don't.* New York, NY: Harper Collins.

Collins, K. (2004). *Growing readers: Units of study in the primary classroom.* Portland, ME: Stenhouse.

Commission on Effective Teachers and Teaching (CETT). (2011). *Transforming teaching: Connecting professional responsibility with student learning.* Available at http://www.nea.org/assets/docs/Transformingteaching2012.pdf

Connelly, F. M., & Clandinin, D. J. (1988). *Teachers as curriculum planners: Narratives of Experience.* New York, NY: Teachers College Press.

Cooley, C. H. (1902). *Human nature and social order.* New York, NY: Charles Scribner.

Coskie, T., Robinson, L., Riddle Buly, M., & Egawa, K. (2005). What makes an effective literacy coach. *Voices from the Middle, 12*(4), 60–61. Available at https://literacyleads.wikispaces.com/file/view/Effective+Coach.pdf

Council for the Accreditation of Educator Preparation (CAEP). (2013, June 11). *CAEP accreditation standards and evidence: Aspirations for educator preparation.* Washington, DC: Author.

Council of Chief State School Officers. (2011, April). *Interstate Teacher Assessment and Support Consortium (InTASC) model core teaching standards: A resource for state dialogue.* Washington, DC: Author. Available at http://www.ccsso.org/Documents/2011/InTASC_Model_Core_Teaching_Standards_2011.pdf

Cox, A. R. (1992). *Foundations for literacy: Structures and techniques for multisensory teaching of basic written language skills.* Cambridge, MA: Educators Publishing Service.

Crews, D. (1991). *Truck*. New York, NY: Greenwillow Books.

Cummins, J. (1979). Linguistic interdependence and the educational development of bilingual children. *Review of Educational Research, 49*(2), 222–251.

Cummins, J. (1980). The cross-lingual dimensions of language proficiency: Implications for bilingual education and the optimal age issue. *TESOL Quarterly, 14*(2), 175–187.

Cummins, J., Bismilla, V., Chow, P., Cohen, S., Giampapa, F., Leoni, L., Sandhu, P., & Sastri, P. (2005). Affirming diversity in multilingual classrooms. *Educational Leadership, 63*(1), 38–43.

Cunningham, A. E., Perry, K. E., Stanovich, K. E., & Stanovich, P. J. (2004). Disciplinary knowledge of K–3 teachers and their knowledge calibration in the domain of early literacy. *Annals of Dyslexia, 54*(1), 139–166.

Cunningham, A. E., & Stanovich, K. E. (2003). Reading can make you smarter! *Principal, 83*, 34–39

Cunningham, K. (2013). We are what we repeatedly do: Creating a close reading culture in a K–8 school. *Connecticut Reading Association Journal, 2*(1), 21–28.

Cunningham, K. (2014). Partnering to strengthen the teaching of foundational literacy skills. In J. Ferrara, J. L. Nath, & I. N. Guadarrama (Eds.), *Creating visions for university–school partnerships* (pp. 259–282). Charlotte, NC: Information Age.

Cunningham, K., & Enriquez, G. (2013). Bridging core-readiness with social justice through social justice picture books. *New England Reading Association Journal, 48*(2), 28–37.

Cunningham, P. M. (2000). *Phonics they use: Words for reading and writing* (3rd ed.). New York, NY: HarperCollins.

Cunningham, P. M., & Allington, R. L. (2010). *Classrooms that work: They can all read and write* (5th ed.). Boston, MA: Allyn and Bacon.

Cunningham, P. M., & Hall, D. P. (1994). *Making big words: Multilevel, hands-on spelling and phonic activities.* Torrance, CA: Good Apple.

Daniels, H. (2002). *Literature circles: Voice and choice in book clubs and reading groups.* Portland, ME: Stenhouse.

Danielson, C. (2011). Evaluations that help teachers learn. *Educational Leadership, 68*(4), 35–39.

Darling-Hammond, L., Chung Wei, R., Andree, A., Richardson, N., & Orphanos, S. (2009). *Professional learning in the learning profession: A status report on teacher development in the United States and abroad.* Dallas, TX: National Staff Development Council.

Darling-Hammond, L., & McLaughlin, M. W. (1995). Policies that support professional development in an era of reform. *Phi Delta Kappan, 76*(8), 597–604.

Dearing, E., Kreider, H., Simpkins, S., & Weiss, H. (2006). Family involvement in school and low-income children's literacy performance: Longitudinal associations between and within families. *Journal of Educational Psychology, 98*, 653–664.

Delpit, L. (1995). *Other people's children: Cultural conflict in the classroom.* New York, NY: The New Press.

Deno, S. L. (1985). Curriculum-based measurement: The emerging alternative. *Exceptional Children, 52*(3), 219–232.

Dewey, J. (1933). *How we think.* Buffalo, NY: Prometheus Books. (Original work published 1910)

DeWitt, P. (2014, October 5). *5 reasons leaders need to encourage teacher voice* [Web log post]. Available at http://blogs.edweek.org/edweek/finding_common_ground/2014/10/5_reasons_leaders_need_to_encourage_teacher_voice.html

Diaz-Strom, M. D. (2000). *Carmen's colors.* New York, NY: Lee & Low.

Donaldson, G. A. (2007). What do teachers bring to leadership? *Educational Leadership, 65*(1), 26–29.

Donovan, M. S., & Cross, C. T. (2002). *Minority students in special education and gifted education.* Washington, DC: National Academy Press.

Dooley, K. (2009). Intercultural conversation: Building understanding together. *Journal of Adolescent and Adult Literacy, 52*(6), 497–506.

Dorn, L. J., & Soffos, C. (2001). *Scaffolding young writers: A writers' workshop approach.* Portland, ME: Stenhouse.

Drago-Severson, E. (2004). *Helping teachers learn: Principal leadership for adult growth and development.* Thousand Oaks, CA: Corwin.

DuBard, N. E., & Martin, K. M. (1994). *Teaching language-deficient children: Theory and application of the Association Method for Multisensory Teaching.* Cambridge, MA: Educators Publishing Service.

DuBois, W. E. B. (1953). *The souls of black folk.* New York, NY: Fawcett.

DuFour, R. (2004). What is a professional learning community? *Educational Leadership, 61*(8), 6–11.

Duke, N. K., & Pearson, P. D. (2002). Effective practices for developing reading comprehension. In A. E. Farstrup & S. J. Samuels (Eds.), *What research has to say about reading instruction* (3rd ed., pp. 205–242). Newark, DE: International Reading Association.

Dweck, D. S. (2006). *Mindset: The new psychology of success.* New York, NY: Random House.

Echevarría, J., Vogt, M., & Short, D. (2008). *Making content comprehensible for English learners.* New York, NY: Pearson.

Edwards, P. A. (2008, March). *Engaging hard to reach parents. Increasing parent involvement at your school.* Winding Brook Conference Centre. Available at https://readingrecovery.org/images/pdfs/Conferences/NC08/Handouts/Edwards_Engaging_Hard_To_Reach_Parents.pdf

Edwards, P. A. (2009). *Tapping parent potential.* New York, NY: Scholastic.

Edwards, P. A. (2011). Differentiating parent supports. In S. Redding, M. Murphy, & P. Sheley (Eds.), *Handbook on family and community engagement* (pp. 113–116). Lincoln, IL: Academic Development Center.

Edwards, P. A., Paratore, J. R., & Sweeney, J. S. (2014). Working with parents and the community. In S. B. Wepner, D. S. Strickland, & D. J. Quatroche (Eds.), *The administration and supervision of reading programs* (5th ed., pp. 214–222). New York, NY: Teachers College Press.

Elya, S. M. (2006). *Home at last.* New York, NY: Lee & Low.

Enfield, M. L., & Greene, V. (1997). *Project read*. Bloomington, MN: Language Circle Enterprise.

Eunice Kennedy Shriver National Institute of Child Health and Human Development, NIH, DHHS. (2001). *Put reading first: The research building blocks for teaching children to read*. Washington, DC: U.S. Government Printing Office.

Fan, X., & Chen, M. (2001). Parental involvement and students' academic achievement: A meta-analysis. *Educational Psychology Review, 13*(1), 1–22.

Farrell, D. (1983). Exit, voice, loyalty, and neglect as responses to job dissatisfaction: A multidimensional-scaling study. *Academy of Management Journal, 26*, 596–607.

Figueredo, D.H. (2011). *What can fly?* New York, NY: Lee & Low.

Fillmore, L. W., & Fillmore, C. J. (2012). What does text complexity mean for English learners and language minority students? In K. Hakuta, & M. Santos (Eds.), *Understanding language: Language, literacy, and learning in the content areas* (pp. 64–74). Palo Alto, CA: Stanford University. Available at http://ell.stanford.edu/publication/what-does-text-complexity-mean-english-learners-and-language-minority-students

Fisher, D., & Frey, N. (2008). *Better learning through structured teaching: A framework for the gradual release of responsibility*. Alexandria, VA: ASCD.

Fisher, D., & Frey, N. (2012). Close reading in elementary schools. *The Reading Teacher, 66*(3), 179–188.

Flaitz, J. (2013). *Evaluation of the Manhattanville College Changing Suburbs Institute® Professional Development Schools program: A report to JPMorgan Chase Foundation.* Unpublished report.

Flinders, D. J. (1988). Teacher isolation and the new reform. *Journal of Curriculum and Supervision, 4*(1), 17–29.

Flood, J., & Lapp, P. (1994). Teacher book clubs: Establishing literature discussion groups for teachers (issues and trends). *The Reading Teacher, 47*(7), 574–576.

Fountas, I. C., & Pinnell, G. S. (1996). *Guided reading: Good first teaching for all children*. Portsmouth, NH: Heinemann.

Fountas, I. C., & Pinnell, G. S. (1998). *Teaching phonics and spelling in the reading/writing classroom*. Portsmouth, NH: Heinemann.

Fountas, I. C., & Pinnell, G. S. (2000). *Guiding readers and writers (grades 3–6): Teaching comprehension, genre, and content literacy*. Portsmouth, NH: Heinemann.

Fountas, I. C., & Pinnell, G. S. (2010) *Benchmark literacy assessment system* (2nd ed.). Portsmouth, NH: Heinemann.

Fox, D., & Short, K. (2003). *Stories matter: The complexity of cultural authenticity in children's literature*. Urbana, IL: National Council of Teachers of English.

Frayer, D., Frederick, W. C., & Klausmeier, H. J. (1969). *A schema for testing the level of cognitive mastery*. Madison, WI: Wisconsin Center for Education Research.

Fuchs, D., Mock, D., Morgan, P., & Young, C. (2003). Responsiveness to intervention: Definitions, evidence, and implications for the learning disabilities construct. *Learning Disabilities Research and Practice, 18*, 157–171.

Fullan, M. (2010). *All systems go: The change imperative for whole systems reform.* San Francisco, CA: Corwin.

Gangi, J. M. (2008). The unbearable whiteness of literacy instruction: Realizing the implications of the proficient reader research. *Multicultural Review, 17*(2), 30–35.

Gangi, J. M., & Ferguson, A. (2006). African American literature: Books to stoke dreams. *The Tennessee Reading Teacher, 34*(2), 29–38.

Ganske, K. (2013). *Word journeys: Assessment-guided phonics, spelling, and vocabulary instruction* (2nd ed.). New York, NY: The Guilford Press.

Garet, M. S., Porter, A., Desimone, L., Birman, B., & Yoon, K. S. (2001, Winter). What makes professional development effective? Results from a national sample of teachers. *American Educational Research Journal, 38*(4), 915–945.

Gee, J. P. (1996). *Social linguistics and literacies: Ideology in Discourses* (2nd ed.). London, UK: Taylor and Francis.

Gee, J. P. (2011). *Social linguistics and literacies: Ideology in discourses* (4th ed.). New York, NY: Taylor and Francis.

Genishi, C. (2002). Young English language learners: Resourceful in the classroom. Research in review. *Young Children, 57*(4), 66–72.

Genishi, C., & Dyson, A. (2009) *Children, language and literacy: Diverse learners in diverse times.* New York, NY: Teachers College Press.

George, M. (2002). Professional development for a literature-based middle school curriculum. *The Clearing House, 75*(6), 327–331.

Gere, A. R., Aull, L., Dickinson, H., Gerben, C., Green, T., Moody, S., McBee Orzulak, M., Damian, M., Perales, E., & Thomas, E. E. (2008). *English Language Learners: A policy research brief produced by the National Council of Teachers of English.* Available at http://www.ncte.org/library/nctefiles/resources/policyresearch/ellresearchbrief.pdf

Gewertz, C. (2012). Common core's focus on "close reading" stirs worries. *EducationWeek, 31*(20), 6.

Gibson, S. A. (2008). An effective framework for primary-grade guided writing instruction. *The Reading Teacher, 62*(4), 324–334.

Goldenberg, C. (2013, Summer). Unlocking the research on English learners. *American Educator, 37*(2), 4–11, 38.

Goleman, D. (1995). *Emotional intelligence: Why it can matter more than IQ.* New York, NY: Bantam.

Goleman, D. (2000, March). Leadership that gets results. *Harvard Business Review, 78*(2), 78–90.

Goleman, D. (2004, January). What makes a leader? *Harvard Business Review, 82*(1), 82–91.

Goleman, D., Boyatzis, R. E., & McKee, A. (2004). *Primal leadership: Learning to lead with emotional intelligence.* Cambridge, MA: Harvard Business Press.

Goleman, D., McKee, A., & Boyatzis, R. E. (2002). *Primal Leadership: Realizing the power of emotional intelligence.* Cambridge, MA: Harvard Business Review Press.

Gómez, D. W., Ferrara, J., Santiago, E., Fanelli, F., & Taylor, R. (2012). Full-service community schools: A district's commitment to educating the whole child. In A. Honigsfeld & A. Cohan (Eds.), *Breaking the mold of education for culturally and linguistically diverse students: Innovative and successful practices for the 21st century* (pp. 65–73). Lanham, MD: Rowman and Littlefield Education.

Gómez, D. W., Lang, D. E., & Lasser, S. M. (2010). Avenidas nuevas: New pathways for modeling and supporting home-based literacy strategies with Hispanic parents. In A. Honigsfeld & A. Cohan (Eds.), *Breaking the mold of school instruction and organization: Innovative and successful practices for the twenty-first century* (pp. 123–135). Lanham, MA: Rowman & Littlefield.

Google (2015). *Google Keep.* Available at https://play.google.com/store/apps/details?id=com.google.android.keep&hl=en

Guralnik, D. B. (Ed.). (1960). *Webster's New World Dictionary of the American Language (1960)*. New York, NY: The World Publishing Co.

Guth, N. D., & Pettengill, S. S. (2005). *Leading a successful reading program: Administrators and reading specialists working together to make it happen.* Newark, DE: International Reading Association.

Hack, C., Hepler, S., & Hickman, J. (1993*). Children's literature in the elementary school* (5th ed.). New York, NY: Holt, Rinehart & Winston.

Hanover Research. (2012, March). *Best practices for including multiple measures in teacher evaluation.* Washington, DC: Author. Available at http://www.hanover-research.com/wp-content/uploads/2012/05/Best-Practices-for-Including-Multiple-Measures-in-Teacher-Evaluations-Membership.pdf

Hargreaves, A. (1996). Revisiting voice. *Educational Researcher, 25*(1), 12–19.

Harrison, J. (2013). Professional learning and the reflective practitioners. In S. Dymoke (Ed.), *Reflective teaching and learning in the secondary school* (2nd ed., pp. 6–46). London, UK: Sage. Available at http://www.sagepub.com/upm-data/49808_02_Dymoke_Ch_01.pdf

Harvey, S., & Goudvis, A. (2007). *Strategies that work: Teaching comprehension for understanding and engagement* (2nd ed.). Portland, ME: Stenhouse Publishers.

Heath, S. B. (1983). *Ways with words: Language, life, and work in communities and classrooms.* Cambridge, UK: Cambridge University Press.

Heath, S. B. (2004). Learning, language, and strategic thinking through the arts. *Reading Research Quarterly, 39*, 338–341.

Helgeland, B. (Director). (2013). *42* [Motion picture]. United States: Warner Bros.

Henderson, A., Mapp, K., Johnson, V., & Davies, D. (2007). *Beyond the bake sale: The essential guide to family-school partnerships.* New York, NY: The New Press.

Henderson, E. (1990). *Teaching spelling* (Rev. ed.). Boston, MA: Houghton Mifflin.

Herman, R. (1993). *The Herman method for reversing reading failure.* Sherman Oaks, CA : Herman Method Institute.

Hirsh, S. (2009). A new definition. *Journal of Staff Development, 30*(4), 10–16.

Holdaway, D. (1979). *The foundations of literacy.* New York, NY: Scholastic.

Holland, D., Lachicotte, W., Skinner, D., & Cain, C. (1998). *Identity and agency in cultural worlds.* Cambridge, MA: Harvard University Press.

Honig, A. S. (1994, Winter). Helping children become more caring and cooperative. *New York State Association for the Education of Young Children Reporter, 30*(2), 1.

Honigsfeld, A. (2009). ELL programs: Not "one size fits all." *Kappa Delta Pi Record, 45*(4), 166–171.

Hoyt, L. (1999). *Revisit, reflect, retell: Strategies for improving reading comprehension.* Portsmouth, NH: Heinemann.

Howard, T. C. (2001). Powerful pedagogy for African American students; a case of four teachers. *Urban Education, 36*(2), 179–202.

Hudelson, S. (1989). *Write on: Children writing in ESL.* Englewood Cliffs, NJ: Prentice Hall Regents.

Hull, G., & Moje, E. (2012). What is the development of literacy the development of? *Understanding Language.* Palo Alto, CA: Stanford University. Available at http://ell.stanford.edu/sites/default/files/pdf/academic-papers/05-Hull%20%26%20Moje%20CC%20Paper%20FINAL.pdf

Immigrate to Manitoba, Canada. (n.d.). *Immigration planning guide: Conduct an internal and external environmental scan.* Available at http://www2.immigratemanitoba.com/browse/regionalcommunities/plan_guide/community-int.ext.html

Intercultural Development Research Association. (Producer). (2014, August). *IDRA CN 144 – PTA Comunitarios are born in their communities* [Audio podcast]. Available at http://www.idra.org/The_News/Currently/PTA_Comunitarios_are_Born_in_their_Communities_%28podcast%29/

International Dyslexia Association. (2014). *Multisensory structured language teaching. Just the facts.* Baltimore, MD: Author. Available at http://www.interdys.org/ewebeditpro5/upload/MSLTeachingRev0914.pdf

International Reading Association. (2000). *Providing books and other print materials for classroom and school libraries: A position statement of the International Reading Association.* Newark, DE: International Reading Association. Available at http://www.reading.org/Libraries/position-statements-and-resolutions/ps1039_libraries_2.pdf

International Reading Association. (2002). *Family-school partnerships: Essential elements for literacy instruction in the United States.* Newark, DE: Author.

International Reading Association. (2004). *The role and qualifications of the reading coach in the United States.* Newark, DE: Author.

International Reading Association. (2010). *Standards 2010: Reading specialist/literacy coach.* Newark, DE: Author.

Invernizzi, M., Meier, J., & Juel, C. (2005). *Phonological awareness literacy screening 1-3 technical reference.* Charlottesville, VA: University Printing.

Jadama, L. M. (2014). Impact of subject matter knowledge of a teacher in teaching and learning process. *Middle Eastern & African Journal of Educational Research, 2,* 20–29.

Jesse, L. G. (2007). The elements of a professional learning community: Professional learning communities will change how you and your staff view learning. *Leadership Compass, 5*(2), 1–3. Available at https://www.naesp.org/resources/2/Leadership_Compass/2007/LC2007v5n2a4.pdf

Johns, J. L. (2008). *Basic reading inventory: Student word lists, passages, and early literacy assessments* (10th ed.). Dubuque, IA: Kendell Hunt.

Johns, J. L., & Lenski, S. (2001). *Improving reading: Strategies and resources*. Dubuque, IA: Kendell Hunt.

Joyce, B. R., & Showers, B. (2002). *Student achievement through staff development* (3rd ed.). Alexandria, VA: Association for Supervision and Curriculum Development.

Jung, C. G. (1971). Psychological types. *Collected works of C.G. Jung, volume 6*. Princeton, NJ: Princeton University Press.

Katz, L. G., & Raths, J. D. (1985). Dispositions as goals for teacher education. *Teaching and Teacher Education, 1*(4), 301–307.

Keene, E. O., & Zimmermann, S. (2007). *Mosaic of thought: Teaching comprehension in a reader's workshop* (2nd ed.). Portsmouth, NH: Heinemann.

Keller, T. (2012, November 12). *Ohio schools experience change in student demographics*. Available at http://online.notredamecollege.edu/masters-education-degree/ohio-schools-student-demographics/

Kelly, R. (2013). Encouraging a growth mindset to help lead change. *Academic Leader, 29*(8), 1, 6.

King, M. L. (1963). *Letter from Birmingham Jail*. Available at http://www.uscrossier.org/pullias/wp-content/uploads/2012/06/king.pdf

King-Thorius, K. A., & Sullivan, A. L. (2013). Interrogating instruction and intervention in RTI research with students identified as English language learners. *Reading & Writing Quarterly, 29*, 64–88.

Kneebone, E. (2014, July). *The growth and spread of concentrated poverty, 2000 to 2008–2012*. Available at http://www.brookings.edu/research/interactives/2014/concentrated-poverty#/M10420

Knight, J. K. (1995). Starting over: An overview. In C. W. McIntyre & J. S. Pickering (Eds.), *Clinical studies of multisensory structured language education* (pp. 231–232). Salem, OR: International Multisensory Structured Language Education Council.

Korgstad, J. M. (2014, July). *A view of the future through kindergarten demographics*. Pew Research Center. Available at http://www.pewresearch.org/fact-tank/2014/07/08/a-view-of-the-future-through-kindergarten-demographics/

Korgstad, J. M., Gonzalez-Barrera, A., & Lopez, M. H. (2014, July). *Children 12 and under are fastest growing group of unaccompanied minors at U. S. border*. Pew Research Center. Available at http://www.pewresearch.org/fact-tank/2014/07/22/children-12-and-under-are-fastest-growing-group-of-unaccompanied-minors-at-u-s-border/

Krashen, S. D. (1981). Bilingual education and second language acquisition theory. *Schooling and language minority students: A theoretical framework*, 51–79. Evaluation, Dissemination and Assessment Center California State University, Los Angeles, California Office of Bilingual Bicultural Education. California State Department of Education Sacramento, California.

Krashen, S. D. (1999, May). *Bilingual education: Arguments for and (bogus) arguments against.* Georgetown University Roundtable on Languages and Linguistics, Washington, DC.

Ladson-Billings, G. (1994). *The dreamkeepers: Successful teachers for African-American children.* San Francisco, CA: Jossey-Bass.

Lake, M. D. (2005). *Pop pop and grandpa.* New York, NY: Lee & Low.

L'Allier, S., Elish-Piper, L., & Bean, R. M. (2010). What matters for elementary literacy coaching? Guiding principles for instructional improvement and student achievement. *The Reading Teacher, 63*(7), 544–554.

Laman, T. T., & Van Sluys, K. (2008). Being and becoming: Multilingual writers' practices. *Language Arts, 85*(4), 265–274.

Lambert, L. (1998). *Building leadership capacity in schools.* Alexandria, VA: Association for Supervision and Curriculum Development.

Lareau, A. (1987). Social class differences in family-school relationships: The importance of cultural capital. *Sociology of Education, 60*(2), 73–85.

Learning Point Associates. (2004). *A closer look at the five essential components of effective reading instruction: A review of scientifically based reading research for teachers.* Naperville, IL: Learning Point Associates. Available at http://www.learningpt.org/pdfs/literacy/components.pdf

Lee, H. V. (1996). *I had a hippopotamus.* New York, NY: Lee & Low.

Lee, J., & Bowen, N. K. (2006). Parent involvement, cultural capital, and the achievement gap among elementary school children. *American Educational Research Journal, 43*(2), 193–218.

Lee & Low Books. (2012). *Why hasn't the number of multicultural books increased in 18 years?* Available at http://blog.leeandlow.com/2013/06/17/why-hasnt-the-number-of-multicultural-books-increased-in-eighteen-years/

LeFevre, A. L., & Shaw, T. V. (2012). Latino parent involvement and school success: Longitudinal effects of formal and informal support. *Education and Urban Society 44*(6), 707–723.

Lenhart, A., Kahne, J., Middaugh, E., Macgill, A., Evans, C., Vitak, J. (2008). *Teens, video games, and civics.* Washington, DC: Pew Research Center. Available at http://www.pewinternet.org/2008/09/16/teens-video-games-and-civics/

Leslie, L., & Caldwell, J. S. (2010). *Qualitative reading inventory* (5th ed.). Upper Saddle River, NJ: Pearson.

Leu, D. J., Forzani, E., & Kennedy, C. (2014). Providing classroom leadership in new literacies: Preparing students for their future. In S. B. Wepner, D. S. Strickland, & D. J. Quatroche (Eds.), *The administration and supervision of reading programs* (5th ed.) (pp. 200–213). New York, NY: Teachers College Press.

Lewis, C. (2001). *Literary practices as social acts: Power, status, and cultural norms in the classroom.* New York, NY: Routledge.

Linan-Thompson, S., & Vaughn, S. (2007). *Research-based methods of reading instruction for English language learners.* Alexandria, VA: ASCD.

Lindamood, C. H., & Lindamood, P. C. (1975). *Auditory discrimination in depth.* Austin, TX.: PRO-ED. (Original work published 1969)

Literacyleadershipteam:Guidanceforschoolimprovementplan.(2011).Unpublisheddocument.Availableathttp://www.broward.k12.fl.us/schoolimprove1/Documents/LiteracyLeadershipTeam.pdf

Llorens, M. B. (1994). Action research: Are teachers finding their voice? *The Elementary School Journal, 95*(1), 3–10.

Lobel. A. (1972). *Frog and toad together.* New York, NY: Harper Collins.

Long, K. (2014, September). Eight qualities of a great teacher mentor. *CTQCollaboratory.* Available at http://www.edweek.org/tm/articles/2014/09/30/ctq_long_mentor.html?r=1327098762&preview=1

Lortie, D. C. (1975). *Schoolteacher: A sociological study.* Chicago, IL: University of Chicago Press.

Lovelace, S., & Wheeler, T. (2006). Cultural discontinuity between home and school language socialization patterns: Implications for teachers. *Education, 127*(2), 303–309.

Luke, A. (1997). Genres of power? Literacy education and the production of capital. In R. Hasan & G. Williams (Eds.), *Literacy in Society* (pp. 308–338). London, UK: Longman Press.

Lyman, F. (1987). Think-pair-share: An expanding teaching technique. *MAA-CIE Cooperative News, 1*(1), 1–2.

Lyons, C. A., & Pinnell, G. S. (2001). *Systems for change in literacy education: A guide for professional development.* Portsmouth, NH: Heinemann.

MacGinitie, W. H., MacGinitie, R. K., Maria, K., Dreyer, L. G., & Hughes, K. E. (2000). *Gates-MacGinitie reading tests* (4th ed.). Rolling Meadows, IL: The Riverside Publishing Company.

Madden, M., Lechart, A., Duggan, M., Cortesi, S., & Gasser, U. (2013). *Teens and technology 2013.* Washington, DC: Pew Research Center. Available at http://www.pewinternet.org/2008/09/16/teens-video-games-and-civics/

Mahoney, K., MacSwan, J., & Thompson, M. (2005). The condition of English language learners in Arizona: 2005. In D. Garcia & A. Molnar (Eds.), *The condition of preK–12 education in Arizona, 2005* (pp. 1–24). Tempe, AZ: Education Policy Research Laboratory, Arizona State University.

McCarrier, A., Pinnell, G. S., & Fountas, I. (2000). *Interactive writing: How language and literacy come together, K–2.* Portsmouth, NH: Heinemann.

McCawley, P. F. (2009, August). *Methods for conduction of an educational needs assessment: Guidelines for cooperative extension system professionals* (BUL 879). Moscow, ID: University of Idaho Extension. Available at http://www.cals.uidaho.edu/edcomm/pdf/bul/bul0870.pdf

McGee, L. M., & Richgels, D. J. (1996). *Literacy's beginnings: Supporting young readers and writers* (2nd ed.). Boston, MA: Allyn and Bacon.

McKee, A., Boyatzis, R., & Johnston, F. (2008). *Becoming a resonant leader: Develop your emotional intelligence, renew your relationships, sustain your effectiveness.* Cambridge, MA: Harvard Business Review Press.

McKeon, D. (2004). When meeting "common" standards is uncommonly difficult. *Educational Leadership, 51*(8), 45–49.

McMasters, K. L., Jung, P. G., Brandes, D., Pinto, V., Fuchs, D., Kearns, . . . Yen, L. (2014). Customizing a research-based reading practice: Balancing the importance of implementation fidelity with professional judgment, *The Reading Teacher, 68*(3), 173–183.

McTighe, J., & Wiggins, G. (2005). *Understanding by design.* New York, NY: Pearson.

McWhorter, J. (2000). *Spreading the word: Language and dialect in America.* Portsmouth, NH: Heinemann.

Menken, K., & Look, K. (2000, February). *Meeting the needs of linguistically and culturally diverse students. Schools in the middle.* Washington, DC: National Association of Secondary School Principals.

Mertler, C. A. (2006). *Action research: Teachers as researchers in the classroom.* Thousand Oaks, CA: Sage.

MetLife. (2009). *The MetLife survey of the American teacher: Collaborating for student success.* New York, NY: Metropolitan Life Insurance Company.

Michael-Luna, S., & Canagarajah, S. (2008). Multilingual academic literacies: Pedagogical foundations for code meshing in primary and higher education. *Journal of Applied Linguistics, 4*(1), 55–77.

Microsoft. (2015). OneNote. Available at http://www.onenote.com/

Miller, D. (2012). *Reading with meaning: Teaching comprehension in the primary grades* (2nd ed.). Portland, ME: Stenhouse.

Mindich, D., & Lieberman, A. (2012). *Building a learning community: A tale of two schools.* Stanford, CA: Stanford Center for Opportunity Policy in Education. Available at http://learningforward.org/docs/publicationssection/2012phase4report.pdf

Mitch, C. (2014, Spring). Learning to lead: How education and emotions are transforming the workplace. *Penn GSE,* 10–12.

Mitchell, K. (2012). English is not ALL that matters in the education of secondary multilingual learners and their teachers. *International Journal of Multicultural Education, 14*(1), 1–21.

Moats, L. C. (1999). *Teaching reading is rocket science: What expert teachers of reading should know and be able to do* (ED445323). Washington, DC: American Federation of Teachers.

Moats, L. C. (2010). *From speech to print: Language essentials for teachers* (2nd ed.). Baltimore, MD: Brooks Publishing.

Moje, E. B., & Luke, A. (2009). Literacy and identity: A review of perspectives on identity and their impact on literacy studies. *Reading Research Quarterly, 44*(4), 415–437.

Moll, L., Amanti, K., Neff, D., & Gonzales, N. (1992). Funds of knowledge for teaching: Using qualitative approaches to connect homes and classrooms. *Theory into practice, 31*(2), 132–141.

Montemayor, A. M. (2013, March). PTA Comunitario as a family leadership model. *IDRA Newsletter.* San Antonio, TX: Intercultural Development Research Association. Available at http://www.idra.org/IDRA_Newsletter/March_2013_Parents_for_Community_Engagement/PTA_Comunitario_as_a_Family_Leadership_Model/

Moran, M. C. (2007). *Differentiated literacy coaching.* Alexandria, VA: Association for Supervision and Curriculum Development.

Morrow, L. M., & Weinstein, C. S. (1986). Encouraging voluntary reading: The impact of a literature program on children's use of library centers. *Reading Research Quarterly, 21,* 330–346.

Mraz, M., & Kissel, B. (2014). Professional development in early childhood education: Models and recommendations. In L. E. Martin, S. Kragler, D. J. Quatroche, & K. L. Bauserman (Eds.), *Handbook of professional development in education: Successful models and practices, PreK–12* (pp. 174–188). New York, NY: The Guilford Press.

Murphey, D., Cooper, M. & Forry, N. (2013, November). *The youngest Americans: A statistical portrait of infants and toddlers in the United States.* Child Trends. Publication #2013-48.

Myers & Briggs Foundation. (n.d.). *MBTI® basics.* Available at http://www.myersbriggs.org/my-mbti-personality-type/mbti-basics/the-16-mbti-types.asp#ENTJ

Myers, I. B., McCaulley, M. H., Quenk, N. L., & Hammer, A. L. (1998). *MBTI Manual (A guide to the development and use of the Myers Briggs type indicator)* (3rd ed.). Mountain View, CA: Consulting Psychologists Press.

National Center for Education Statistics. (2012). *Digest of education statistics, table 44.* Washington, DC: U.S. Department of Education.

National Council for the Accreditation of Teacher Education. (2010–2014). *NCATE Glossary.* Available at http://www.ncate.org/Standards/UnitStandards/Glossary/tabid/477/Default.aspx

National Council of Teachers of English. (1992). *Guideline on teaching storytelling: A position statement from the committee on storytelling.* Available at http://www.ncte.org/positions/statements/teachingstorytelling

National Council of Teachers of English. (2011). The need for teacher communities: An interview with Linda Darling-Hammond. *The Council Chronicle, 21*(2), 12–14. Urbana, IL: NCTE.

National Governors Association Center for Best Practices & Council of Chief State School Officers. (2010). *Common Core State Standards language arts.* Washington, DC: Author.

Nelson, C. A. (2012). *Building capacity to transform literacy learning.* National Center for Literacy Education/National Council of Teachers of English. Available at http://www.ncte.org/library/NCTEFiles/About/NCLE/NCLEshortlitreview.pdf

Nelson, S. D. (2009). *Quiet hero: The Ira Hayes story.* New York, NY: Lee & Low.

Neuman, S. B. (1999). Books make a difference: A study of access to literacy. *Reading Research Quarterly, 34,* 286–301.

Neuman, S. B., & Roskos, K. (1997). Literacy knowledge in practice: Contexts of participation for young writers and readers. *Reading Research Quarterly, 32,* 10–32.

Nichols, B. (2010, August). *Differentiate leadership.* Available at connectedprincipals.com/archives/144

Nichols, M. (2009). *Expanding comprehension with multigenre text sets*. New York, NY: Scholastic.

Nieto, S. (2002). *Language, culture, and teaching: Critical perspectives for a new century*. Mahwah, NJ: Lawrence Erlbaum Associates Publishers.

Numeroff, L. J. (1985). *If you give a mouse a cookie*. New York, NY: Harper Collins.

O'Brien, A. S. (2003). *A special day*. New York, NY: Lee & Low.

O'Day, J. (2009). Good instruction is good for everyone—or is it? English language learners in a balanced literacy approach. *Journal of Education for Students Placed at Risk, 14*(1), 97–119.

Opitz, M. P., & Ford, M. P. (2001) *Reading readers: Flexible and innovative strategies for guided reading*. Portsmouth, NH: Heinemann.

O'Sullivan, M. (2001). *Community mapping: Toward cultural awareness*. Unpublished manuscript prepared for the UNITE workgroup on Pre-service Teacher Education Programs for Urban Schools.

Parkes, B. (2000). *Read it again: Revisiting shared reading*. Portland, ME: Stenhouse.

Partnership for Assessment of Readiness for College and Careers. (2011). *PARCC model content frameworks: English language arts/literacy grades 3–11*. Available at http://www.parcconline.org/sites/parcc/files/PARCCMCFE -LALiteracyAugust2012_FINAL.pdf

Partnership for Reading: National Institute for Literacy; National Institute of Child Health and Human Development; US Department of Education. (2001). *Put reading first: The research building blocks for teaching children to read*. Washington, DC: U.S. Government Printing Office.

Pashiardis, P. (1996). Environmental scanning in educational organizations: Uses, approaches, sources and methodologies. *International Journal of Educational Management, 10*(3), 5–9.

Paterson, K. (2003). What does it mean to be truly literate? *Language Arts, 81*(1), 8–9.

Pearson, P. D., & Gallagher, M. C. (1983). The instruction of reading comprehension. *Contemporary Educational Psychology, 8*(3), 317–344.

Pérez, A. I. (2013). *My very own room*. New York, NY: Lee & Low.

Petrides, K. V. (2010). Trait emotional intelligence theory. *Industrial and Organizational Psychology: Perspectives on Science and Practice, 3*, 136–139.

Pew Research Center. (2013). *Social networking use*. Available at http://www.pewresearch.org/data-trend/media-and-technology/social-networking-use/

Philips, S. U. (1992). *The invisible culture: Communication in classroom and community on the Warm Springs Indian Reservation*. Long Grove, IL: Waveland Press.

Pinar, B. (2012). *What is curriculum theory?* (2nd ed.). New York, NY: Routledge.

Popovics, A. J. (1990). Environmental scanning: A process to assist colleges in strategic planning. *College Student Journal, 24*, 78–80.

Price, P. C. (2006, Fall). Are you as good a teacher as you think? *Thought & Action*, 7–14. Available at http://www.nea.org/assets/img/PubThoughtAndAction /TAA_06_02.pdf

Quiroz, B., Greenfield, P., & Altchech, M. (1999). Bridging cultures with a parent teacher conference. *Educational Leadership, 56*(7), 68–70.

Ray, B., & Seely, C. (1998). *Fluency through TPR storytelling* (2nd ed.) Berkeley, CA: Command Performance Language Institute.

Rea, D. M., & Mercuri, S. P. (2006). *Research-based strategies for English language learners: How to reach goals and meet standards, K–8.* Portsmouth, NH: Heinemann.

Reeves, D. B. (2006). *The learning leader: How to focus school improvement for better results.* Alexandria, VA: Association for Supervision and Curriculum Development.

Reeves, D. B. (2009). *Leading change in your school: How to conquer myths, build commitment, and get results.* Alexandria, VA: Association for Supervision and Curriculum Development.

Remillard, J. (2001). *Studying neighborhoods in learning to teach.* Unpublished manuscript prepared for the UNITE workgroup on Pre-service Teacher Education Programs for Urban Schools.

Resnick, L. B. (1995). From aptitude to effort: A new foundation for our schools. *Daedalus, 124*(4), 55–62.

Reutzel, D. R., Jones, C. D., Fawson, P. C., & Smith, J. A. (2008). Reconsidering silent sustained reading. *Journal of Educational Research, 102*(1), 37–50.

Reynolds, J. (2004). *Living in an igloo.* New York, NY: Lee & Low.

Rideout, V. (2012). *Social media, social life: How teens view their digital lives.* New York, NY: Common Sense Media. Available at file:///Users/kegancunningham/Downloads/socialmediasociallife-final-061812.pdf

Rideout, V., Foeher, U., & Roberts, D. (2010). *Generation M²: Media in the lives of 8- to 18-year-olds.* Menlo Park, CA: The Henry J. Kaiser Family Foundation. Available at https://www.commonsensemedia.org/research/social-media-social-life-how-teens-view-their-digital-lives

Ritchey, K. D., & Goeke, J. L. (2006). Orton-Gillingham and Orton-Gillingham–based reading instruction: A review of the literature. *Journal of Special Education, 40*(3), 171–183.

Robb, L. (2003). *Literacy links: Practical strategies to develop the emergent literacy at-risk children need.* Portsmouth, NH: Heinemann.

Robison, L. (2014, July). *Changing demographics in Ohio require continued focus on early literacy.* Available at http://edexcellence.net/articles/changing-demographics-in-ohio-require-continued-focus-on-early-literacy

Roderick, M., Nagaoka, J., & Coca, V. (2009). College readiness for all: The challenge for urban high schools. *Future Child, 19*(1), 185–210.

Rodgers, A., & Rodgers, E. (2014). Effective literacy coaching for teachers: Context and practice. In S. B. Wepner, D. S. Strickland, & D. J. Quatroche (Eds.), *The administration and supervision of reading programs* (5th ed., pp. 103–128). New York, NY: Teachers College Press.

Rodgers, E. M., & Pinnell, G. S. (Eds.). (2002). *Learning from teaching in literacy education: New perspectives on professional development.* Portsmouth, NH: Heinemann.

Rogers, C. (2002). Defining reflection: Another look at John Dewey and reflective thinking. *Teachers College Record, 101*(4), 842–866.

Rogers, R., Kramer, M. A., Mosley, M., Fuller, C., Light, R., Nehart, M., & Thomas, P. (2005). The long haul: Professional development as social change. *Language Arts, 82*(5), 347–358.

Rusbult, C. E., & Zembrodt, I. M. (1983). Responses to dissatisfaction in romantic involvements: A multidimensional-scaling analysis. *Journal of Experimental Social Psychology, 19*, 274–293.

Rush, M. (2015). List of skills you need in order to be a successful teacher. *Houston Chronicle Chron.com* Available at http://work.chron.com/list-skills-need-order-successful-teacher-27287.html

Santiago, E., Ferrara, J., & Blank, M. (2008). A full-service school fulfills its promise. *Educational Leadership 65*(7), 44–47.

Santiago, E., Ferrara, J., & Quinn, J. (2012). *Whole child, whole school.* Lanham, MD: Rowman & Littlefield Education.

Schleppegrell, M. J. (2004). *The language of schooling: A functional linguistics perspective.* Mahwah, NJ: Lawrence Erlbaum.

Schlichte, J., Yssel, N., & Merbler, J. (2005). Pathways to burnout: Case studies in teacher isolation and alienation. *Preventing School Failure, 50*(1), 35–40.

Schön, D. A. (1983). *The reflective practitioner: How professionals think in action.* New York, NY: Basic Books.

Schön, D. A. (1987). *Educating the reflective practitioner.* San Francisco, CA: Jossey-Bass.

Schwarzer, D., Haywood, A., & Lorenzen, C. (2003). Fostering multiliteracy in a linguistically diverse classroom. *Language Arts, 80*(6), 453–460.

Shanklin, N. L. (2006, September). What are the characteristics of effective literacy coaching? *Literacy Coaching Clearinghouse,* 1–3. Available at http://files.eric.ed.gov/fulltext/ED530356.pdf

Shoebottom, P. (1996). *Language differences: A guide to learning English.* Frankfurt International School, Oberursel, Germany. Available at http://esl.fis.edu/grammar/langdiff/index.htm.

Short, K., & Burke, C. (1991). *Creating curriculum: Teachers and students as a community of learners.* Portsmouth, NH: Heinemann.

Silva, T. (1993) Toward an understanding of L2 writing: The ESL research and its implications. *TESOL Quarterly, 27*(4), 657–677.

Sims, R. (1982). *Mirrors, windows, and sliding glass doors.* Available at http://www.rif.org/us/literacy-resources/multicultural/mirrors-windows-and-sliding-glass-doors.htm

Skerrett, A. (2012). Languages and literacies in translocation: Experiences and perspectives of a transnational youth. *Journal of Literacy Research, 44*(4), 364–395.

Slingerland, B. H., & Aho, M. (1994–1996). *Slingerland reading program.* Cambridge, MA: Educators Publishing Service.

Sloan, W. M. (2008, May). Collaborating over coffee: Creating a successful school-business partnership. *Association for Supervision and Curriculum Development Education Update, 50*(5), 1, 3.

Sneed, D., & Fonseca, J. (2005). *Punched paper.* New York, NY: Lee & Low.

Spalding, R. B., & North, M. E. (2012). *Writing road to reading: The Spalding method for teaching speech, spelling, writing, and reading* (6th ed.). New York, NY: HarperCollins.

Steiner, L., & Kowal, J. (2007, September). *Issue brief: Principal as instructional leader: Designing a coaching program that fits.* Washington, DC: The Center for Comprehensive School Reform and Improvement. (ERIC EDU 499255) Available at http://files.eric.ed.gov/fulltext/ED499255.pdf

Sterrett, E. A. (2001). *The manager's pocket guide to Emotional Intelligence.* Amherst, MA: HRD Press.

Stoll, L., Bolam, R., McMahon, A., Wallace, M., & Thomas, S. (2006). Professional learning communities: A review of the literature. *Journal of Educational Change, 7*(4), 221–258.

Strauss, V. (2014, September 5). America's suburban schools facing new pressures. *The Washington Post.* Available at http://www.washingtonpost.com/blogs/answer-sheet/wp/2014/09/05/americas-suburban-schools-facing-new-pressures/

Street, B. V. (1999). The meanings of literacy. In D. A Wagner, R. L. Venezky & B. V. Street (Eds.), *Literacy: An international handbook* (pp. 34–40). Boulder, CO: Westview Press.

Suen, A. (2000). *100 days.* New York, NY: Lee & Low.

Sweeney, D. (2003). *Learning along the way: Professional development by and for teachers.* Portland, ME: Stenhouse.

Talbert-Johnson, C. (2006). Preparing highly qualified teacher candidates for urban schools: The importance of disposition. *Education and Urban Society, 39*(1), 147–160.

Tallerico, M. (2014). District issues: Administrators at all levels involved in teachers' professional development. In L. E. Martin, S. Kragler, D. J. Quatroche, & K. L. Bauserman (Eds.), *Handbook of professional development in education: Successful models and practices, PreK–12* (pp. 125–144). New York, NY: The Guilford Press.

Tan, S. (2007). *The arrival.* New York, NY: Arthur A. Levine Books.

Tatum, A. W. (2012, March). *Executive summary: Literacy practices for African-American male adolescents.* Students at the Center Series: Teaching and Learning in the Era of the Common Core. A Jobs for the Future Project. Available at http://www.studentsatthecenter.org/sites/scl.dl-dev.com/files/field_attach_file/Exec_Tatum_040212.pdf

Taylor, R. L., & Wasicsko, M. M. (2000, November). *The dispositions to teach.* Paper presented at the meeting of Southern Regional Association of Teacher Educators, Lexington, KY. Available at https://coehs.nku.edu/content/dam/coehs/docs/dispositions/resources/The_Dispositons_to_Teach.pdf

Teachers College Reading and Writing Project. (2014). *Teachers College reading and writing project assessments.* Available at http://readingandwritingproject.org/resources/assessments/running-records

TeamWeek3. (n.d.). *State standards and federal mandates for literacy instruction for English language learners.* Available at http://www.docstoc.com/docs/155500177/TeamWeek3docx-UOPLTACulturallyResponsive---Learning-Team-A

Thelamour, B., & Jacobs, D. L. (2014). Homework practices of English and non-English-speaking parents. *Urban Education 49*(5), 528–542.

This I Believe, Inc. (2005–2014). *This I believe: A public dialogue about belief, one essay at a time.* Available at http://thisibelieve.org/

Thomas, W. P., & Collier, V. (2003). The multiple benefits of dual language. *Educational Leadership, 61*(2), 61–64.

Thomas, W. P., & Collier, V. (2012) *Dual language education for a transformed world.* Albuquerque, NM: Fuente Press.

Thornton, H. (2006). Dispositions in action: Do dispositions make a difference in practice? *Teacher Education Quarterly, 33*(2), 53–68.

Tjemkes, B. V., & Furrer, O. (2011). Behavioral responses to adverse situations in strategic alliances in T. K. Das (Ed.), *Behavioral perspectives on strategic alliances* (pp. 227–249). Charlotte, NC: Information Age Publishing,

Tomlinson, C. A., & Imbeau, M. (2010). *Differentiated classroom: Responding to the needs of all learners.* Alexandria, VA: ACSD.

Treadway, L. (2000). *Community mapping.* Unpublished manuscript prepared for Contextual Teaching and Learning Project, Ohio State University and U. S. Department of Education.

Trelease, J. (2006). *The read-aloud handbook.* New York, NY: Penguin Books.

Trelease, J. (2009). *Why read aloud to children?* Available at http://www.trelease-on-reading.com/read-aloud-brochure.pdf

Tyler, G. (2007). *First day of school.* New York, NY: Lee & Low.

Tyler. R. (1975). Specific approaches to curriculum development. In J. Schaffarzick & D. Hampson (Eds.), *Strategies for curriculum development* (pp. 17–33). Berkeley, CA: McCutchan.

United States Census Bureau. (2001). *Population 5 years and over who spoke a language other than English at home by language group and English-speaking ability. Appendix Table 1.* Available at http://www.census.gov/hhes/socdemo/language/data/acs/ACS-12.pdf

United States Census Bureau. (2012). 2012 Statistical Abstract, Section 1, Population. Available at http://www.census.gov/compendia/statab/

University of Oregon. (n.d.). *Dynamic Indicators of Basic Early Literacy Skills* (D.I.B.E.L.S.) (6th ed.). Available at https://dibels.uoregon.edu/market/assessment/dibels

University of Tennessee. (2001, Summer). *Urban institute community mapping guide,* Unpublished manuscript, University of Tennessee, Knoxville, TN.

Uppsala University. (n.d.). *Assessing teaching skills in higher education.* Uppsala, Sweden: Uppsala University Office for Development of Teaching and Interactive Learning (UPI). Available at http://www.uadm.uu.se/upi/arkiv/rapporter/Assessing%20Teaching%20Skills.pdf

Urzúa, C. (1986). A children's story. In P. Rigg & D. S. Enright (Eds.), *Children and ESL: Integrating perspectives* (pp. 93–112). Washington, DC: Teachers of English to Speakers of Other Languages.

Urzúa, C. (1987). "You stopped too soon": Second language children composing and revising. *TESOL Quarterly, 21*(2), 279–304.

U.S. Department of Education. (2009a). *American Recovery and Reinvestment Act of 2009: Using ARRA funds provided through Part B of the Individuals with Disabilities Education Act (IDEA) to drive school reform and improvement.* Washington, DC: Author. Available at http://www2.ed.gov/policy/gen/leg/recovery/guidance/idea-b-reform.pdf

U.S. Department of Education. (2009b). *Guidance: Using Title I, Part A ARRA funds for grants to local educational agencies to strengthen education, drive reform, and improve results for students.* Washington, DC: Author. Available at http://www2.ed.gov/policy/gen/leg/recovery/guidance/titlei-form.pdf

U.S. Department of Education. (2010). *Race to the top fund: Purpose.* Available at http://www2.ed.gov/programs/racetothetop/index.html

U. S. Department of Education, Office of Elementary and Secondary Education. (2010, June). *Guidance on school improvement grants under section 1003(g) of the Elementary and Secondary Education Act.* Available at http://www2.ed.gov/programs/sif/index.html

USLegal. (2001–2015). Teaching skills law & legal definition. Available at http://definitions.uslegal.com/t/teaching-skills/

Van Sluys, K., & Reinier, R. (2006). "Seeing the possibilities": Learning with, from, and about multilingual classroom communities. *Language Arts, 83*(4), 321–331.

Vygotsky, L. (1980). Zone of proximal development. *Mind in society: The development of higher psychological processes.* Boston, MA: Harvard University Press.

Walqui, A. (1999, July). *Professional development for teachers of English language learners.* Paper presented at a conference sponsored by the National Educational Research Policy and Priorities Board, the Office of Educational Research and Improvement, and the Office of Bilingual Education and Minority Languages Affairs, Washington, DC.

Walsh, E. S. (2010). *Mouse paint/ Pintura de ratón.* Boston, MA: HMH Books.

Wells, A. S., & Ready, D. (2014, May 25). Suburbs at a crossroads. *Newsday,* A36.

Wepner, S. B. (2011). How to become a collaborative leader. In S. B. Wepner & D. Hopkins (Eds.), *Collaborative leadership in action: Partnering for success in schools* (pp. 166–183). New York, NY: Teachers College Press.

Wepner, S. B., Clark Johnson V., Henk, W., & Lovell, S. (2013). Deans' interpersonal/negotiating skills. *Academic Leader, 29*(3), 2–3.

Wepner, S. B., Ferrara, J., Rainville, K. N., Gómez, D. W., Lang, D. E., & Bigaouette, L. (2012). *Changing suburbs, changing students: Helping school leaders face the challenges.* Thousand Oaks, CA: Corwin.

Wepner, S. B., Gómez, D. W., & Ferrara, J. (2013). Beyond campus walls for preparing new teachers to work with Hispanic students. *Excelsior: Leadership in Teaching and Learning, 8*(1), 95–105.

Wepner, S. B., Henk, W., & Lovell, S. (2015, March). Developing deans as effective leaders for today's changing educational landscape. *Journal of Higher Education Management, 30*(1), 51–64.

Wepner, S. B., & Quatroche, D. J. (2014). Reading specialists as leaders of literacy. In S. B. Wepner, D. S. Strickland, & D. J. Quatroche (Eds.), *The administration and supervision of reading programs* (5th ed., pp. 75–102). New York, NY: Teachers College Press.

Wepner, S. B., & Seminoff, N. E. (1993, September/October). Storyboarding. *School Leader, 34*–35, 48.

Wilkins-Fontenot, K. (n.d.). *Emotional intelligence: Relating to yourself and others.* Available at http://hrs.wsu.edu/utils/File.aspx?fileid=2811

Wilson, B. (1988). *Wilson Reading System.* Millbury, MA: Wilson language Training.

Wilson, B. (2005). *Fundations.* Oxford, MA: Wilson Language Corporation.

Wisconsin Center for Education Research. (2014a). WIDA *Performance standards listening and reading, K–12.* Madison, WI: Author. Available at https://www.wida.us/standards/CAN_DOs/

Wisconsin Center for Education Research. (2014b). *WIDA performance standards speaking and writing, K–12.* Madison, WI: Author. Available at https://www.wida.us/standards/CAN_DOs/

Wong-Fillmore, L., & Fillmore, C. (2012). *What does text complexity mean for English learners and language minority students? Understanding language: Language, literacy and learning in the content areas.* Available at http://ell.stanford.edu/sites/default/files/pdf/academic-papers/06-LWF%20CJF%20Text%20Complexity%20FINAL_0.pdf

Wood, D., Bruner, J. S., & Ross, G. (1976). The role of tutoring in problem solving. *Journal of Child Psychology & Psychiatry & Allied Disciplines, 17*(2), 89–100.

Zacarian, D. (2013). *Mastering academic language.* Thousand Oaks, CA: Corwin.

Zemelman, S., Daniels, H., & Hyde, A. (2012). *Best practice: Bringing standards to life in America's classrooms* (4th ed.). Portsmouth, NH: Heinemann.

Zwiers, J., & Crawford, M. (2011*). Academic conversations: Classroom talk that fosters critical thinking across disciplines.* Portland, ME: Stenhouse.

Zwiers, J., O'Hara, S., & Pritchard, R. (2014). *Common core standards in diverse classrooms: Essential practices for developing academic language and disciplinary literacy.* Portland, ME: Stenhouse Publisher.

Index

Note: Page numbers by f indicate cited figures in the text.

About the Authors

Shelley B. Wepner is dean and professor in the School of Education of Manhattanville College. She was a reading teacher/specialist, Title I teacher, and K–8 curriculum supervisor in three school districts before becoming a faculty member and administrator in higher education. She has served as editor of *The Reading Instruction Journal* of the New Jersey Reading Association, column editor for *The Reading Teacher* of the International Reading Association, and chairperson of the Technology and Teacher Education Committee of the American Association of Colleges for Teacher Education. She has published more than 140 articles, book chapters, award-winning software packages, and books, which are most recently related to connections between K–12 education and higher education and leadership skills for effectively supporting teacher education and literacy development. Her most recent book publications are *Changing Suburbs, Changing Students: Helping School Leaders Face the Challenges* (2012) and the 5th edition of *The Administration and Supervision of Reading Programs* (2014).

Diane W. Gómez is an associate professor and chairperson of the Department of Educational Leadership and Special Subjects in the School of Education of Manhattanville College. She has served as a Professional Development School liaison in two full-service community schools of the Manhattanville Changing Suburbs Institute districts. Before becoming a faculty member and administrator in higher education, she was a high school Spanish and ESL teacher in public, parochial, and special education residential treatment schools in New York State and New York City. She has written several articles related to professional development schools, dual-language programs, and English learners, and has presented papers and workshops at national and international professional organization conferences. Her most recent book publications are *Changing Suburbs, Changing Students: Helping School Leaders Face the Challenges* (2012) and chapters in three of the five volumes of the Breaking the Mold series (2010, 2012, 2013).

Katie Egan Cunningham is an assistant professor in the Literacy Department in the School of Education of Manhattanville College. She was an elementary school teacher and literacy specialist in New York City before becoming a faculty member in higher education. Katie is the author of *Story: Still the Heart of Literacy Learning* to be published in fall 2015. She is coeditor of *The Language and Literacy Spectrum*, the journal of the New York State Reading Association, with her literacy colleagues. She is also coauthor of the children's and young adult literature site *The Classroom Bookshelf*, and has written several articles and book chapters on children's literature, new technologies, and professional development schools. She has also served as a Professional Development School liaison in a full-service community school of the Manhattanville Changing Suburbs Institute districts, and serves as a literacy consultant throughout the New York area, supporting teachers, literacy leaders, and administrators.

Kristin N. Rainville is an assistant professor in the Department of Leadership and Literacy at Sacred Heart University. Kristin is a former elementary classroom teacher, literacy coach, and state-level administrator. As a faculty member at Manhattanville College, Kristin served as a Professional Development School liaison in one of the Changing Suburbs Institute® districts. Kristin is a consultant throughout the New York, Connecticut, and New Jersey areas, supporting teachers and literacy coaches. Kristin's research and writing focus is on literacy leadership, whether through literacy coaching, classroom instruction, action research, or teacher candidate preparation. She has published in *The Reading Teacher* and *Reading & Writing Quarterly*. Kristin is coeditor of *The Language and Literacy Spectrum*, the journal of the New York State Reading Association, with her literacy colleagues. Kristin is also a coauthor of *Changing Suburbs, Changing Students: Helping School Leaders Face the Challenges* (2012).

Courtney Kelly is an associate professor in the Literacy Department in the School of Education of Manhattanville College. Courtney taught middle and high school reading and English in Texas, Massachusetts, and Cali, Colombia, before earning an MA in Latin American literature and culture and a PhD in language, literacy, and culture at the Ohio State University. During her time in Ohio, she worked with young people in changing school districts, serving as the coordinator of an after-school program designed to promote meaningful interactions between immigrant middle school students and their mainstream peers. She has shared her research on multilingual literacies and new technologies through presentations at international conferences and publications in international journals. While at Manhattanville, she has also completed outreach projects at two professional development schools, supervising graduate students in literacy in their work with culturally and linguistically diverse students.